Beneath Apple ProDOS

For users of ProDOS 8

Fourth Printing, November 1988

by Don D. Worth and Pieter M. Lechner

QUALITY SOFTWARE

21000 Devonshire #114
Chatsworth, CA 91311

Apple Books from Quality Software

Beneath Apple DOS — $19.95
by Don Worth & Pieter Lechner

Understanding the Apple II — $22.95
by Jim Sather

Understanding the Apple IIe — $24.95
by Jim Sather

Apple Utility Software from Quality Software

Bag of Tricks 2 (includes diskette) — $49.95
by Don Worth & Pieter Lechner

Production Editor: Kathryn M. Schmidt
Original Diagrams: Don Worth & Pieter Lechner
Art Director: Vic Grenrock
Illustrations By: George Garcia
Compositor: American Typesetting, Inc.

ISBN 0-912985-05-4 Library of Congress Number: 84-61383

5 4

Printed in the United States of America

This book is dedicated to my sister, Betsy, who said she had room on her bookshelf for another one of my books.

Don D. Worth

This book is dedicated to my Father and Mother, with a deep sense of appreciation and gratitude.

Pieter M. Lechner

CONTENTS

CONTENTS

Acknowledgements

The authors wish to thank Quality Software for their able assistance in producing this book. Special thanks to Bob Christiansen, Bob Pierce, Kathy Schmidt, George Garcia, Vic Grenrock, and Jeff Weinstein for their unique and special contributions.

CHAPTER 1

INTRODUCTION

Beneath Apple ProDOS is intended to serve as a companion to the manuals provided by Apple Computer, Inc. for ProDOS, providing additional information for the advanced programmer or for the novice Apple user who wants to know more about the structure of disks. It is not the intent of this manual to replace the documentation provided by Apple. Although, for the sake of continuity, some of the material covered in the Apple manuals is also covered here, it will be assumed that the reader is reasonably familiar with the contents of Apple's *ProDOS User's Manual* and *BASIC Programming With ProDOS*. Since all chapters presented here may not be of use to each Apple owner, each has been written

to stand on its own. Readers of our earlier book, *Beneath Apple DOS*, will notice that we have retained the basic organization of that book in an attempt to help them familiarize themselves with *Beneath Apple ProDOS* more quickly.

The information presented here is a result of intensive disassembly and annotation of various versions of ProDOS by the authors. It also uses as a reference various application notes and preliminary documentation from Apple. Although no guarantee can be made concerning the accuracy of the information presented here, all of the material included in *Beneath Apple ProDOS* has been thoroughly researched and tested.

There were several reasons for writing *Beneath Apple ProDOS*:

- To show how to access ProDOS and/or the Disk II drive directly from machine language.
- To help you fix damaged disks.
- To correct errors and omissions in the Apple documentation.
- To allow you to customize ProDOS to fit your needs.
- To provide complete information on diskette formatting.
- To document the internal logic of ProDOS.
- To present a critical, non-Apple perspective of ProDOS.
- To provide more examples of ProDOS programming.
- To help you to learn about how an operating system works.

When Apple introduced ProDOS Version 1.0.1 in January 1984. three manuals were available: the *ProDOS User's Manual* documents the use of ProDOS utilities; the *BASIC Programming With ProDOS* manual describes the command language supported by the BASIC Interpreter and how to write BASIC programs which access the disk; and the *ProDOS Technical Reference Manual (for the Apple II family)* documents the assembly language interfaces to ProDOS. It should be stated that this technical reference manual represents the best internal documentation Apple has ever provided to users of one of their operating systems. Unfortunately, the *ProDOS Technical Reference Manual* documents a prerelease version of ProDOS, and is not entirely accurate for the current release at the time of this writing. In addition, many sections require further explanation before the interfaces they describe can be used at all. For example, the discussion of how one adds a command to the BASIC Interpreter omits several vital pieces of information which are documented fully in *Beneath Apple ProDOS*. In addition, none of the Apple documentation addresses diskette formatting or direct access of the Disk II family of controllers from assembly language. *Beneath Apple ProDOS* was written in an attempt to improve upon the documentation base established by Apple. Most of the topics covered by Apple's technical manual are covered here also, but they are explained in a different and, we hope, clearer way, based upon a programmer's understanding of the code in the ProDOS Kernel and the BASIC Interpreter. We have also added substantial information on diskette formatting and repair, the internal logic and structure of ProDOS, and customizing techniques, as well as providing several example programs and quick reference materials.

In addition to the ProDOS specific information provided, many of the discussions also apply to other operating systems in the Apple II and Apple III family of machines. For example, disk formatting at the track and sector level is for the most part the same. Also, the format of a ProDOS volume is nearly identical to that of an Apple III SOS volume.

With the introduction of the Apple IIGS in late 1986, a 16-bit version of ProDOS was introduced. Designed similarly to the original ProDOS, it was named ProDOS 16, while the original ProDOS became known as ProDOS 8. ProDOS 16 was destined to be short-lived, and in late 1988 Apple replaced it with GS/OS, a 16-bit operating system compatible with ProDOS only in the sense that GS/OS has the ability to directly use disks originally formatted for any operating system, including and especially ProDOS. This book does not attempt to describe either ProDOS 16 or GS/OS. ProDOS 8 remains the standard operating system for the Apple IIe and the Apple IIc.

For those readers who would like to have a detailed description of every bit of code in ProDOS 8, a supplement to this book is available and can be ordered directly from Quality Software. Please see page 8-8.

CHAPTER 2

TO BUILD A BETTER DOS

From June 1978 to January 1984, the primary disk operating system for the Apple II family was Apple DOS. Throughout its first six years of existence, DOS has gone through a number of changes, culminating in its final version, DOS 3.3. DOS was originally designed primarily to support the BASIC programmer, but has since been adopted by assembly language programmers and by the majority of Apple users for a variety of applications.

THE DEFICIENCIES OF DOS

Although it is a flexible and easy to use operating system, DOS suffers from many weaknesses. Among these are:

- **DOS is slow.** Since each byte read from the disk is copied between memory buffers up to three times, a large portion of the actual overhead in reading data from the disk is in processor manipulation after the data has been read. To circumvent this, several "fast DOS" packages have been marketed by third parties which heavily modify DOS to prevent multiple buffering under certain circumstances.
- **DOS is device dependent.** When DOS was developed, the only mass storage device for the Apple was the Disk II diskette drive. Now that diskette drives with increased capacity and hard disks are available, a more device independent file organization is needed. DOS is limited in the number of files which can be stored on a diskette as well as their maximum size. These are significant drawbacks when a hard disk with five million bytes or more is used.

- Over the years, new hardware has been introduced by Apple and other manufacturers which DOS does not intrinsically support. The Apple IIe with its 80-column card and the Thunderclock are examples.

- **DOS is difficult to customize.** There are few external “hooks” provided to allow system programmers the opportunity to personalize the operating system to special applications. For example, a new command cannot be added to DOS without version dependent patches.

- DOS file structures and system calls are **incompatible** with other operating systems. Each operating system Apple has announced in the past has had its own way of organizing data on a diskette. There is no compatibility between DOS, SOS and the Apple Pascal system. This means that special utilities must be written to move data between these systems and that applications developed in one environment will not run without major modifications under any other system.

- DOS does not provide a consistent mechanism for supporting multiple peripherals which can generate hardware **interrupts.** In the past, various manufacturers have implemented interrupt handlers on their own, often resulting in incompatibilities between their devices.

- DOS provides little standardization of **memory use** and of operating system interfaces. Most “interesting” locations within DOS are internalized and therefore not officially available to the programmer. Also, since there is no standard way to set aside portions of memory for specific applications, it is difficult to put a program in a “safe” place so that it may co-reside with another application.

- Although DOS allows most of its commands to be executed from within a BASIC program, additional function is needed. Under DOS, there is no way to conveniently read a file directory from a BASIC program, or to save and restore Applesoft’s variables, for example. Likewise, the implementation of program CHAINing is not integrated into DOS.

- Additional functions under DOS which would also be desirable (to name only a few) are: a display of the amount of freespace left on a diskette; a way to show the address and length parameters stored with a binary file; and a way to create unbootable data disks to increase storage space for user files.

ENTER ProDOS

In January 1984, Apple introduced a new disk operating system for its Apple II family of computers. ProDOS is intended to replace DOS 3.3 as the standard Apple II operating system, and it is now being shipped with all new Disk II drives instead of DOS. Although, on the surface, ProDOS is very similar in appearance to DOS 3.3, it represents a major redesign and is a new and separate system. From the beginning, ProDOS addresses all of DOS's weaknesses mentioned above:

- ProDOS is up to **eight times faster** than DOS in disk access. A new "direct read" mode has been implemented which allows multisector reads to be performed directly from the disk to the programmer's buffer without multiple buffering within ProDOS itself. When performing direct reads, ProDOS can transfer data from the diskette at a rate of eight kilobytes per second (at best, DOS can read one kilobyte per second). Even when reading small amounts of data from the disk, ProDOS does less multiple buffering than does DOS.

- ProDOS provides a **device independent** interface to "foreign" mass storage devices. The concept of a hierarchically organized disk "volume" was created to allow for large capacity devices, and vectors are provided to allow device drivers for non-standard disks to be integrated into ProDOS. Directories may be dynamically expanded to unlimited size to allow for large numbers of files, and an individual file may now occupy up to 16 million bytes of space on a volume. The largest volume which can be supported is 32 million bytes.

- Device **driver support** has also been provided for calendar/clock peripherals, allowing time and date stamping of files, and support for the Apple IIe and IIc 80-column hardware is a part of ProDOS.

- Learning from its mistakes with DOS, Apple has externalized as many ProDOS functions as possible through well defined **system calls**. In addition to standard file management system calls, interfaces are provided to support user written commands to the BASIC Interpreter, and to invoke a ProDOS command from within an assembly language program.

- The ProDOS file and volume structure is nearly identical to that of the Apple III **SOS** operating system. There are even strong similarities between ProDOS system calls and those on Apple's Macintosh! A ProDOS volume may be accessed from SOS directly without the need for a special utility program. ProDOS system calls are a large subset of those offered under SOS, and applications may be developed which will easily port between the two operating systems.

- ProDOS defines a protocol which **interrupting** devices may use to coexist harmoniously in the same machine. Up to four interrupt drivers may be installed in ProDOS, and each device need not know that the others exist.

- Most system locations of general interest have been placed in externally accessible areas of memory called **global pages**. Through a global page, a user written program can obtain the current ProDOS version number, the most recent values entered on a ProDOS command line, or the configuration of the current hardware including the machine type, memory size, and contents of the peripheral card slots. In addition, a voluntary system has been provided to "fence off" portions of memory for special uses by marking a memory bit map in the system global page.

- New support has been provided under ProDOS for **BASIC** programmers. A BASIC program can now read a directory file, make a "snapshot" of its variables on disk and later restore them, and chain between programs, preserving the variables.

- The **CATALOG** command under ProDOS displays the address and length values of binary files as well as the space remaining on a disk volume.

MORE ProDOS ADVANTAGES

In addition to addressing needs which grew out of DOS, Apple has also come up with **other enhancements** with ProDOS:

- A new "smart" RUN command ("–") has been added which will automatically perform the function of a RUN, EXEC or BRUN as appropriate depending upon the type of file being RUN.

- The assembly language interface has been expanded to include obtaining and updating statistical information about a file, moving the end of file mark in a file, allowing line-at-a-time reads versus byte stream reads, determining the names of diskettes mounted in online drives, and creating new files or directories. In addition, entry points are included to allow applications to pass control from program to program and to allocate memory.

- The language independent, file management portion of ProDOS (the Kernel), is a separate unit from the BASIC support routines. Applications may be written which reclaim the memory normally occupied by BASIC support routines.

- All ProDOS utilities are menu oriented with enhanced user interfaces.

- Owners of the Extended 80-column card in an Apple IIe have access to a 64K "RAM/electronic disk drive" under ProDOS. Data stored there may be accessed almost instantaneously allowing much more efficient loading and storing of programs and data.

- Applesoft string "garbage collection" has been rewritten under ProDOS, and is now many times faster and more efficient.

- Files may be restricted or "locked" by type of access. Read only files may be established, or files which may be written but not destroyed, for example.

- The binary save (BSAVE) command has been enhanced under ProDOS. BSAVEs into existing binary files whose A and/or L keywords are omitted will use the current values of the target file. Also, other file types besides BIN files may be BLOADed and BSAVEd, allowing direct modification at a byte-by-byte level. (For example, one can BLOAD a text file and examine it in memory, making modifications to the hex image.)

- The record length of a random access text file is now stored with the file, allowing subsequent BASIC programs to access it without knowing its record length.

- Data disk volumes may now be created which do not contain an image of the operating system. ProDOS makes more efficient use of the disk, resulting in slightly more user storage for files.

- More information about a file is stored in the directory entry under ProDOS than under DOS. The length of a binary or Applesoft file, for example, is stored in the directory, not in the file itself.

- The manner in which the ProDOS BASIC Interpreter intercepts a BASIC program's command lines has been improved and is more reliable. It is now very difficult to "disconnect" ProDOS as could occur under DOS.

- More file types (256) are available under ProDOS. Some are "user definable."

WHAT YOU GIVE UP WITH ProDOS

ProDOS is not for everyone, however. There are a number of **disadvantages** to moving from DOS to ProDOS:

- Most assembly language programs which ran under DOS will have to be rewritten for ProDOS. The file management interfaces are completely different, and the "PRINT control-D" mechanism which worked from assembly language under DOS no longer works under ProDOS. This means that most commercial applications, such as word processors, compilers, and spreadsheets, will not be available for ProDOS until they are converted. This state of affairs will change, however, since ProDOS is now the "official" operating system for Apple II computers.

- Apple's older version of BASIC, Integer BASIC, is not supported under ProDOS. Indeed, Applesoft must be in the motherboard ROMs for the ProDOS BASIC Interpreter to work at all. This means that only the ProDOS Kernel, used in a standalone, run-time environment, will run on an original, Integer Apple II. It is likely that someone (probably not Apple) will soon market an Integer BASIC interpreter for ProDOS, however.

- ProDOS requires 64K to support BASIC programming and commands. It can be made to run in 48K for run-time assembly language applications, but 64K is required to run the BASIC Interpreter which incorporates all of the ProDOS commands (e.g. CATALOG, BLOAD, etc.).

- Under BASIC, less memory is available to the program. Under DOS, HIMEM was set at $9600 with three file buffers built into DOS. Under ProDOS, HIMEM is at $9600 with no file buffers built in. Thus, as soon as a ProDOS BASIC program opens a file, HIMEM is moved down and 1K less memory is available. Likewise, since the Kernel occupies the Language Card (or bank switched memory), this space may not be used for other purposes. (DOS could be relocated into the language card to make more space available to BASIC programs. Also, Applesoft enhancement aid programs typically were loaded into the language card's alternate 4K bank under DOS. This is where ProDOS stores its Quit code now.)
- ProDOS only maintains a single directory prefix for all volumes, rather than remembering a default prefix for each volume. Hence, diskette swapping and access to multiple volumes at once can be cumbersome.
- Although the pathname for a file may be 64 characters, the actual name of a file may be only 15 characters, and may not include any special characters or blanks (other than "period"). 30 characters were permitted under DOS.
- Under DOS, up to 16 files may be opened concurrently by a BASIC program. Under ProDOS, only eight files may be opened at once. Also, an open file "cost" 595 bytes under DOS; under ProDOS, a 1024-byte buffer is allocated.
- BASIC programs which are computationally oriented will run about four percent slower on ProDOS than they did under DOS. This is because the ProDOS BASIC Interpreter leaves Applesoft TRACE running (invisibly) at all times so that it can monitor the execution of the program and perform garbage collection and disk commands. On the other hand, if strings or disk accesses are used, this degradation of performance will be more than offset by improvements in these areas.
- Several DOS commands have been removed, including NOMON, MON, and VERIFY. There is now no way to see the commands in an EXEC file as they are executed.
- If a ProDOS directory is destroyed, it is harder to reconstruct than was the DOS CATALOG track. More information is stored in the directory making it harder to identify a file's type

by examining its data blocks. Also, since seedling files do not have index blocks (similar to DOS Track/Sector Lists), they are almost impossible to find once their directory entries are gone.

OTHER DIFFERENCES BETWEEN ProDOS AND DOS

There are a few other minor differences between ProDOS and DOS which are worth noting:

- The BRUN command now calls the target program rather than jumping to it as did DOS. The invoked program may return to ProDOS via a return subroutine.
- CLOSE will not produce an error message if the file named is not currently open.
- APPEND implies WRITE. It is not necessary to follow an APPEND command with a WRITE command in a BASIC program.
- ASCII text in ProDOS directory entries or TXT files is stored with the most significant bit **off**.

CHAPTER 3

DISK II HARDWARE AND DISKETTE FORMATTING

This chapter will explain how data is stored on a floppy diskette using a disk drive (Disk II family or equivalent). Much of the information in this chapter is applicable not only to ProDOS but also to other operating systems on the Apple computer (DOS, PASCAL, CP/M). Because ProDOS isolates device specific code, the contents of this chapter should not be considered a prerequisite for understanding succeeding chapters.

For system housekeeping, ProDOS divides external storage devices into blocks. Each **block** contains 512 bytes of information. It is device independent in that each device has its own driver. This driver enables ProDOS to read and write blocks, and additionally to obtain the status of a device. The device itself may actually store information in a number of ways and not necessarily in blocks. Blocks can be thought of as a conceptual unit of data that was created in software, having little or no relation to how data is actually stored on an external storage device. In fact, the standard Disk II stores information in a track and sector format. The device driver provides a mapping between these tracks and sectors, and the blocks. Since a sector contains 256 bytes, two **sectors** are required for each block. There are 560 sectors on a diskette and therefore 280 blocks. Chapter 4 deals with how ProDOS allocates these blocks to create files.

TRACKS AND SECTORS

As stated above, a diskette is divided into tracks and sectors. This is done during the initialization or formatting process. A **track** is a physically defined circular path which is concentric with the hole in the center of the diskette. Each track is identified by its distance from the center of the disk. Similar to a phonograph stylus, the read/write head of the disk drive may be positioned over any given track. The tracks are similar to the grooves in a record, but they are not connected in a spiral. Much like playing a record, the diskette is spun at a constant speed while the data is read from or written to its surface with the read/write head. Apple formats its diskettes into 35 tracks, numbered from 0 to 34, track 0 being the outermost track and track 34 the innermost. Figure 3.1 illustrates the concept of tracks, although they are invisible to the eye on a real diskette.

It should be pointed out, for the sake of accuracy, that the disk arm can position itself over 70 distinct locations or **phases**. To move the arm from one track to the next, two phases of the stepper motor which moves the arm must be cycled. This implies that data might be stored on 70 tracks, rather than 35. Unfortunately, the resolution of the read/write head is such that attempts to use these phantom **half** tracks create so much cross-talk that data is lost or overwritten. Although standard ProDOS uses only full tracks (even phases), some copy protected disks use half tracks (odd phases) or combinations of the two. This will work provided that no data is closer than two phases from other data. See APPENDIX B for more information on copy protection schemes.

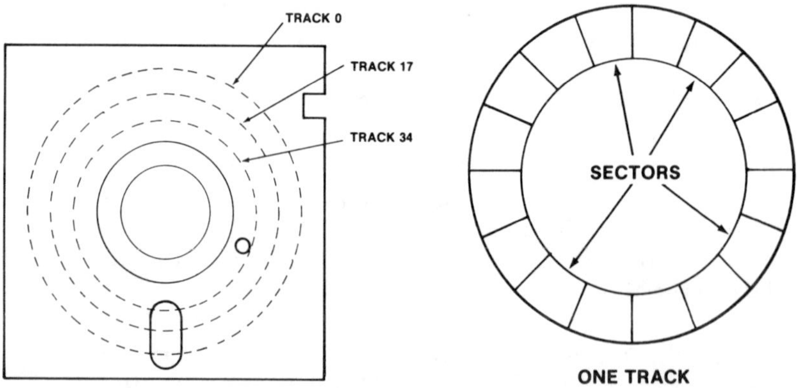

Figure 3.1 Tracks and Sectors

A **sector** is a subdivision of a track. It is the smallest unit of "updatable" data on the diskette. While ProDOS reads or writes data a block at a time (two sectors), the device driver operates on one sector at a time. This allows the device driver to use only a small portion of memory as a buffer during read or write operations. Apple has used two different track formats to date. The initial operating system divided the track into 13 sectors, but all recent operating systems use 16 sectors. The sectoring does not use the index hole, provided on most diskettes, to locate the first sector of the track. The implication is that the software must be able to locate any given track and sector with no help from the hardware. This scheme, known as **soft sectoring**, takes a little more space for storage but allows flexibility, as evidenced by the previous change from 13 sectors to 16 sectors per track. The following table categorizes the amount of data stored on a diskette under ProDOS. Both system and data diskettes are categorized.

DISKETTE ORGANIZATION	
TRACKS	35
SECTORS PER TRACK	16
SECTORS PER DISKETTE	560
BYTES PER SECTOR	256
BYTES PER DISKETTE	143,360
USABLE* BLOCKS FOR DATA STORAGE	
ProDOS System Diskette	221
ProDOS Data Diskette	273
USABLE* BYTES PER DISKETTE	
ProDOS System Diskette	113,152
ProDOS Data Diskette	139,776

*System Diskette includes PRODOS and BASIC.SYSTEM files only.

TRACK FORMATTING

Up to this point we have broken down the structure of data to the track and sector level. To better understand how data is stored and retrieved, we will start at the bottom and work up.

As this manual is about software (ProDOS), we will deal primarily with the function of the hardware rather than explain how it performs that function. For example, while data is in fact stored as a continuous stream of analog signals, we will deal with discrete **digital** data, i.e. a "0" or a "1". We recognize that the hardware converts analog data to digital data, but how this is accomplished is beyond the scope of this manual. For a full and detailed explanation of the hardware, please refer to Jim Sather's excellent book, *Understanding the Apple II*, published by Quality Software.

Data bits are recorded on the diskette in precise intervals. The hardware recognizes each of these intervals as either a "0" or a "1" We will define these intervals to be **bit cells**. A bit cell can be thought of as the distance the diskette moves in four machine cycles, which is about four microseconds. Using this representation, data written on and read back from the diskette takes the form shown in Figure 3.2. The data pattern shown represents a binary value of 101.

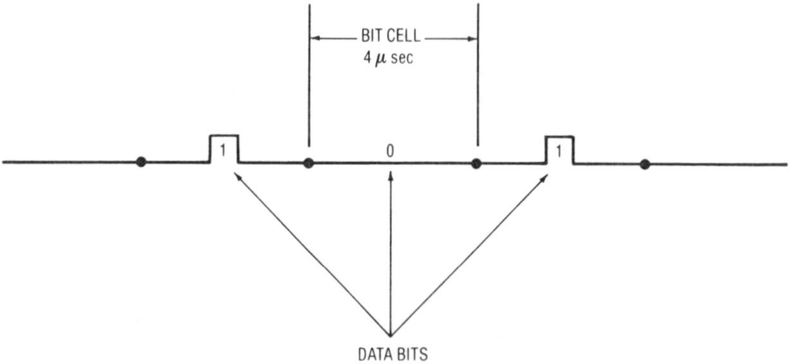

Figure 3.2 Bits on Diskette

A byte as recorded on the disk consists of eight (8) consecutive bit cells. The **most significant bit** cell is usually referred to as bit cell 7, and the **least significant** is **bit** cell 0. When reference is made to a specific data bit (i.e. data bit 5), it is with respect to the corresponding bit cell (bit cell 5). Data is written and read serially, one bit at a time. Thus, during a write operation, bit cell 7 of each byte is written first, and bit cell 0 is written last. Correspondingly, when data is being read back from the diskette, bit cell 7 is read first and bit cell 0 is read last. Figure 3.3 illustrates the relationship of the bits within a byte.

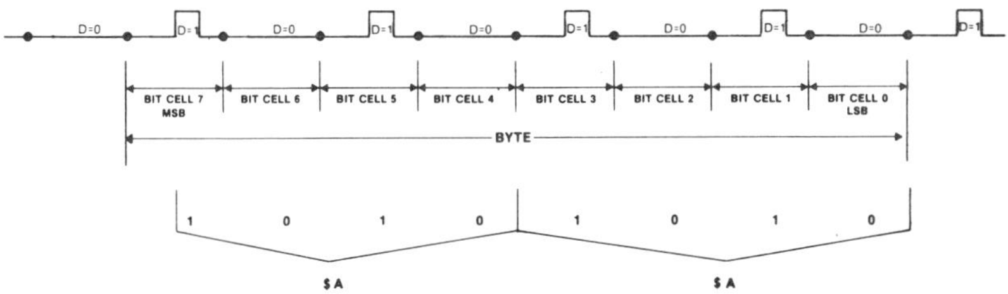

Figure 3.3 One Byte on Diskette

To graphically show how bits are stored and retrieved, we must take certain liberties. The diagrams are a representation of what functionally occurs within the disk drive. For the purposes of our presentation, the hardware interface to the diskette will be represented as an 8-bit **data register**. Since the hardware involves considerably more complication, from a software standpoint it is reasonable to use the data register, as it accurately embodies the function of data flow to and from the diskette. For a further discussion of the hardware, please see APPENDIX D.

Figure 3.4 shows the three bits, 101, being read from the diskette data stream into the data register. Of course another five bits would be read to fill the register.

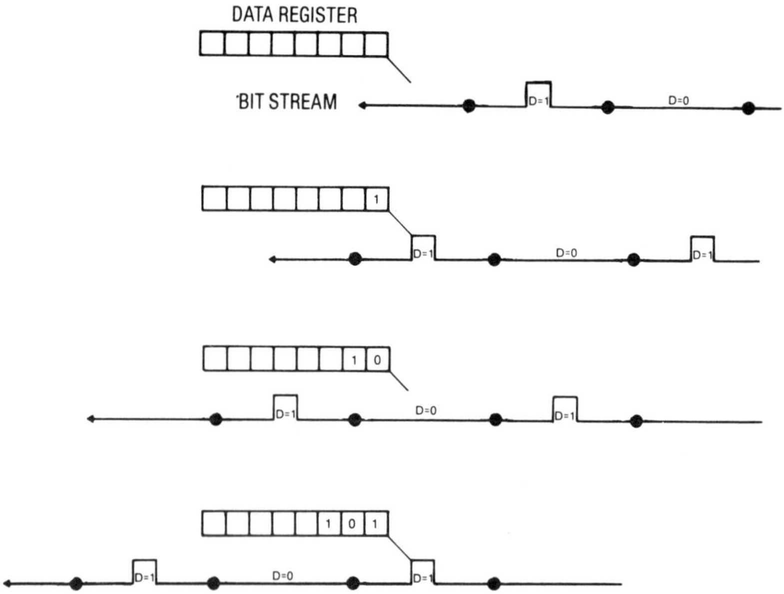

Figure 3.4 Reading Data from a Diskette

Writing data can be depicted in much the same way (see Figure 3.5). It should be noted that, while in write mode, zeroes are being brought into the data register to replace the data being written. It is the task of the software to make sure that the register is loaded and instructed to write in 32-cycle (microsecond) intervals. If not, zero bits will continue to be written every four cycles, which is in fact exactly how self-sync bytes are created. Self-sync bytes will be covered in detail shortly.

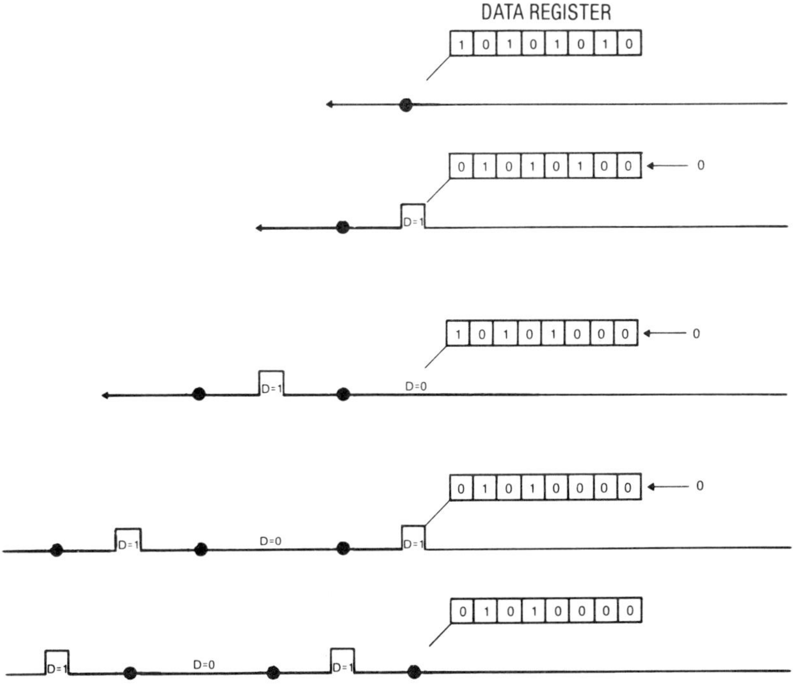

Figure 3.5 Writing Data to a Diskette

A **field** is made up of a group of consecutive bytes. The number of bytes varies, depending upon the nature of the field. The two types of fields present on a diskette are the **Address Field** and the **Data Field**. They are similar in that they both contain a prologue, a data area, a checksum, and an epilogue. Each field on a track is separated from adjacent fields by a number of bytes. These areas of separation are called **gaps** and are provided for two reasons. First, they allow the updating of one field without affecting adjacent fields (on the Apple, only data fields are updated). Secondly, they allow the computer time to decode the address field before the corresponding data field can pass beneath the read/write head.

All gaps are primarily alike in content, consisting of self-sync hexadecimal FF's, and vary only in the number of bytes they contain. Figure 3.6 is a diagram of a portion of a typical track, broken into its major components.

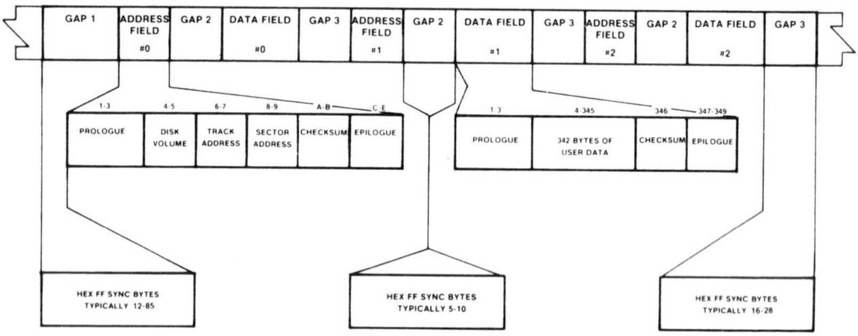

Figure 3.6 Track Format

Self-sync or auto-sync bytes are special bytes that make up the three different types of gaps on a track. They are so named because of their ability to automatically bring the hardware into synchronization with data bytes on the disk. The difficulty in doing this lies in the fact that the hardware reads bits, and the data must be stored as 8-bit bytes. It has been mentioned that a track is literally a continuous stream of data bits. In fact, at the bit level, there is no way to determine where a byte starts or ends, because

Down By The Old Bit Stream

each bit cell is exactly the same, written in precise intervals with its neighbors. When the drive is instructed to read data, it will start wherever it happens to be on a particular track. That could be anywhere among the 50,000 or so bits on a track. The hardware finds the first bit cell with data in it and proceeds to read the following seven data bits into the 8-bit register. In effect, it assumes that it had started at the beginning of a data byte. Of course, in reality, it could have started at any of the "1" bits of the byte. Pictured in Figure 3.7 is a small portion of a track.

0 1 1 0 1 0 1 1 1 0 1 0 1 1 0 0 1 1 1 1 0 1 1 0 1 1 1 0 1 0 1

Figure 3.7 An Example Bit Stream on the Diskette

From looking at the data, there is no way to tell what bytes are represented, because we don't know where to start. This is exactly the problem that self-sync bytes overcome.

A **self-sync byte** is defined to be a hexadecimal FF with a special difference. It is, in fact, a 10-bit byte rather than an 8-bit byte. Its two extra bits are zeroes. Figure 3.8 shows the difference between a normal data hex FF that might be found elsewhere on the disk and a self-sync hex FF byte.

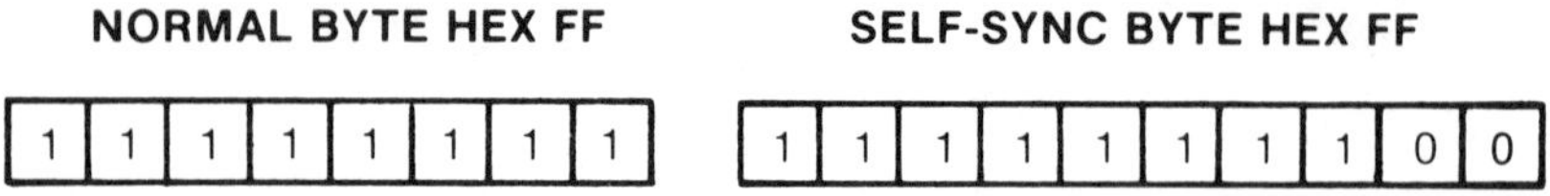

Figure 3.8 Comparison Between a Normal Byte and a Self-Sync Byte

A self-sync byte is generated by using a 40-cycle (microsecond) loop while writing an FF. A bit is written every four cycles, so two of the zero bits brought into the data register while the FF was being written are also written to the disk, making the 10-bit byte. It can be shown, using Figure 3.9, that four self-sync bytes are sufficient to guarantee that the hardware is reading valid data. The reason for this is that the hardware requires the first bit of a byte to be a "1". Pictured at the top of the figure is a stream of four self-sync bytes followed by a normal FF. Each row below that demonstrates what the hardware will read should it start reading at any given bit in the first byte. In each case, by the time the four sync bytes have passed beneath the read/write head, the hardware will be **synced** to read the data bytes that follow. As long as the disk is left in read mode, it will continue to correctly interpret the data unless there is an error on the track.

Figure 3.9 Self-Sync Bytes

We can now discuss the particular portions of a track in detail. The three gaps will be covered first. Unlike some other disk formats, the size of the three gap types will vary from drive to drive and even from track to track. During the formatting process, ProDOS will start with large gaps and keep making them smaller until an entire track can be written without overlapping itself. A minimum number of self-sync bytes is maintained for each gap type. The result is fairly uniform gap sizes within each particular track.

Gap 1 is the first data written to a track during initialization. Its purpose is twofold. The gap originally consists of 128 self-sync bytes, a large enough area to insure that all portions of a track will contain data. Since the speed of a particular drive may vary, the total length of the track in bytes is uncertain, and the percentage occupied by data is unknown. The initialization process is set up, however, so that even on drives of differing speeds, the last data field written will overlap Gap 1, providing continuity over the entire physical track. Unlike earlier operating systems, ProDOS will let you know if your drive is too fast or too slow. The remaining portion of Gap 1 must be approximately 75% as long as a Gap 3 on that track, enabling it to serve as a Gap 3 type for Address Field number 0 (See Figure 3.6 for clarity).

Gap 2 appears after each Address Field and before each Data Field. Its primary purpose is to provide time for the information in an Address Field to be decoded by the computer before a read or write takes place. If the gap was too short, the beginning of the Data Field might spin past while ProDOS was still determining if this was the sector to be read. The 200 cycles that five self-sync bytes provide seems ample time to decode an Address Field. When a Data Field is written, there is no guarantee that the write will occur in exactly the same spot each time. This is due to the fact that the drive which is rewriting the Data Field may not be the one which originally formatted or wrote it. Since the speed of the drives can vary, it is possible that the write could start in mid-byte (see Figure 3.10). For this reason, the length of Gap 2 varies from five to ten bytes. This is not a problem as long as the difference in positioning is not great. To insure the integrity of Gap 2 when writing a data field, five self-sync bytes are written prior to writing the Data Field itself. This serves two purposes. Since

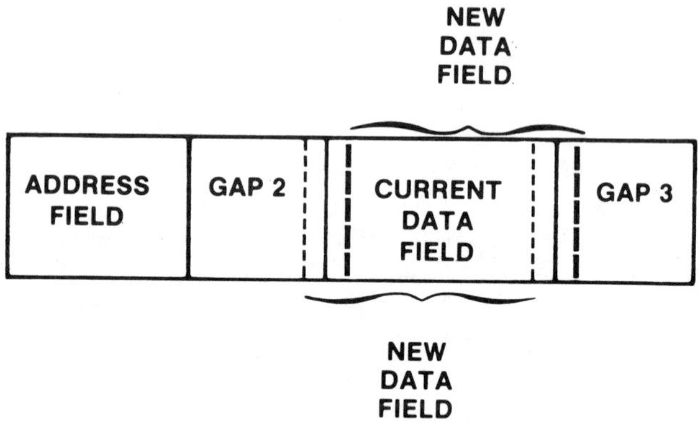

Figure 3.10 ProDOS Doesn't Always Write in the Same Place

relatively little time is spent decoding an address field, the five bytes help place the Data Field near its original position. Secondly, and more importantly, the five self-sync bytes are the minimum number required to guarantee read-synchronization. It is probable that, in writing a Data Field, at least one sync byte will be destroyed. This is because, just as in reading bits on the track, the write may not begin on a byte boundary, thus altering an existing byte. Figure 3.11 illustrates this.

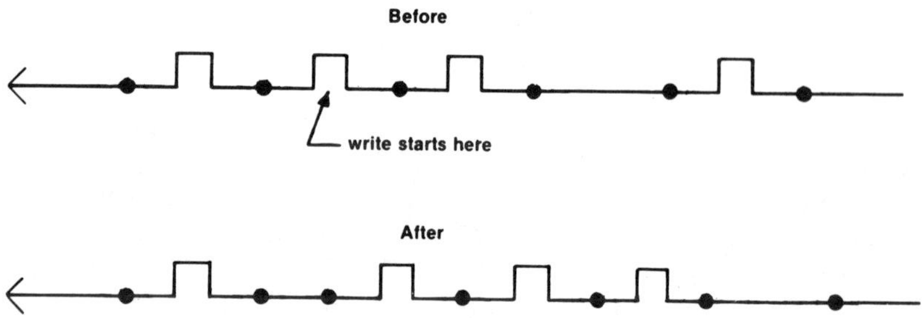

Figure 3.11 Writing Out of Sync

Gap 3 appears after each Data Field and before each Address Field. It is longer than Gap 2 and care is taken to make sure it ranges from 16 to 28 bytes in length. It is quite similar in purpose to Gap 2. Gap 3 allows the additional time needed to manipulate the data that has been read before the next sector is to be read. The length of Gap 3 is not as critical as that of Gap 2. If the following Address Field is missed, ProDOS can always wait for the next time it spins around under the read/write head (one revolution of the disk at most). Since Address Fields are never rewritten, there is no problem with Gap 3 providing synchronization, since only the first part of the gap can be overwritten or damaged (see Figure 3.10 for clarity).

ADDRESS FIELDS

An examination of the contents of the two types of fields is in order. The Address Field contains the **address** or identifying information about the Data Field which follows it. The volume, track, and sector number of any given sector can be thought of as its "address," much like a country, city, and street number might identify a house. As shown previously in Figure 3.6, there are a number of components which make up the Address Field. A more detailed illustration is given in Figure 3.12.

PROLOGUE	VOLUME	TRACK	SECTOR	CHECKSUM	EPILOGUE
D5 AA 96	XX YY	XX YY	XX YY	XX YY	DE AA EB

Figure 3.12 Address Field

Each byte of the Address Field is encoded into two bytes when written to the disk. APPENDIX C describes the "4 and 4" method used for Address Field encoding.

The **prologue** consists of three bytes which form a unique sequence, found in no other component of the track. This fact enables ProDOS to locate an Address Field with almost no possibility of error. The three bytes are $D5, $AA, and $96. The $D5 and $AA are reserved (never written as data), thus insuring the uniqueness of the prologue. The $96, following this unique string, indicates that the data following constitutes an Address Field (as opposed to a Data Field). The address information follows next, consisting of the **volume***, **track**, and **sector** number and a checksum. This information is absolutely essential for ProDOS to know where it is positioned on a particular diskette. The **checksum** is computed by exclusive-ORing the first three pieces of information, and is used to verify its integrity. Lastly follows the **epilogue**, which contains the three bytes $DE, $AA and $EB. The $EB is only partly written during initialization, and is therefore never verified when an Address Field is read. The epilogue bytes are sometimes referred to as **bit-slip marks**, which provide added assurance that the drive is still in sync with the bytes on the disk. These bytes are probably unnecessary, but do provide a means of double checking.

DATA FIELDS

The other field type is the Data Field. Much like the Address Field, it consists of a **prologue**, **data**, **checksum**, and an **epilogue** (refer to Figure 3.13). The prologue differs only in the third byte. The bytes are $D5, $AA, and $AD, which again form a unique sequence, enabling ProDOS to locate the beginning of the sector data. The data consists of 342 bytes of encoded data. (The encoding scheme used is quite complex and is documented in detail in APPENDIX C.) The data is followed by a checksum byte, used to verify the integrity of the data just read. The epilogue portion of the Data Field is absolutely identical to the epilogue in the Address Field and serves the same function.

Figure 3.13 Data Field

*Volume number is a leftover from earlier operating systems and is not used by ProDOS.

DISK II BLOCK AND SECTOR INTERLEAVING

Because the disk drive is such an integral part of the Apple II family of machines, it is important that it perform efficiently. One major factor in disk drive performance is how the data is arranged on the diskette. Because the diskette spins and the head that reads and writes the data is stationary, it is necessary to wait for a particular portion of a given track to pass by. This waiting (rotational delay) can add significant time to a disk access if the data is poorly arranged. **Interleaving** (or skewing) is the arranging of data at the block or sector level to maximize access speed. It effectively places a gap between blocks or sectors that will normally be accessed sequentially, allowing sufficient time for internal housekeeping before the next one appears. In general, if blocks or sectors are poorly arranged on a track, it is usually necessary to wait an entire revolution of the diskette before the next desired block or sector can be accessed.

The first versions of Apple's operating system used **physical interleaving** on the disk. (That is, sectors were written in a particular order on the diskette.) A number of different schemes were used in an attempt to maximize performance. This worked reasonably well but, because different methods were used for different operations, performance suffered. Later versions

standardized the physical interleaving (as sequential), and used a software method to try to maximize performance. An attempt was also made to standardize some operations, but performance still was not optimal as evidenced by a proliferation of "fast" DOS's.

ProDOS provides an impressive improvement over Apple's earlier operating systems. Several factors account for the dramatic improvement. The routine to read data is significantly faster, minimizing the delay occurring between read operations. The data is dealt with in larger pieces (512 bytes vs. 256 bytes), lowering the number of requests to the code that actually reads and writes data (Device Driver). And almost all operations involve files stored on sequential blocks. As a disk begins to get full, this will not always be possible and some files will be discontinuous; but for the most part, all operations (loading ProDOS or Applesoft BASIC, reading or writing to files or a directory) involve data in contiguous pieces. This greatly simplifies the problem of finding an optimal interleaving for disk accesses.

In ProDOS, the interleaving is done in software. The 16 sectors are in numerically ascending order on the diskette (0, 1, 2, . . . 15), and are not physically interleaved at all. An algorithm is used to translate block numbers into physical sector numbers used by the ProDOS device driver. For example, if the block number requested were 2, this would be translated to track 0, physical sectors 8 and A.* Figure 3.14 illustrates the concept of **software interleaving** and Table 3.1 shows the mapping of physical sectors to blocks for a Disk II or compatible drive.

There are two kinds of interleaving to consider in the case of ProDOS. First, there is the interleaving of the two sectors that make up a block. This will be referred to as **intra-block** or "within block" interleaving. Second, there is the interleaving between blocks on a given track. This will be referred to as **inter-block** or "between block" interleaving. It should be noted that we are concerned primarily with delays within ProDOS and the Disk II Device Driver, and not with delays that may be present in various application packages.

*Those familiar with DOS 3.3 should note that physical sector numbers and DOS 3.3 sector numbers are not the same. Most "disk utilities" use DOS 3.3 sector numbers and not physical sector numbers. The bottom of Table 3.1 shows how DOS 3.3 sector numbers are related to ProDOS block numbers.

Table 3.1 ProDOS Block Conversion Table for Diskettes

	PHYSICAL SECTOR							
	0&2	4&6	8&A	C&E	1&3	5&7	9&B	D&F
TRACK 0	000	001	002	003	004	005	006	007
TRACK 1	008	009	00A	00B	00C	00D	00E	00F
TRACK 2	010	011	012	013	014	015	016	017
TRACK 3	018	019	01A	01B	01C	01D	01E	01F
TRACK 4	020	021	022	023	024	025	026	027
TRACK 5	028	029	02A	02B	02C	02D	02E	02F
TRACK 6	030	031	032	033	034	035	036	037
TRACK 7	038	039	03A	03B	03C	03D	03E	03F
TRACK 8	040	041	042	043	044	045	046	047
TRACK 9	048	049	04A	04B	04C	04D	04E	04F
TRACK A	050	051	052	053	054	055	056	057
TRACK B	058	059	05A	05B	05C	05D	05E	05F
TRACK C	060	061	062	063	064	065	066	067
TRACK D	068	069	06A	06B	06C	06D	06E	06F
TRACK E	070	071	072	073	074	075	076	077
TRACK F	078	079	07A	07B	07C	07D	07E	07F
TRACK 10	080	081	082	083	084	085	086	087
TRACK 11	088	089	08A	08B	08C	08D	08E	08F
TRACK 12	090	091	092	093	094	095	096	097
TRACK 13	098	099	09A	09B	09C	09D	09E	09F
TRACK 14	0A0	0A1	0A2	0A3	0A4	0A5	0A6	0A7
TRACK 15	0A8	0A9	0AA	0AB	0AC	0AD	0AE	0AF
TRACK 16	0B0	0B1	0B2	0B3	0B4	0B5	0B6	0B7
TRACK 17	0B8	0B9	0BA	0BB	0BC	0BD	0BE	0BF
TRACK 18	0C0	0C1	0C2	0C3	0C4	0C5	0C6	0C7
TRACK 19	0C8	0C9	0CA	0CB	0CC	0CD	0CE	0CF
TRACK 1A	0D0	0D1	0D2	0D3	0D4	0D5	0D6	0D7
TRACK 1B	0D8	0D9	0DA	0DB	0DC	0DD	0DE	0DF
TRACK 1C	0E0	0E1	0E2	0E3	0E4	0E5	0E6	0E7
TRACK 1D	0E8	0E9	0EA	0EB	0EC	0ED	0EE	0EF
TRACK 1E	0F0	0F1	0F2	0F3	0F4	0F5	0F6	0F7
TRACK 1F	0F8	0F9	0FA	0FB	0FC	0FD	0FE	0FF
TRACK 20	100	101	102	103	104	105	106	107
TRACK 21	108	109	10A	10B	10C	10D	10E	10F
TRACK 22	110	111	112	113	114	115	116	117
	0&E	D&C	B&A	9&8	7&6	5&4	3&2	1&F
	DOS 3.3 SECTOR							

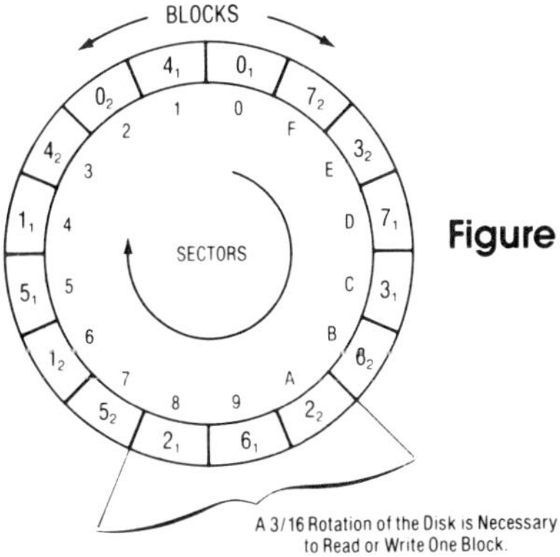

Figure 3.14 Block Interleaving (Track 0)

INTRA-BLOCK INTERLEAVING

When ProDOS accesses a block, it must of course access the two sectors that make up that block. There is a small delay after the device driver has accessed the first sector, before it can access the second sector. This delay is different for Read and Write operations. The Read operation is so fast that the disk can read two sectors in a row. However, the Write operation takes longer, so for optimal performance there must be a gap between the two sectors that make up a block. If there wasn't a gap, an entire revolution of the diskette would be required for each block written. A single sector provides a sufficient gap, so intra-block interleaving (within the block) consists of **one sector**. The result is that ProDOS is able to write to a given block as rapidly as is possible. Some time is lost when reading a block, but no other interleaving scheme would provide the same overall efficiency. Intra-block interleaving is illustrated in Figure 3.15.

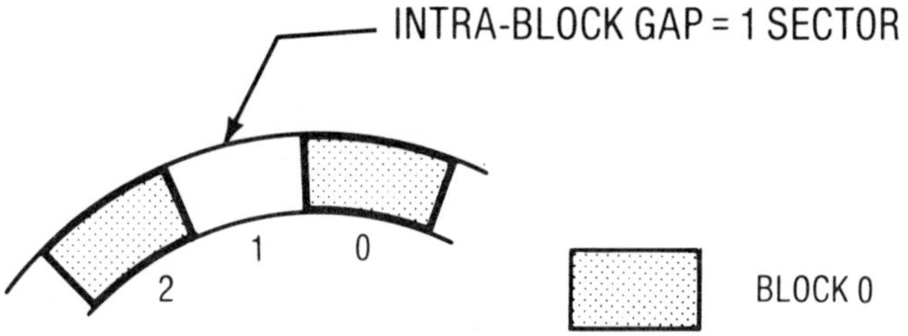

Figure 3.15 Intra-Block Interleaving (Within Block)

INTER-BLOCK INTERLEAVING

When ProDOS accesses a number of blocks as required in most disk operations (i.e. reading or writing a directory or a file), another kind of interleaving is involved. There will be a delay between accesses, but it is now between blocks rather than sectors. There is relatively little difference in delay time in the MLI itself between reading and writing—almost all the difference occurs in the device driver. However, when ProDOS writes a block that is already allocated (i.e. part of an existing directory or file), it always reads that block before writing to it. This requires an entire revolution of the diskette regardless of how the interleaving is done. It turns out that, just as for intra-block operations, a **single sector** is a sufficient gap for reading blocks. Inter-block interleaving is illustrated in Figure 3.16.

READING OR WRITING A BLOCK

Assume that we wish to access block 2. ProDOS passes the request to the device driver which in turn converts the block number into its track and sector representation (see Figure 3.14). The arm is moved to the proper track (0) and then a sector is read. This could be any sector, because the diskette is spinning. Sectors are continually read until sector 8 is found. The following two sectors are then read (9 and A) which completes the read of block 2 (sectors 8 and A). Depending on where we start on the track, we could read between 3 and 18 sectors. The same process occurs when writing a single block, with one small difference. After sector 8 is located and written to, the delay required to ready the data for sector A will cause us to miss reading sector 9. This does not alter the amount of rotation necessary to complete the task. To summarize, the time required to either read or write a single block consists of two factors. (We are assuming the track has already been located). First, there is the time required to **locate** the first sector of the block—this is variable and ranges between 0 and the time of one full rotation of the diskette. Second is the time required to actually **read or write** the two sectors that make up the block—this is fixed and always requires 3/16 rotation of the diskette.

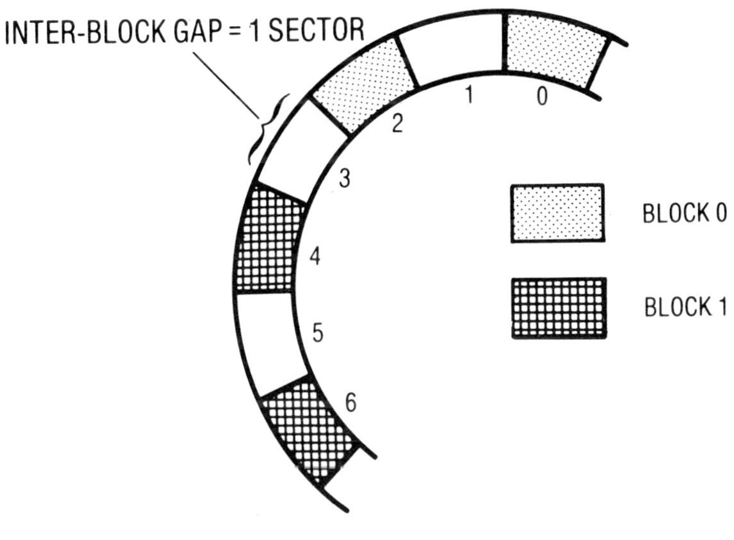

Figure 3.16 Inter-Block Interleaving (Between Block)

READING OR WRITING CONSECUTIVE BLOCKS

Let's examine what occurs when a number of blocks are accessed during reading or writing of a typical file. We will assume the file is reasonably large and takes up a number of blocks. We will confine our observation to a single track, in which eight blocks comprise the file of interest. We will assume track 2, which contains blocks 10 through 17 (as in Figure 3.17), and we will further assume that the blocks will be accessed sequentially. When the read/write head moves to track 2, we will start reading sectors until the appropriate sector is found (0 in this case). Then each sector is read until all eight blocks are found. This will require exactly **two revolutions** of the disk. Writing takes significantly longer because each block is read before being written to. Therefore, once the first sector of the block in question is located, one entire revolution is necessary to write each block. Upon writing a block, ProDOS is able to locate the next block immediately, read it, wait through one revolution and write it. A total of **ten revolutions** is required to write an entire track as opposed to two revolutions to read it.

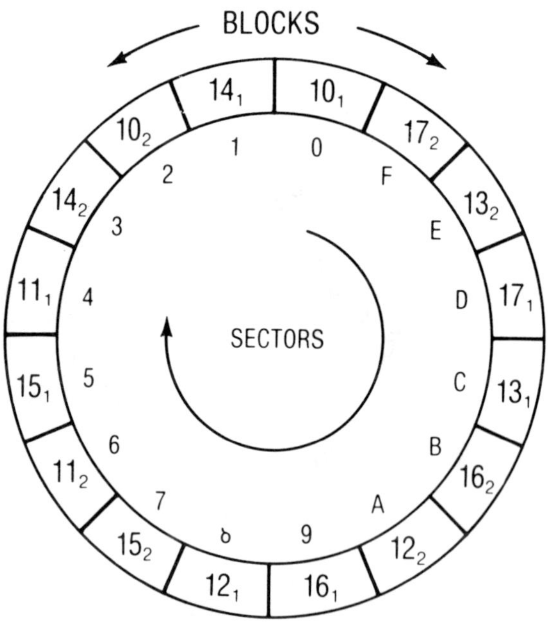

Figure 3.17 Example: The Block Interleaving of Track 2

CHAPTER 4

VOLUMES, DIRECTORIES, AND FILES

As was described in Chapter 3, a 16-sector diskette consists of 560 data areas of 256 bytes each, called sectors. These sectors are arranged on the diskette in 35 concentric rings, called tracks, of 16 sectors each. The way ProDOS allocates these tracks of sectors is the subject of this chapter.

THE DISKETTE VOLUME

ProDOS defines a **volume** to be any (usually direct access) individual mass storage media. The discussion which follows assumes this media to be a single 35-track diskette, but all of the structures presented here are identical for other diskette sizes and even for a hard disk such as the Apple ProFile. Another interesting point is that the structure of a ProDOS volume is almost identical to that of an Apple III SOS volume. This fact allows greater data compatibility between the two operating systems.

To make the allocation of sectors more manageable, ProDOS pairs them up to form 512-byte **blocks**. Since there are 16 sectors per track and 560 sectors per diskette volume, there are eight blocks per track and 280 blocks per volume. These blocks are numbered from 0 to 279 (decimal) or $0000 to $0117 (hexadecimal). The arrangement of blocks on a diskette is shown in Figure 4.1. Of course, on a real diskette, skewing (discussed in Chapter 3) would reorder the blocks on any given track, but, for the purposes of this discussion, the blocks can be assumed to be stored sequentially.

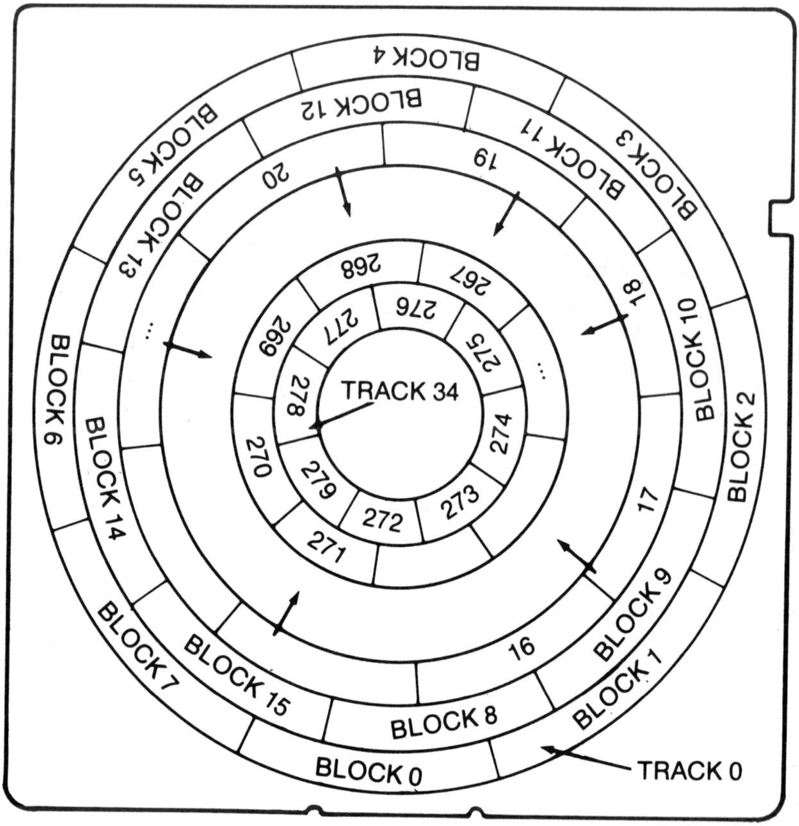

Figure 4.1 Blocks on a Diskette

A file, be it BAS, BIN, TXT, or SYS type, consists of one or more blocks containing data. Since a block is the smallest unit of allocatable space on a ProDOS volume, a file will use up at least one block even if it is less than 512 bytes long; the remainder of the block is wasted. Thus, a file containing 600 characters (or bytes) of data will occupy one entire block and 88 bytes of another with 424 bytes wasted. Knowing that there are 280 blocks on a diskette, one might expect to be able to use up to 280 times 512 or 143,360 bytes of space on a diskette for files. Actually, the largest file that can be stored is 271 blocks long (or 138,752 bytes). The reason for this is that some of the blocks on the diskette volume must be used for what is called **overhead**.

VOLUME OVERHEAD

Overhead blocks contain the image of the ProDOS bootstrap loader (which is loaded by the ROM on your diskette controller card and, in turn, loads the ProDOS system files into memory), a list of file names and locations of the files on the diskette, and an accounting of the blocks which are free for use by new files or for expansions of existing ones. An example of the way ProDOS uses blocks is given in Figure 4.2.

Notice that in the case of this diskette volume, system overhead (that part of the diskette which does not actually contain files) falls entirely on track 0 of the diskette (blocks 0 through 7). In fact, there is room for one block's worth of file data on track 0 (block 7). The first block (block 0) is always devoted to the image of the bootstrap loader. (Block 1 is the SOS bootstrap loader.) Following these, and always starting at block 2, is the **Volume Directory**. The Volume Directory is the "anchor" of the entire volume. On any diskette (or hard disk for that matter) for any version of ProDOS, the first or "key" block of the Volume Directory is always in the same place—block 2. Since files can end up anywhere on the diskette, it is through the Volume Directory key block that ProDOS is able to find them. Thus, just as the card catalog is used to locate a book in a library, the Volume Directory is the master index to all of the files on a volume. In addition to describing the name, attributes and placement of each file, it also contains the block number of the **Volume Bit Map** which will be described

```
/EXAMPLE

 NAME            TYPE  BLOCKS  MODIFIED          CREATED           ENDFILE SUBTYPE

 BASFILE          BAS       1  <NO DATE>         <NO DATE>             109
 TXTFILE          TXT       1  <NO DATE>         <NO DATE>               9 R=     64
 BINFILE          BIN       1  <NO DATE>         <NO DATE>              48 A=$03D0

BLOCKS FREE:  270      BLOCKS USED:    10     TOTAL BLOCKS:   280
```

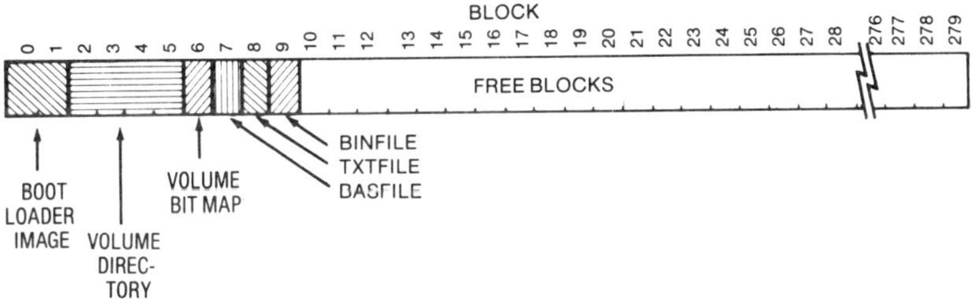

Figure 4.2 Block Usage on an Example Diskette

next. The first four bytes of every Volume Directory block are reserved for "pointers" to (the block numbers of) the previous Volume Directory block and the next Volume Directory block. This structure is called a doubly-linked list and is handy in that, from any block, it is easy to move forward or backward through the directory entries. The Volume Directory and Volume Bit Map are diagrammed in Figure 4.3.

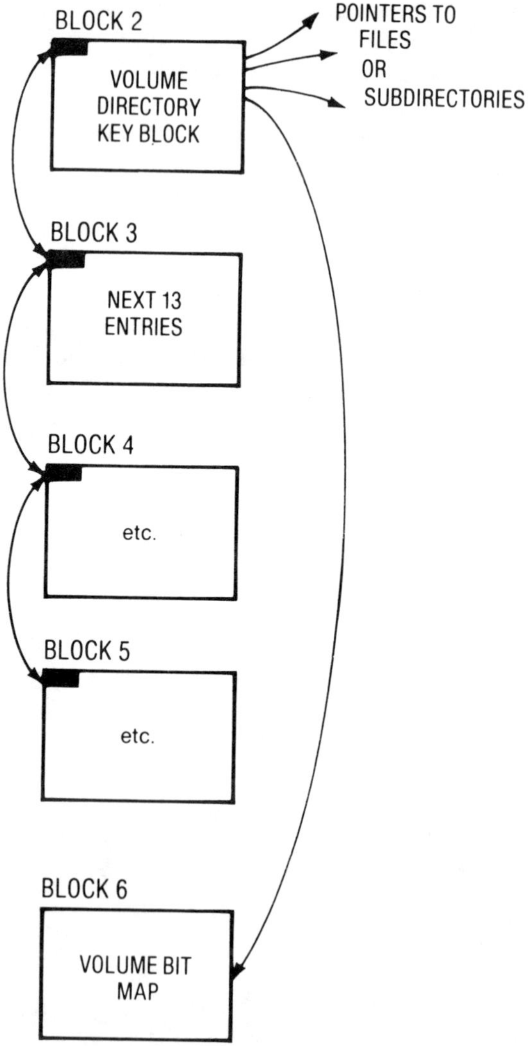

Figure 4.3 Linking of Volume Directory and Volume Bit Map

VOLUME SPACE ALLOCATION—THE VOLUME BIT MAP

When a diskette volume is first formatted, only the first seven blocks described above are marked in use. All of the remainder of the diskette blocks are considered "free" for use with files yet to be created. Each time a new block is required for a file, the free block with the lowest number is used. To keep track of which blocks have been used and which are free, ProDOS maintains one block as the Volume Bit Map. The Volume Bit Map is located by following a pointer in the Volume Directory, however, it is almost always in block 6. It consists of 512 bytes, each byte representing eight blocks on the volume. If the bytes are examined in binary form, each consists of eight bits having a value of one or zero. Thus, if block zero is in use as it always is, then the first byte's first bit is set to zero. If the ninth block (block 8) is free, then the first bit of the second byte is set to one. Since there are many more bits in the Volume Bit Map (4096 bits in all) than there could ever be blocks on a diskette, only the first 280 (or 35 bytes) are used. For a 5-megabyte hard disk, like the Apple ProFile, 1241 bytes are needed; in this case, since the number of blocks on the volume is stored in the Volume Directory, ProDOS automatically knows to expect a bigger Volume Bit Map—one which is three blocks long. Bits which do not correspond to a real block (because it would be past the end of the volume) are set to zero. An example of a Volume Bit Map for the volume mapped in Figure 4.2, is given in Figure 4.4. Notice that, since three 1-block files have been allocated, a total of ten blocks are marked "in use."

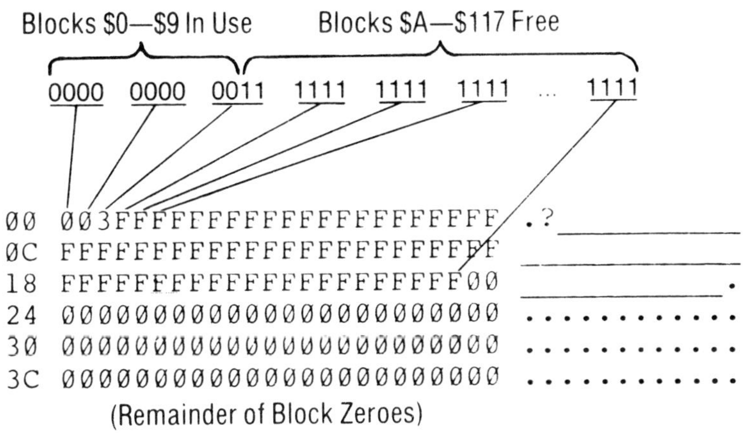

Figure 4.4 Example Volume Bit Map

THE VOLUME DIRECTORY

When ProDOS must find a specified file by name, it first reads block 2 of the diskette, the **key block** of the Volume Directory. If the file name is not found in this block, the next directory block is read, following the pointer in the third and fourth bytes of the current block. Typically, the Volume Directory blocks occupy blocks 2 through 5 of a volume. Of course, as long as a block number pointer exists, linking one block to the next, and the first Volume Directory block is block 2, ProDOS does not really care where the rest of the directory blocks are located. Figure 4.5 diagrams the Volume Directory for the example given in Figure 4.2. The figure shows the "next block" pointer (bytes +2 and +3 in the block) of block 2 in the Volume Directory, as an arrow pointing to block 3. Each block, in turn, has block numbers in the same relative location (+0,+1 and +2,+3) which point backward to the previous block and forward to the next block respectively. If no previous or next block exists, a block number of zero is used to indicate this (block 0, being part of the boot image, would never be a valid block number for a directory or file block, so this is a safe convention). The first block in the Volume Directory (the key block) contains a special entry called the **header** which describes the directory itself and the characteristics of the volume, etc. This is followed by 12 file descriptive

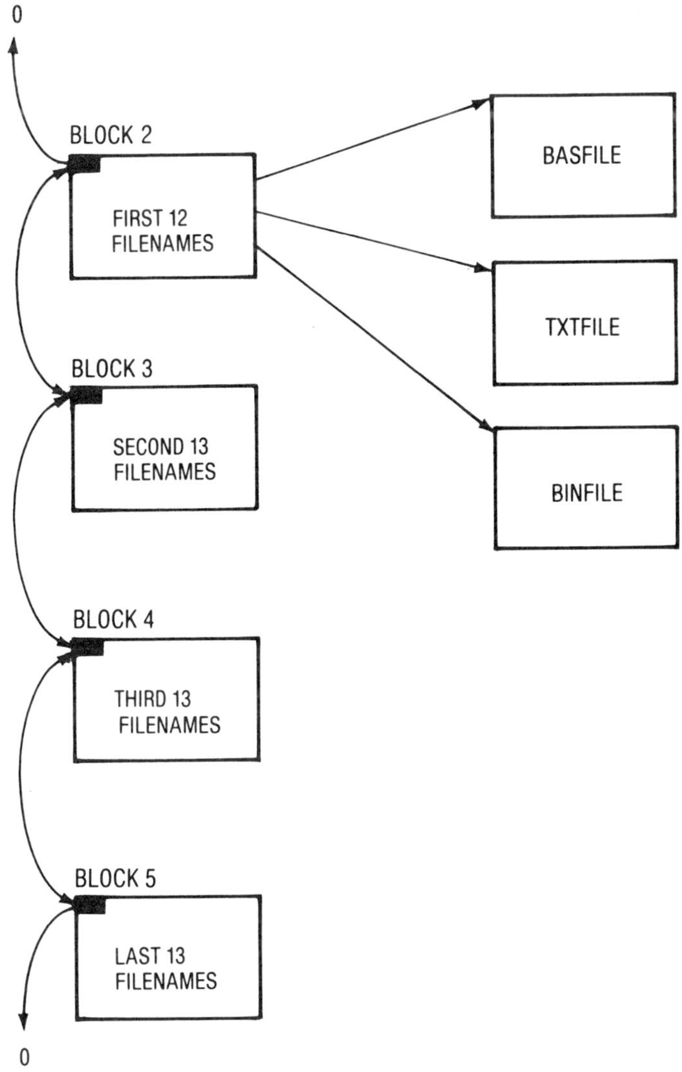

Figure 4.5 The Volume Directory

entries. All Volume Directory blocks other than the key block contain descriptions of up to 13 files each. (In practice, these entries can also be used to describe subdirectories, but this will be covered in detail later in the chapter.) Thus, with four Volume Directory blocks, a total of 4 times 13 less 1 (for the Volume Directory Header entry) or 51 files may be described.

THE VOLUME DIRECTORY HEADER

The Volume Directory Header is the first entry in the first block of the Volume Directory. As such, its first byte follows the four bytes of next/previous block pointers, so its first byte is at +$04. A description of its format follows:*

BLOCK BYTE	DESCRIPTION
$04	STORAGE_TYPE/NAME_LENGTH: The first nibble (top four bits) of this byte describes the type of entry. In this case, this is a Volume Directory Header so this nibble is $F. The low four bits are the length of the name in the next field (the volume name).
$05-$13	VOLUME_NAME: A 15-byte field containing the name of this volume. The actual length is defined by NAME_LENGTH above; the remainder of the field is ignored. No "/" is present as the first character since this is only used to delimit different level names but is not part of the names themselves.
$14-$1B	Reserved for future use. Usually zeroes.
$1C-$1F	CREATION: The date and time of the creation (formatting) of this volume. This field is zero if no date was assigned. The format of the field is as follows: BYTE 0 and 1—yyyyyyymmmmddddd year/month/day BYTE 2 and 3—000hhhhh00mmmmmm hours/minutes where each letter above represents one binary bit. This is the standard form for all create and modify date/time stamps in directories.
$20	VERSION: The ProDOS version number under which this volume was formatted. This field tells later versions of ProDOS not to expect to find any fields which were defined by Apple after this version of ProDOS was released. This field indicates the level of upward compatibility between versions. Under ProDOS 1.0, its value is zero.

*Unless otherwise indicated, all multiple byte numeric values, such as block numbers, EOF marks, etc., are stored least significant byte first, most significant byte last (LO/HI).

$21 MIN_VERSION: Minimum version of ProDOS which can access this volume. A value in this field implies that significant changes were made to the field definitions since prior versions of ProDOS were in use and these older versions would not be able to successfully interpret the file structure of this volume. This field indicates the level of downward compatibility between versions. Under ProDOS 1.0, its value is zero.

$22 ACCESS: The bits in the flag byte define how the directory may be accessed. The bit assignments are as follows:

$80 — Volume may be destroyed (reformatted)
$40 — Volume may be renamed
$20 — Volume directory has changed since last backup
$02 — Volume directory may be written to
$01 — Volume directory may be read

All other bits are reserved for future use.

$23 ENTRY_LENGTH: Length of each entry in the Volume Directory in bytes (usually $27).

$24 ENTRIES_PER_BLOCK: Number of entries in each block of the Volume Directory (usually $0D). Note that the Volume Directory Header is considered to be an entry.

$25-$26 FILE_COUNT: Number of active entries in the Volume Directory. An active entry is one which describes a file or subdirectory which has not been deleted. This count does not include the Volume Directory Header. Note that this field's name is a bit misleading since the count also includes subdirectory entries.

$27-$28 BIT_MAP_POINTER: The block number of the first block of the Volume Bit Map described earlier. This value is usually 6.

$29-$2A TOTAL_BLOCKS: The total number of blocks on this volume. $0118 is for a 35-track diskette (280 decimal). This number may be used to compute the number of blocks in the Volume Bit Map as described earlier.

FILE DESCRIPTIVE ENTRIES

Each file (or subdirectory) on a volume has a File Descriptive Entry in the Volume Directory or another directory. These entries all have the same format:

BYTE OFFSET	DESCRIPTION
$00	STORAGE_TYPE/NAME_LENGTH: The first nibble (top four bits) of this byte describes the type of entry. Currently assigned values are: $0 = Deleted entry. Available for reuse $1 = File is a seedling (only one data block) $2 = File is a sapling (2 to 256 data blocks) $3 = File is a tree (257 to 32768 data blocks) $D = File is a subdirectory $E = Reserved for Subdirectory Header entry $F = Reserved for Volume Directory Header entry The low four bits are the length of the file or subdirectory name in the next field. When a file is deleted, a $00 is stored in this byte.
$01-$0F	FILE_NAME: A 15-byte field containing the name of this file. The actual length is defined by NAME_LENGTH above; the remainder of the field is ignored.
$10	FILE_TYPE: Primary file type. The hexadecimal value of this byte gives the file type as shown in the following table:

TYPE	NAME	DESCRIPTION
$00		Typeless file
$01	BAD	Bad block(s) file
$04	TXT	Text file (ASCII text, msb off)
$06	BIN	Binary file (8-bit binary image)
$0F	DIR	Directory file
$19	ADB	AppleWorks data base file
$1A	AWP	AppleWorks word processing file
$1B	ASP	AppleWorks spreadsheet file
$EF	PAS	ProDOS PASCAL file

$F0	CMD	ProDOS added command file
$F1-$F8		User defined file types 1 through 8
$FC	BAS	Applesoft BASIC program file
$FD	VAR	Applesoft stored variables file
$FE	REL	Relocatable object module file (EDASM)
$FF	SYS	ProDOS system file

All other types are either SOS file types or are reserved by Apple for future use. See reference page 1 at the back of the book for a complete list.

$11-$12 KEY_POINTER: The block number of the key block of the file. In the case of a seedling file, this is the block number of the only data block. For saplings, this is the block number of the index block. For tree files, this is the block number of the master index block. (More on these file structures later.) If the file is a subdirectory file, this is the block number of its first block.

$13-$14 BLOCKS_USED: The total number of blocks used by this file including index blocks and data blocks. If the file is a subdirectory, this is the number of directory blocks.

$15-$17 EOF: The location of the end of the file (EOF) as a 3-byte offset from the first byte. This can also be thought of as the length in bytes of a sequential file.

$18-$1B CREATION: The date and time of the creation of this file. This field is zero if no date was assigned. The format of the field is as follows:

BYTE 0 and 1—yyyyyyymmmmddddd year/month/day
BYTE 2 and 3—000hhhhh00mmmmmm hours/minutes

where each letter above represents one binary bit. This is the standard form for all create and modify date/time stamps in directories.

$1C VERSION: The ProDOS version number under which this file was created. This field tells later versions of ProDOS not to expect to find any fields which were defined by Apple after this version of ProDOS was released. This field indicates the level of upward compatibility between versions. Under ProDOS 1.0, its value is zero.

$1D MIN_VERSION: Minimum version of ProDOS which can access this file. A value in this field implies that significant changes were made to the file structure definition since prior versions of ProDOS were in use, and these older versions would not be able to successfully interpret the file structure of this file. This field indicates the level of downward compatibility between versions. Under ProDOS 1.0, its value is zero.

$1E ACCESS: The bits in this flag byte define how the file may be accessed. The bit assignments are as follows:

$80 —File may be destroyed
$40 —File may be renamed
$20 —File has changed since last backup
$02 —File may be written to
$01 —File may be read

All other bits are reserved for future use. An unlocked file's ACCESS is usually $C3. If a file is locked, ACCESS will be set to $01. Subdirectory files which have a non-zero FILE_COUNT field will be locked until all files described by them are deleted.

$1F-$20 AUX_TYPE: Auxiliary type field whose contents depend upon FILE_TYPE. Common uses are as follows:

TYPE	USE
TXT	Random access record length (L from OPEN)
BIN	Load address for binary image (A from BSAVE)
BAS	Load address for program image (when SAVEd)
VAR	Address of compressed variables image (when STOREd
SYS	Load address for system program (usually $2000)

$21-$24 LAST_MOD: Date and time at which file was last modified. This field is zero if no date was assigned. Format is identical to CREATION above.

$25-$26 HEADER_POINTER: Block number of the key block for the directory which describes this file.

Figure 4.6 is an example of a typical Volume Directory block for the example introduced with Figure 4.2. In this case, there are only three files on the diskette so only the first three directory entries are filled in. The remaining directory entries have never been used and contain zeroes.

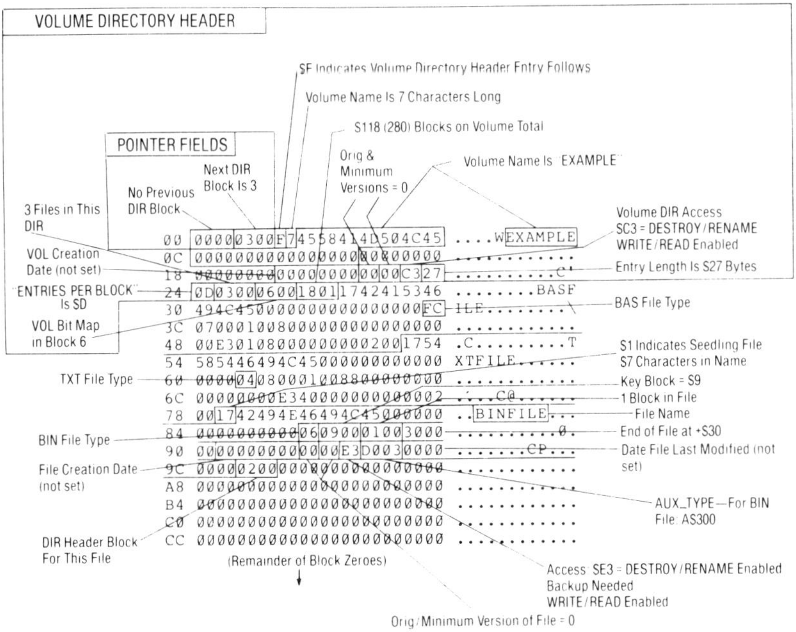

Figure 4.6 Example Volume Directory Block

FILE STRUCTURES

One of ProDOS's major jobs is to keep track of the blocks which make up a file. When programming, the user need never know that a file is actually made up of one or more blocks scattered far and wide all over the diskette volume. ProDOS must make the file appear to the programmer to be a continuous stream of sequential data.

So far the files shown in the examples here have had only one block. This was done to avoid complicating the discussion of the Volume Directory. In practice, however, very few files are 512 bytes or less in length. ProDOS defines three file structures to handle files of different sizes:

The Seedling —for files of 512 bytes or less
The Sapling —for files with more than 512 bytes but less than 128K bytes of data
The Tree —for files with more than 128K bytes of data up to 16 megabytes (16,777,216 bytes).

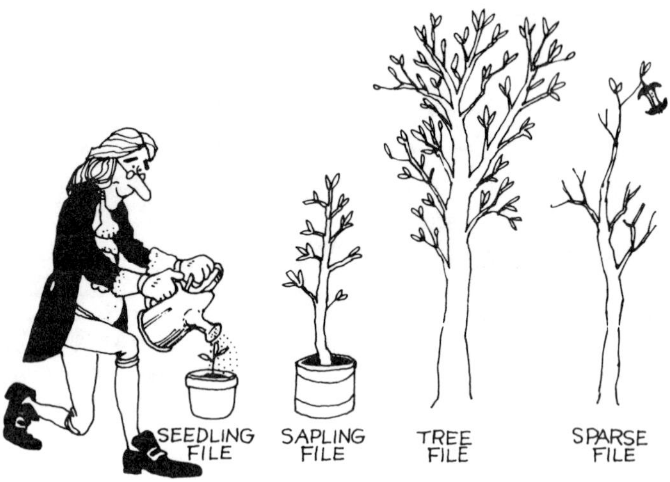

Examples of **seedling** files have already been shown. A seedling file consists of a single **data block** whose number is stored in the KEY_POINTER field in the file entry of the directory. Thus, a seedling file, by definition, costs only one block of storage (and a file descriptive entry).

For the purposes of this discussion, let us assume that we had run the following Applesoft BASIC program against our example disk volume from Figure 4.2.

```
10 PRINT CHR$(4);"OPEN TXTFILE,L64"
20 FOR I=0 TO 2
30 PRINT CHR$(4);"WRITE TXTFILE,R";I
40 PRINT "RECORD";I
50 NEXT I
60 PRINT CHR$(4);"CLOSE TXTFILE"
70 END
```

This program creates the TXT file, "TXTFILE", with a record length of 64 bytes. It then writes three records containing the strings "RECORD0", "RECORD1", and "RECORD2". The total size of this file is then 3 times 64 or 192 bytes. Since this is less than 512 bytes, the file is stored as a seedling.

Now, assume that statement 20 is changed to read:

```
20 FOR I=0 TO 100
```

and the program is rerun. The file it creates will now contain 101 records of 64 bytes each, so the total size is 6464 bytes. As the ninth record is written (RECORD8), ProDOS discovers that the original seedling block is full. There is no room in the directory to store another block number, so ProDOS creates what is called an **index block**. This block contains the block numbers of each data block in the file in the order that they should be accessed. Using an index block, ProDOS can describe the file in a sequential and orderly way, even though its data blocks may not be physically contiguous (next to one another on the diskette). For example, if the previous data block in a file was 47, it is not necessary to store the data which follows it in block 48. Instead, any free block located anywhere on the diskette may be used simply by placing its block number next to 47's in the index block.

Thus, in our example, a new block is allocated to be the index block ($A), another new block is allocated to be the second data block ($B), both the original data block's number and the new data block's number are placed in the new index block, and, finally, the directory entry for the file is updated so that it now points to the index block instead of the seedling data block. Of course, the STORAGE_TYPE field in the directory entry must also be changed to indicate that this is now a **sapling** file and is no longer a seedling. Index block entries which are not associated with any data block yet (such as those beyond the end of file position) are set to zeroes. Since a block is 512 bytes long and block numbers require a 2-byte field, this index block can store pointers to up to 256 data blocks representing up to 131,072 bytes of data (128K). Obviously, most files will fall within this class of file structure. A diagram of the general form of a sapling file is given in Figure 4.7.

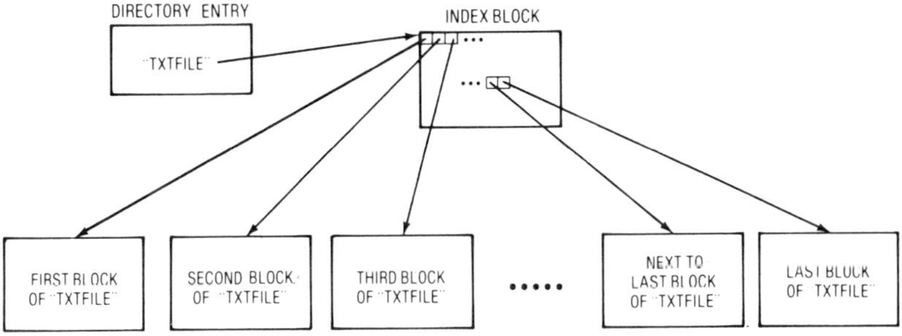

Figure 4.7 Sapling File Organization

The index block for TXTFILE is given in Figure 4.8. Notice that the first block of the file is still block 8, the original data block of the old seedling version of TXTFILE. Notice also that in an index block, the least significant byte of the block numbers are stored in the first half of the block, and the most significant byte (in this example all MSB's are $00) in the last half. This was done to simplify indexing into the block (the 6502 index registers can only index up to 256 bytes at a time). Thus, to find any given block, one

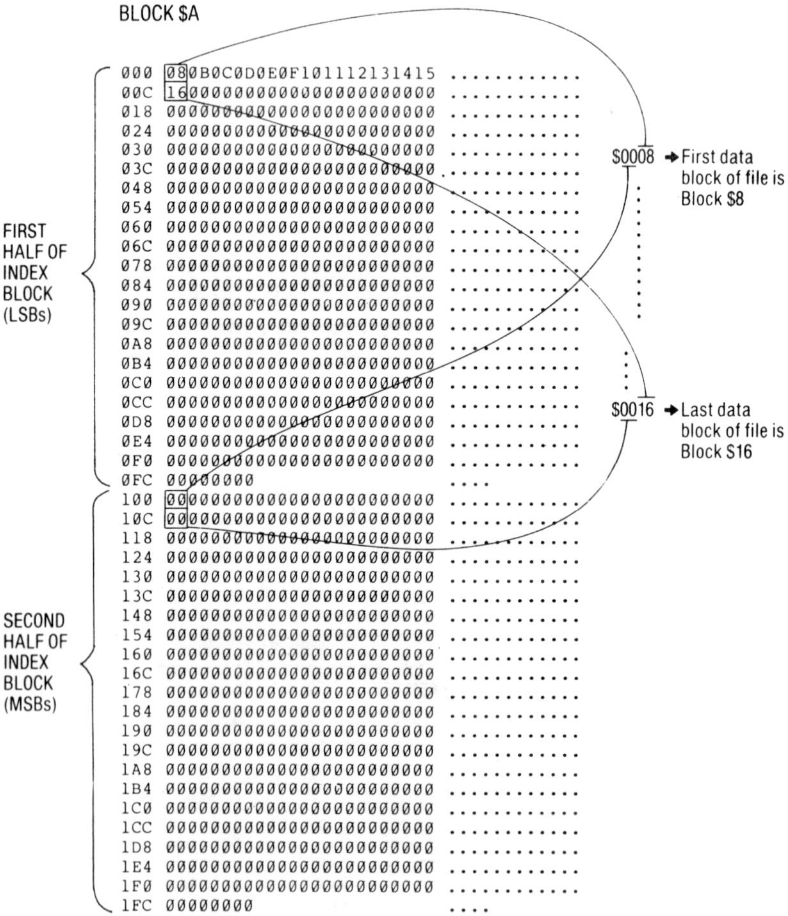

Figure 4.8 Example Sapling Index Block

must assemble a block number by picking the Nth byte and the N + 256th byte in the index block where N is the relative block desired.

Suppose that we now modify our program again so that 2144 records will be written. This pushes the total file size up to 137,216, more than can be described by a single index block. ProDOS must "promote" the file to the next level of the hierarchy, a **tree** file. A tree file consists of a single **master index block**, pointed to by the directory entry, which, in turn, contains the block numbers of two or more other index blocks. These lower level index blocks contain the actual data block numbers. This structure is diagrammed in Figure 4.9. Thus, since the master index block can describe 256 "subindex" blocks, and each subindex block can describe 256 data blocks, in principle this structure would support files of up to 32 megabytes! In order to limit block numbers to a 2-byte signed value of 32767, however, an arbitrary upper limit of 16 megabytes was imposed. In other words, a master index block can never be more than half full.

The entire file structure for TXTFILE is depicted in Figure 4.10. Note that the original index block of the sapling file (block $A) became the first subindex block of the tree file. Also, when the changeover was made, the master index block was allocated first

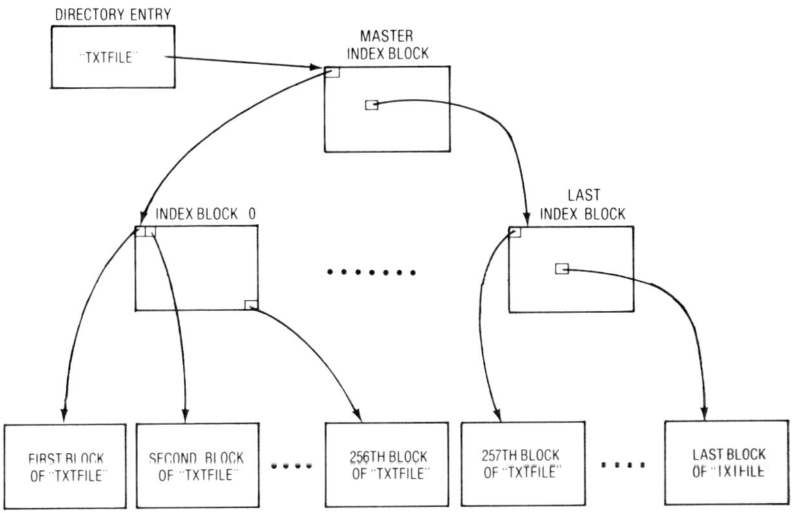

Figure 4.9 Tree File Organization

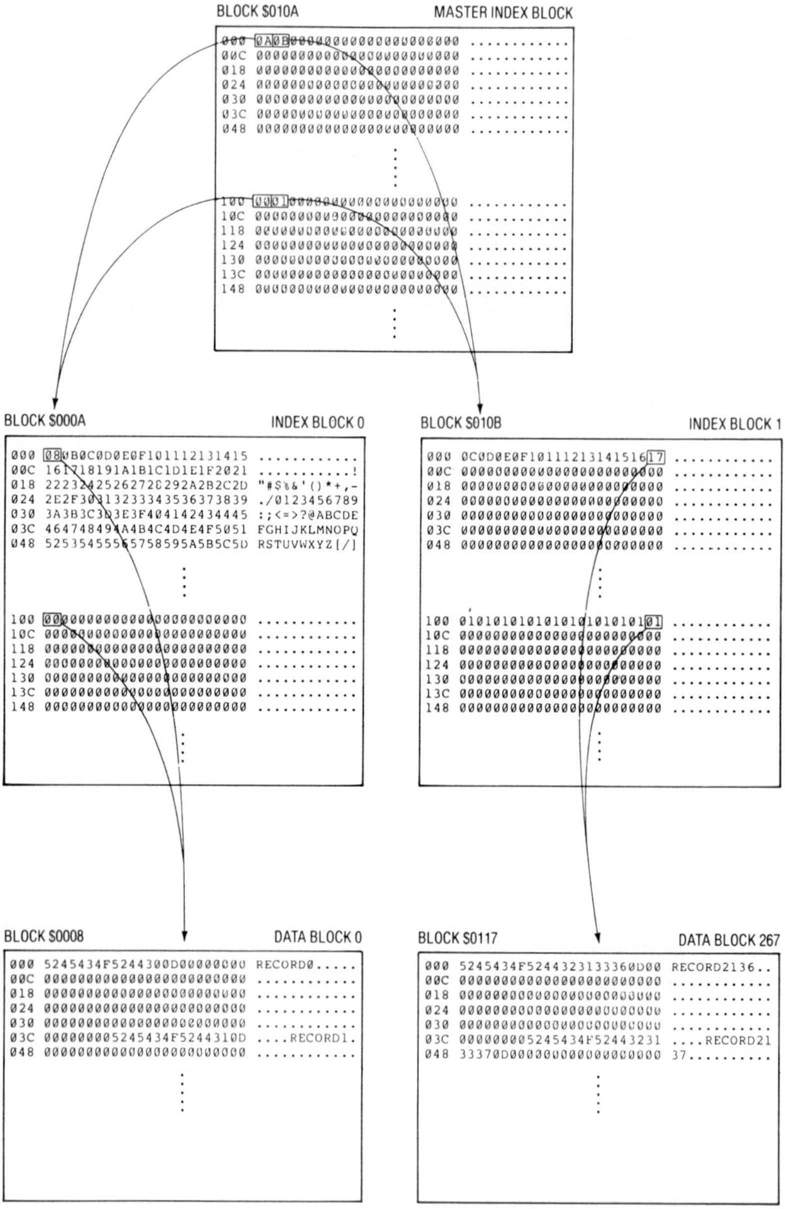

Figure 4.10 Example Tree File

($10A), then the second subindex block ($10B), and finally the data block whose allocation made the file into a tree file ($10C). The last block allocated is for RECORD2136 through RECORD2143 (for a total of 2144 records). This is the last block on the diskette ($117), and, since no blocks were ever freed, the diskette is now full. Although TXTFILE has only two subindex blocks and it is nearly as large as a diskette, this does not imply that all tree files will have two subindex blocks, as will become apparent when sparse files are discussed.

FILE DATA TYPES

Unless they are directories (DIR type files), all files conform to one of the three file structures described above even though the data in files may have different intended uses. A file might contain an Applesoft BASIC program which was SAVEd in addition to being a sapling file. It might be a binary memory image which was BSAVEd and conforms to the seedling structure. Or it might be data for a BASIC program in a TXT file and have the tree characteristic. File types, such as BAS, TXT, or SYS are less important to ProDOS than they are to the programs which use the files. This means that the basic structure of a BAS file is identical to that of a BIN file—only the interpretation of the data differs. ProDOS maintains a consistent set of file types by convention, and to a limited extent, the BASIC command interpreter enforces these conventions (e.g., "FILE TYPE MISMATCH"). You are not prevented, however, from storing an Applesoft BASIC program image in a TXT file if you really work at it!

TXT FILES

The TXT or text file in its **sequential** form is the least complicated file data type (in its random form it is, perhaps, the most complex). A sequential TXT file consists of one or more records, separated from each other by carriage return characters (hex $0D's). This structure is shown and an example file is given in Figure 4.11. Usually, the end of a TXT file is signaled by the End Of File (EOF) position stored in the directory entry for the file.

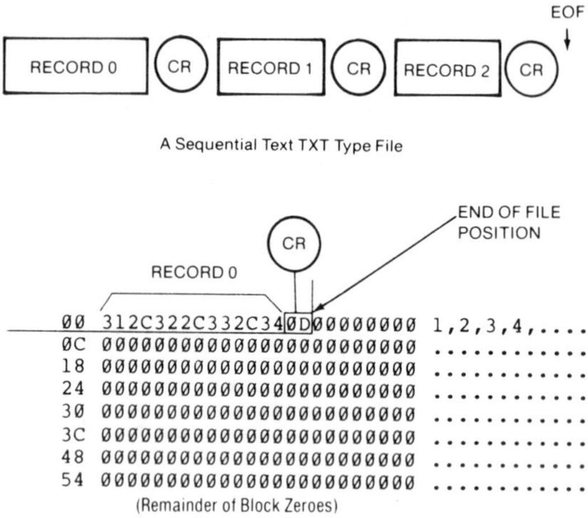

Figure 4.11 Example Sequential Text File Block

Since $0D is used to delimit records, carriage returns should not appear within a record. Usually, only valid ASCII characters are allowed in a TXT file to make them accessible to BASIC programs (i.e. printable text, numerics or special characters; refer to p. 8 of the *Apple II Reference Manual* or p. 16 of the *Apple II Reference Manual for IIe Only*). This restriction makes processing of a TXT file slower and less efficient in the use of disk space than with a BIN or VAR type file, since each digit must occupy a full byte in the file.

When TXT files are accessed **randomly**, or by record number, "holes" can appear between records. In the example given earlier and in Figure 4.12, each record is allotted 64 bytes of space in the file. By doing this, it is easy to find any record by multiplying its number by 64 and using this as a byte offset into the file. The record length is chosen as the maximum amount of space any record might occupy. Thus, records with less than 64 bytes of data, such as the ones in the example, will have wasted space at their end (filled, in this case, with $00s). This wasted space is called padding. The actual data in each record is terminated with a $0D (carriage return) just as in the sequential text file record (allowing BASIC to read it as a single INPUT line). In this way, data within a single record can be accessed as if it was a miniature sequential TXT file. If an attempt is made to sequentially read beyond into the padding, a null string is returned.

When the randomly organized file is OPENed, the record length given with the "L" keyword is stored in the AUX_TYPE field in the directory entry for the file. Then, if later OPENs omit this keyword, the original value can be supplied by ProDOS.

Notice that in the example in Figure 4.12, record 3 has not been initialized. Indeed, none of the other records following RECORD2 have anything but $00s in them. By WRITEing to specific records in a non-sequential order, it is possible to leave very large holes between records which contain data. Such files are called "sparse." If a hole falls within a block which has other records which contain data, it is represented by binary zeroes. But if the hole covers entire blocks, ProDOS does not bother to allocate them at all. There is no point in wasting disk space on holes! Thus, if the next record containing data in our example file was RECORD25, for instance, the

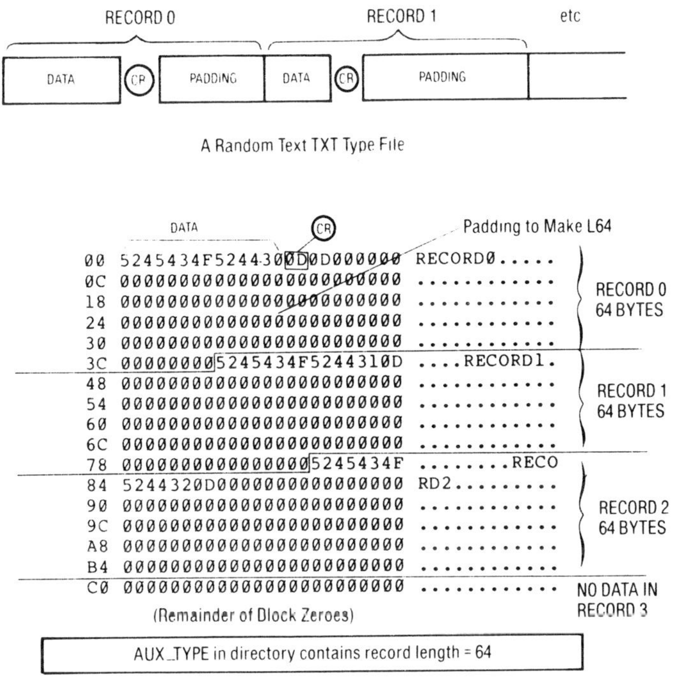

Figure 4.12 Example Random Text File Block

rest of block 0 would contain zeroes (as it does now), no block would be allocated for block 1 or block 2, and block 3 would contain zeroes until the position of RECORD25 was reached. This is diagrammed in Figure 4.13. Notice that the positions of the "phantom" blocks are marked in the file's index block with zeroes. Thus, although the file covers a "data space" of six blocks, only three data blocks are actually allocated. It is possible to create a file with only two data blocks which covers the entire 16-megabyte data space. Such a file would incorporate one master index block with an entry at +0 and at +7F. All the subindex blocks in between would be "phantom," or not allocated and marked with zero pointers. The first index block would contain a single entry at +0 for the first data block. And the last index block would contain a single entry at +FF for the last data block. A 16-megabyte file using only five blocks of disk space!

BIN FILES

The structure of a BIN type file is shown in Figure 4.14. An exact copy of the memory selected is written to the disk block(s). The original address from which the memory was copied is stored in the AUX_TYPE field of the directory entry for the file. The EOF position in the directory records the length of the binary image. These values are those given in the A and L (or E) keywords of the BSAVE command which created the file. ProDOS can be made to BLOAD or BRUN the binary image at a different address by specifying the A (address) keyword when the command is entered, or by changing the address in the directory entry (this is sometimes necessary if the file cannot be BSAVEd from the location where it will run, such as from the screen buffer).

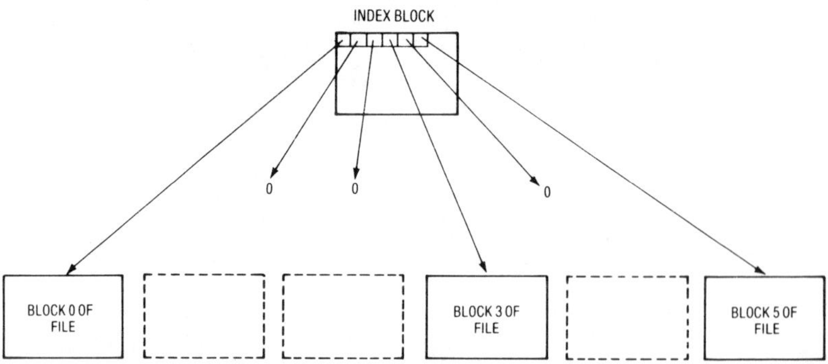

Figure 4.13 A Sparse File

MEMORY IMAGE...

A Binary BIN Type File

$30 Byte Binary Memory Image

```
ØØ 4CØØBE4CØØBEØØØØFFFFØØØØ L.>L.>..__..
ØC FFFFØØØØFFFFØØØØFFFFØØØØ __..__..__..
18 FFFFØØØØFFFFØØØØ59FAØØBE __..__..YZ.>
24 1B4CØ3BE4CØØBE4C59FFEBBF .L.>L.>LY_K?   ——EOF: Marks End of Binary Image
3Ø ØØØØØØØØØØØØØØØØØØØØØØØØ ............
3C ØØØØØØØØØØØØØØØØØØØØØØØØ ............
48 ØØØØØØØØØØØØØØØØØØØØØØØØ ............
54 ØØØØØØØØØØØØØØØØØØØØØØØØ ............
6Ø ØØØØØØØØØØØØØØØØØØØØØØØØ ............
6C ØØØØØØØØØØØØØØØØØØØØØØØØ ............
78 ØØØØØØØØØØØØØØØØØØØØØØØØ ............
84 ØØØØØØØØØØØØØØØØØØØØØØØØ ............
```

(Remainder of Block Zeroes)

AUX_TYPE in Directory Contains Address = $3D0
EOF in Directory Contains Length = $30

Figure 4.14 Example BIN File Block

BAS FILES

A BASIC program is saved to the diskette in a way that is nearly identical to BSAVE. The format of a BAS file is given in Figure 4.15. When the SAVE command is typed, the ProDOS BASIC command interpreter determines the location of the BASIC program in memory and its length by examining Applesoft's zero page addresses. An image of the program is written to the file and, again, the AUX_TYPE and EOF fields of the directory entry represent the address and length. Notice that the character representation of the program is somewhat garbled. This is because, in the interest of saving memory, BASIC "tokenizes" the program. Reserved BASIC words, such as PRINT, IF, END, or CHR$, are replaced with a single hexadecimal code value (set off from other characters by its most significant bit being forced on). A complete treatment of the appearance of a BASIC program in memory is outside of the scope of this manual, but a partial breakdown of the program in Figure 4.15 is given.

PROGRAM MEMORY IMAGE...

An Applesoft BAS Type File

```
10 PRINT CHR$(4);"OPEN TXTFILE,L64"
20 FOR I=0 TO 2
30 PRINT CHR$(4);"WRITE TXTFILE,R";I
40 PRINT "RECORD";I
50 NEXT I
60 PRINT CHR$(4);"CLOSE TXTFILE"
70 END
```

$BA = PRINT

Address of Next Line−1 | Line 10 | $E7 = CHR$ | (4); "O...etc.

```
00 1E080A00BAE72834293B224F ....:G(4);"O
0C 50454E2054585446494C452C PEN TXTFILE,
18 4C363422002908140081490 L64".)....IP
24 30C1320047081E00BAE72834 0A2.G...:G(4
30 293B2257524954452054585 4 );"WRITE TXT
3C 46494C452C52223B49005708 FILE,R";I.W.
48 2800BA225245434F5244223B (.:"RECORD";
54 49005E083200824900780 83C I..2..I.X.<
60 00BAE72834293B22434C4F53 .:G(4);"CLOS
6C 45205458544649 4C4522007E E TXTFILE".
78 084600800000000A00000000 .F..........
84 000000000000000000000000 ............
90 000000000000000000000000 ............
9C 000000000000000000000000 ............
A8 000000000000000000000000 ............
B4 000000000000000000000000 ............
C0 000000000000000000000000 ............
```

Applesoft Program Image

EOF: Marks End of Program Image

(Remainder of Block Zeroes)

AUX_TYPE in Directory Contains Program Start Address = $801
EOF in Directory Contains Program Length = $80

Figure 4.15 Example BAS File Block

OTHER FILE TYPES (VAR, REL, SYS)

Several other file types have been set aside by ProDOS. Many are those found in the SOS operating system (e.g. PCD, PTX, PDA for Pascal etc.). A complete list of file types may be found at the back of the book on reference page 1. Other ProDOS file types include BAD, PAS and CMD. BAD files are obviously intended to mark permanent I/O errors on a disk's surface from accidental use, but there seem to be no utilities within ProDOS which create them. The PAS file type is used to designate a PASCAL AREA on a ProDOS volume.The CMD file is a CI added command file.

AppleWorks file types, ADB, AWP, and ASP, are designed for

the AppleWorks Package, and their structures are specific to that package.

The VAR file type is used to store the contents of a BASIC program's variables using the STORE command. The ProDOS BASIC command interpreter compresses all of the strings together with the numeric variables and saves the resulting chunk of memory as a VAR file. The first five bytes of the file constitute a header which defines the memory image that follows:

VAR FILE HEADER

BYTE OFFSET	LENGTH	DESCRIPTION
+0	(2 bytes)	Combined length of simple and array variables.
+2	(2 bytes)	Length of simple variables only.
+4	(1 byte)	MSB of HIMEM when these variables were STOREd.
+5	(n bytes)	Start of memory image....

The AUX_TYPE field of the directory entry for the file contains the starting address from which the compressed variables were copied. EOF is an indication of the end of the image. When a RESTORE is later issued, the memory image is reloaded, the strings are separated from the rest of the variables, and, if necessary, string pointers are adjusted based on the new HIMEM value.

The REL file type is used with a special form of binary file, containing the memory image of a machine language program which may be relocated anywhere in memory based upon additional information stored with the image itself. Such a file is called a Relocatable Object Module file and is produced as output from the Apple Toolkit Assembler (EDASM). The format for this type of file is given in the documentation accompanying the assembler.

A SYS, or system file, is just like a BIN file except that it nearly always loads at $2000 and implies a reload of the command interpreter after it exits. SYS files are invoked with the "–", or smart RUN command, from the BASIC command interpreter. The interpreter closes all open files, frees all of the memory occupied by itself, and does a standard BRUN at $2000.

DIR FILES—PRODOS SUBDIRECTORIES

Since the Volume Directory has room for just 51 entries, without subdirectories, you would be limited to 51 files per volume. This may not seem to be much of a hardship on a diskette (although it might, since DOS 3.3 allows 105), but on a hard disk with 5 million bytes or more this limit is unthinkable. In order to create a more dynamic and flexible structure, the user is permitted to create subdirectories. A **subdirectory** can be thought of as an extension to the Volume Directory, but there is more to it than that. In the simplest case, a subdirectory is created and an entry which describes it is placed in the Volume Directory. The subdirectory has a structure very similar to the Volume Directory: it has a header entry located at its beginning; its blocks are doubly linked by pointers in the first four bytes of each block; and it can contain file descriptive entries (including entries for "sub-subdirectories"). Unlike the Volume Directory, however, it can be of any length (it starts out with only a single block and more are added as required), its header has a slightly different format, it can be located anywhere on the diskette, and its blocks are not necessary contiguous. A diagram of a typical subdirectory is shown in Figure 4.16. Thus, within a single subdirectory, you can create as many file entries as you have disk blocks! In, practice, however, it is usually more convenient to create multiple subdirectories "dangling" from the Volume Directory, each for a specific purpose (e.g. one for word processing, one for program development, one for spreadsheets, and so on). These subdirectories might even be thought of as miniature "diskettes" within the larger volume. Although it is possible to set up very complex structures using subdirectories (multiple level tree-like networks), usually this is not very efficient or convenient and a single level (all subdirectories linked directly to the Volume Directory) works best.

One of the major concepts around which ProDOS was designed is the notion of a **path** to a file. Ordinarily, if a file is described by the Volume Directory, this path is very simple. ProDOS merely looks up the file in the Volume Directory and that is that. If the file is described by a subdirectory, however, ProDOS insists upon knowing how to find the subdirectory. Of course, ProDOS could systematically search all subdirectories for the file and all subdirectories of the subdirectories, and so on, but this would be very time consuming (especially if you had mistyped the file name and

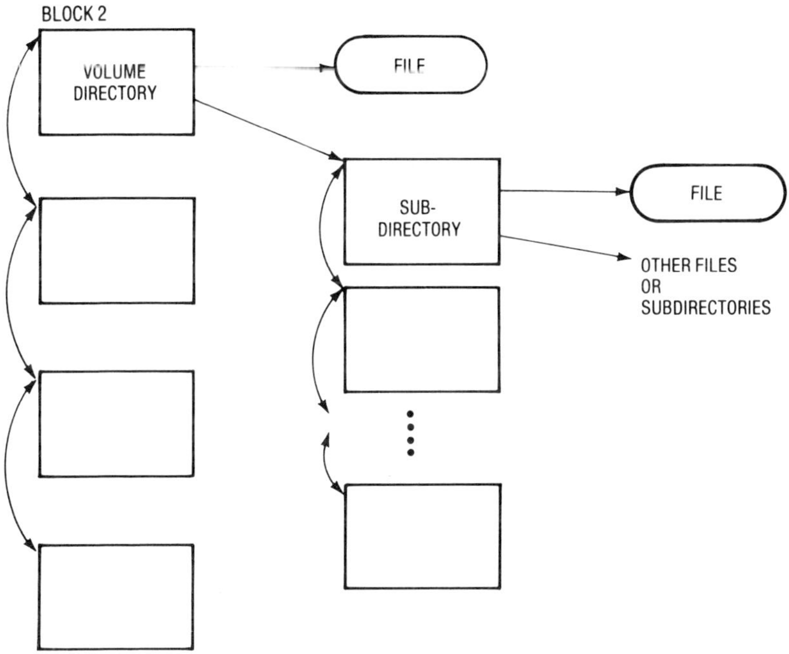

Figure 4.16 A ProDOS Subdirectory

it didn't really exist!). Since the user usually knows which subdirectory contains the file (and, perhaps, which subdirectory describes that subdirectory, etc.) the practice is to tell ProDOS what path to follow to find a file. This is done by first specifying the volume to be searched, thereby naming the Volume Directory, followed by a list of all subdirectories which must be traversed to eventually find the file, and finally by the file name itself. For example, if in Figure 4.16 the volume name is "VOLUME" and the subdirectory name is "SUB" and the file described by the subdirectory is "FILE," the path to find that file would be:

/VOLUME/SUB/FILE

If the file described by the Volume Directory in Figure 4.16 was also called "FILE" there would be no confusion at all, because its pathname would be unique:

/VOLUME/FILE

This points out an additional advantage of subdirectories. It was mentioned earlier that they were like miniature "diskettes," and, just like diskettes, there is no problem in using identical file names within different directories.

To make specifying pathnames easier, the user can specify a default prefix to ProDOS. When a file name is given (without a leading "/" in its name) it is assumed to be an incomplete pathname. To complete it, ProDOS merely attaches the prefix to the beginning. Thus, if the current prefix is:

/VOLUME/SUB/

And a reference was made to "FILE," ProDOS would create the following fully qualified pathname:

/VOLUME/SUB/FILE

Therefore, by specifying a prefix you are, in a sense, stating that you wish to work within a specific "miniature diskette," although you can still access any other file on the volume by giving its complete pathname explicitly.

An example of a typical subdirectory block is given in Figure 4.17. The format of the Subdirectory Header is given below (remember that the first four bytes of each subdirectory block contain the previous and next block numbers respectively):

BLOCK BYTE	DESCRIPTION
$04	STORAGE_TYPE/NAME_LENGTH: The first nibble (top 4 bits) of this byte describes the type of entry. In this case, this is a Subdirectory Header so this nibble is $E. The low 4 bits are the length of the name in the next field (the subdirectory name).
$05-$13	SUBDIR_NAME: A 15-byte field containing the name of this subdirectory. The actual length is defined by NAME_LENGTH above; the remainder of the field is ignored.
$14	$14 must contain $75.
$15-$1B	Reserved for future use.
$1C-$1F	CREATION: The date and time of the creation of this subdirectory. This field is zero if no date was assigned. The format of the field is as follows:

BYTE 0 and 1—yyyyyyymmmmddddd year/month/day
BYTE 2 and 3—000hhhhh00mmmmmm hours/minutes

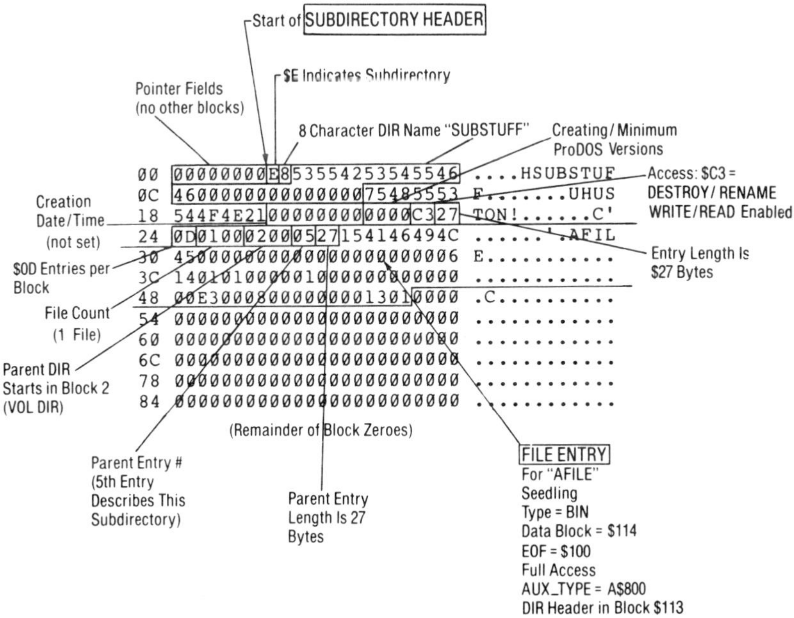

Figure 4.17 Example Subdirectory Block

where each letter above represents one binary bit. This is the standard form for all create and modify date/time stamps in directories.

$20 VERSION: The ProDOS version number under which this subdirectory was created. This field tells later versions of ProDOS not to expect to find any fields which were defined by Apple after this version of ProDOS was released. This field indicates the level of upward compatibility between versions. Under ProDOS 1.0, its value is zero.

$21 MIN_VERSION: Minimum version of ProDOS which can access this subdirectory. A value in this field implies that significant changes were made to the field definitions since prior versions of ProDOS were in use and these older versions would not be able to successfully interpret the structure of this subdirectory. This field indicates the level of downward compatibility between versions. Under ProDOS 1.0, its value is zero.

$22 ACCESS: The bits in the flag byte define how the directory may be accessed. The bit assignments are as follows:

$80—Subdirectory may be destroyed (deleted)
$40—Subdirectory may be renamed
$20—Subdirectory has changed since last backup
$02—Subdirectory may be written to
$01—Subdirectory may be read

All other bits are reserved for future use.

$23 ENTRY_LENGTH: Length of each entry in the Subdirectory in bytes (usually $27).

$24 ENTRIES_PER_BLOCK: Number of entries in each block of the Subdirectory (usually $0D). Note that the Subdirectory Header is considered to be an entry.

$25-$26 FILE_COUNT: Number of active entries in the Subdirectory. An active entry is one which describes a file or subdirectory which has not been deleted. This count does not include the Subdirectory Header. Note that this field's name is a bit misleading since the count also includes other subdirectory entries.

$27-$28 PARENT_POINTER: The block number (within the volume directory or a subdirectory) which contains the file entry for this subdirectory.

$29 PARENT_ENTRY: The number of the file entry within the block number pointed to by the PARENT_POINTER. Given that "ENTRIES PER BLOCK" is $0D, then the PARENT_ENTRY number ranges from $01 to $0D.

$2A PARENT_ENTRY_LENGTH: The length of entries in the parent directory in bytes (usually $27).

EMERGENCY REPAIRS

From time to time the information on a diskette can become damaged or lost. This can create various sýmptoms, ranging from mild side effects, such as the disk not booting, to major problems, such as an input/output (I/O) error in the Volume Directory. A good understanding of the format of a diskette, as described previously, and a few program tools can allow any reasonably sharp Apple II user to patch up most errors on his diskettes.

A first question would be, "how do errors occur?" The most common cause of an error is a worn or physically damaged diskette. Usually a diskette will warn you that it is wearing out by

EMERGENCY REPAIRS ARE EASIER IF YOU HAVE A BACKUP

producing "soft errors." Soft errors are I/O errors which occur randomly. You may get an I/O error message when you CATALOG a disk one time and have it CATALOG correctly if you try again. When this happens, the smart programmer immediately copies the files on the aged diskette to a brand new one and discards the old one or keeps it as a backup.

Another cause of damaged diskettes is the practice of hitting the RESET key to abort the execution of a program which is accessing the diskette. Damage will usually occur when the RESET signal comes just as data is being written onto the disk. Powering the machine off just as data is being written to the disk is also a sure way to clobber a diskette. Of course, real hardware problems in the disk drive, cable, or controller card can cause damage as well.

If the damaged diskette can be CATALOGed, recovery is much easier. A damaged ProDOS bootstrap loader on track 0 can usually be corrected by formatting a fresh diskette and copying the files from the old one to the new one. If only one file produces an I/O ERROR when it is used, it may be possible to copy most of the sectors of the file to another diskette by skipping over the bad sector with an assembler language program which calls the MLI (Machine Language Interface) in the ProDOS Kernel, or with a BASIC program (if the file is a TXT file). Indeed, if the problem is a bad checksum (see Chapter 3), it may be possible to read the bad sector and ignore the error and get most of the data.

An I/O error usually means that one of two conditions has occurred. Either a bad checksum was detected on the data in a sector, meaning that all bytes in the sector which follow the point of damage may be lost; or the sectoring is clobbered such that the sector no longer even exists on the diskette. If the latter is the case, the diskette (or at the very least, the track) must be reformatted, resulting in a massive loss of data. Although a program can be written to format a single track (see APPENDIX A), it is usually easier to copy all readable sectors from the damaged diskette to another formatted diskette and then reconstruct the lost data there.

Disk utilities, such as Quality Software's *Bag of Tricks*, allow the user to read and display the contents of sectors or blocks. *Bag of Tricks* will also allow you to modify the sector data and rewrite it to the same or another diskette. If you do not have *Bag of Tricks* or another commercial disk utility, you can use the ZAP program in APPENDIX A of this book. The ZAP program will read any block of an unprotected disk into memory, allowing the user to examine it or modify the data and then, optionally, rewrite it to a disk. Using such a program is very important when learning about diskette formats and when fixing clobbered data.

Using ZAP, a bad sector within a file can be localized by reading each block listed in the index blocks for that file. If the bad block is in a directory, the pointers of up to 13 files may be lost. When this occurs, a search of the diskette can be made to find "homeless" index blocks (ones which are not otherwise connected to the remaining good directory blocks in that and other directories). As these index blocks are found, new file descriptive entries can be made in the damaged sector which point to these blocks. Of course, it helps to know whether the lost files are seedlings, saplings or trees! When the entire Volume Directory is lost, this process can take hours, even with a good understanding of the format of ProDOS volumes. Such an endeavor should only be undertaken if there is no other way to recover the data. Of course, the best policy is to create backup copies of important files periodically to simplify recovery. More information on the above procedures is given in APPENDIX A.

A less significant but very annoying form of diskette clobber is the loss of free blocks. It is possible, by powering off or hitting RESET at the wrong time, to leave blocks marked in use in the Volume Bit Map which were about to be marked free. These lost blocks can never be recovered by normal means, even when files are deleted, since they do not belong to anyone. The result is a DISK FULL message before the volume is actually full. To reclaim the lost block, it is necessary to compare every block listed in every index block or directory against the Volume Bit Map to see if there are any discrepancies. There are utility programs which will do this automatically, but the best way to solve this problem is to copy all the files on the diskette to another diskette (note that the diskette must be copied on a file by file basis, not as a volume, since a volume copy would copy an image of the diskette, bad Volume Bit Map and all).

If a file is deleted it can usually be recovered, providing that additional block allocations have not occurred since it was deleted. If another file was created after the DELETE command, ProDOS probably has reused some or all of the blocks of the old file. The appropriate directory can be quickly ZAPped to reactivate the file (you will have to guess at the STORAGE_TYPE and NAME_LENGTH values) at +0 in the deleted entry. The file should then be copied to another disk and then the original deleted so that the Volume Bit Map will be correct.

FRAGMENTATION

ProDOS overhead in reading or writing blocks to a volume consists of three main parts:

1. ProDOS computational overhead time (the time to get ready to access the disk).
2. Seek time (moving the disk arm to the proper track).
3. Rotational delay (waiting for the proper sector to appear under the disk head).

In the first respect, ProDOS is an enormous improvement over Apple's earlier operating system, DOS, being up to eight times faster in its operation. This fact only increases the significance of the other two delay areas. Skewing can have an effect on rotational delay to some extent (see Chapter 3), but is much more difficult to control. Seek time, however, can vary greatly depending upon use patterns and the arrangement of files on a volume.

Imagine, for example, a volume on which a great deal of activity has occurred. Many files have been created and deleted over a period of time, leaving "holes" here and there as files are deleted, which are reallocated to existing or new files as necessary. Eventually, a map of the volume looks like a plate of spaghetti! There is nothing really wrong with this — files can be accessed normally — but if parts of an otherwise short file are spread all over the disk volume, ProDOS must spend a lot of time moving the disk read/write head from track to track to pick up all the pieces in the proper order. This costs time. A disk volume in this state of affairs is said to be badly "fragmented." Fragmentation can be even more important on a hard disk since the ratio of seek delay to rotational delay is much greater. Likewise, the best skewing setup in the world can be completely gutted by a fragmented disk, since few sequential file sectors are found together on the same track, and as the arm is moved to a new track there is no telling how long the rotational delay will be.

When disk access time becomes a concern, it is sometimes useful to intelligently move files to specific spots on the disk. To accomplish this, the user must format a new, blank volume and copy the files from the old disk, one by one, to the new disk in an appropriate order. Remember that ProDOS allocates blocks for files in numerically increasing order (from the outside track of the disk to the inside track). Thus, the first file you copy will be placed near the Volume Directory (a good place to be if you want to find that file fast). The last file you copy will go closest to the center hub of the diskette. If your program accesses two files at once, try to place them near one another on the disk. Do not separate them by many other files or you will hear the disk arm "thrashing" back and forth as it first accesses a block in file A and then must access one in file B. While you hear that noise, your program is not doing anything useful! Another thing to remember if your program opens and closes files frequently is that, when it does so, it may access several directories. It is usually a good idea in any case to keep all of your directories squashed down against the Volume Directory (i.e. CREATE all directories before you copy any files onto the new diskette) so that pathname searches will go faster.

CHAPTER 5

THE STRUCTURE OF PRODOS

ProDOS MEMORY USE

ProDOS is an assembly language program which is loaded into RAM memory when the user boots his disk. Although the ProDOS machine language support routines can run by themselves in a machine smaller than 64K (or 48K plus a language card), ProDOS is primarily intended to run only on a full sized 64K or larger Apple II Plus or an Apple IIe or IIc. In a 64K Apple II, ProDOS normally occupies the 16K of bank switched memory (or the Language Card for older Apples) and about 10.5K at the top of main memory ($9600 through $BFFF). The part of ProDOS which occupies the bank switched memory is called the **Kernel**. The part occupying the top of main memory is called the **BASIC Interpreter** (BI). The Kernel consists of support subroutines which may be called by any assembly language program (such as the BASIC Interpreter) to access the disk, either block by block or file by file. The BASIC Interpreter accepts ProDOS commands entered by the user or his programs, and translates them into calls to the Kernel subroutines.* When the BASIC Interpreter is loaded, ProDOS must fool Applesoft BASIC into believing that there is

*It is possible, if the BASIC Interpreter's functions are not required by an application (such as a stand alone arcade-type game), to separate the Kernel from the BASIC Interpreter and not even load the BASIC Interpreter. For the purposes of this discussion, however, we will assume that ProDOS consists of both the Kernel and the BASIC Interpreter. In addition, the ProDOS Kernel may be loaded into the main part of memory if the Apple does not have a language card (48K Apple II), but the BASIC Interpreter may not be used under these circumstances because it cannot be relocated.

actually less RAM memory in the machine than there is. With ProDOS loaded, Applesoft believes that there is only about 38K of RAM. ProDOS does this by adjusting HIMEM after it has loaded the BASIC Interpreter to prevent Applesoft from using the memory ProDOS is occupying. In order to keep track of the memory it is using, ProDOS maintains a "bit map" table which describes every page (256 bytes) in memory and marks it either free or in-use. By examining this table, user written programs can avoid using previously assigned memory, even if later versions of ProDOS are loaded elsewhere.

A diagram of ProDOS's memory is given in Figure 5.1. As can be seen, there are numerous subdivisions of the two basic components mentioned above. In addition, there are two special **global pages** containing addresses and data pertaining to the ProDOS Kernel (SYSTEM GLOBAL PAGE at $BF00) and the BASIC Interpreter (BI GLOBAL PAGE at $BE00) which may be of interest to external user written programs. These global pages will be discussed in more detail later in this chapter.

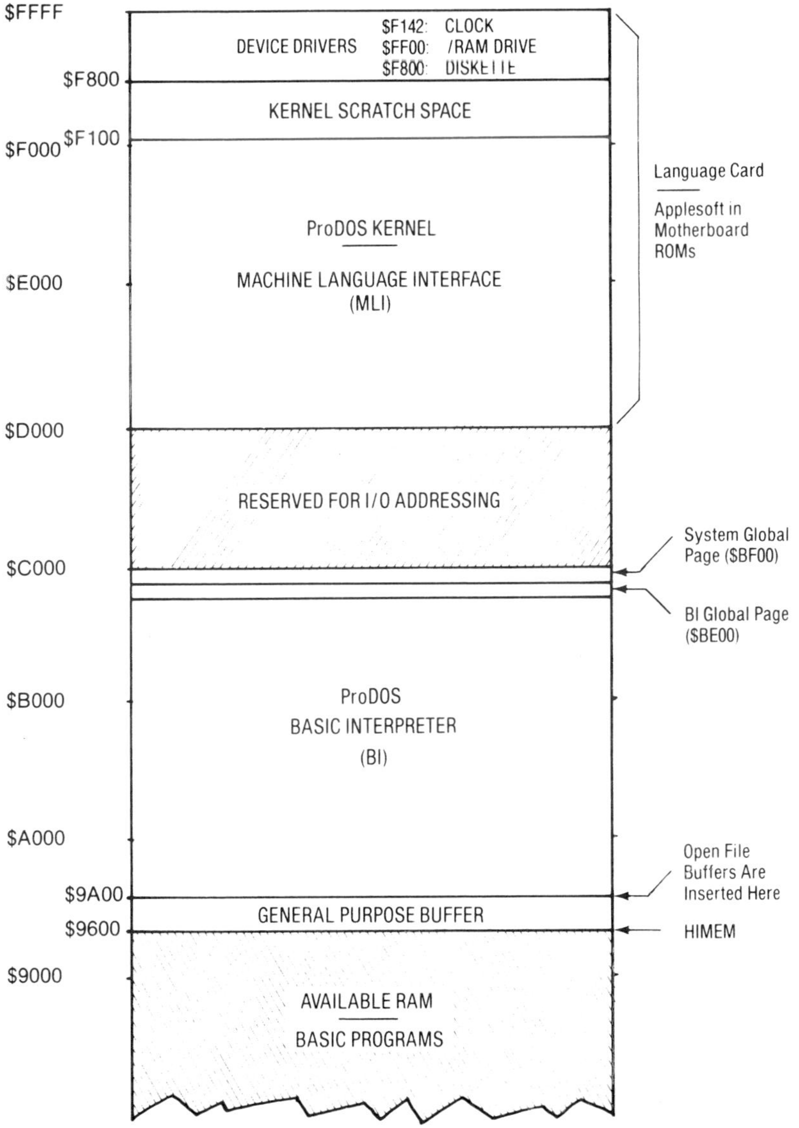

Figure 5.1 ProDOS Memory Usage (64K)

As discussed earlier, ProDOS can be divided into two major components: the Kernel, containing the **Machine Language Interface (MLI)**; and the BASIC Interpreter (BI). In theory, other interpreters could be written and substituted for the BI (to support Pascal or C language development, for example) but at present the only interpreter provided by Apple is the BASIC Interpreter, supporting Applesoft BASIC. There is currently no support for the older Integer BASIC language. In fact, because of the memory utilization of ProDOS, Applesoft must be resident in ROM (since the Kernel resides in the language card). Hence, ProDOS is only supported for Apple II Pluses, IIc's, and IIe's. Use of the term "BASIC Interpreter" should not be confused with the Applesoft BASIC Interpreter in ROM.* Here, "interpreter" means "interpreter of disk access commands," and not "interpreter of BASIC language statements." Although the BI is closely "married" to the Applesoft interpreter in ROM, its primary responsibility is to interpret ProDOS commands which load and save files, display directories, and support file operations in BASIC programs.

The BI normally occupies memory from $9600 to $BEFF. The first 1K ($9600-$9A00) is a general purpose buffer, used during Applesoft string garbage collection and for other purposes. Following this, at $9A00, are the actual machine language instructions and work areas of the BI. Any data which is considered to be of interest to external programs is placed in the BI Global Page at $BE00. As files are opened by BASIC programs, 1024-byte file buffers are allocated and inserted between the general purpose buffer and the BI itself. To do this, the BI must relocate the general purpose buffer and any strings which were allocated by the running BASIC program lower in memory to make room for the file buffers. HIMEM must be lowered accordingly. Thus, the memory available to the BASIC program fluctuates according to the number of open files.

The ProDOS Kernel occupies 12K of the 16K bank switched memory (language card). Most of the remaining 4K bank is not currently used, but is reserved by Apple for future use (the QUIT code occupies three pages currently). The main part of the ProDOS

*Apple's documentation also refers to the BASIC Interpreter as the "BASIC System Program." "BASIC Interpreter" is used here because of frequent references to the "BI," an earlier designation.

Kernel begins at $D000, and contains the Machine Language Interface (MLI) subroutines which allow access to the disk by other programs (such as the BI or user written machine language programs). MLI functions provided include: open a file, create a new file, delete a file, rename a file, determine online volumes, read/write to a file, etc. The Kernel also handles interrupts for devices which can generate them. Access to these subroutines and their data is strictly controlled by the System Global Page which will be described next. Following the Kernel and its scratch space (work areas), is a 2K area devoted to device drivers. In order to provide a device independent interface to peripherals, subroutines are loaded here which can perform block oriented I/O to the Apple diskette drive, the **/RAM** "electronic" 64K memory diskette drive implemented in the Extended 80-Column Text card, and the Thunderclock. Additional device drivers (Hard disk, printer, etc.) must be placed in interface card ROM or in main RAM memory. The entry point addresses of each device driver in use are kept in the System Global Page.

GLOBAL PAGES

The System and BI Global Pages are maintained by ProDOS at fixed locations in main memory ($BF00 and $BE00 respectively). This practice allows important ProDOS data and subroutines to be accessed by external programs via a fixed location. Each time Apple makes a change in ProDOS and reassembles its source code, the addresses of all of the subroutines and variables may change. By putting the addresses of these routines and the variables themselves in fixed locations in memory, dependencies by a user written program on a particular version of ProDOS can be eliminated. Hopefully, all subroutines or data of general interest have been "vectored" through these global pages. If not, the programmer cannot be sure that a subroutine he calls directly will not "move out from under him" in a later version.

The exact format of the System Global Page is given in Chapter 8 but it contains the following information:

1. JMP (Goto) instructions to the main entry of the MLI, a quit vector, a clock/calendar subroutine, etc.
2. Addresses of the device drivers for each slot and drive.
3. A list of all disk drives online, and the slot and drive each occupies.

4. A "bit map" showing which pages of memory are in use and which are free.
5. Addresses of the buffers being used by MLI opened files.
6. Addresses of up to four interrupt handling routines and associated register save areas.
7. Current date, time and file level.
8. A machine ID flag byte giving the model (e.g. Apple IIe) and memory in the machine on which ProDOS is currently running.
9. Various flags indicating MLI status and whether a card occupies any slot.
10. Language card bank switching routines.
11. Interrupt entry and exit routines.
12. ProDOS version number.

The BI global page contains:

1. Addresses of routines in the BI which allow warmstart, command scanning, and error message printing.
2. I/O vectors for PR# and IN# for each slot, and the currently active input and output streams.
3. Default slot and drive.
4. BI status flags indicating whether an EXEC file is active, a BASIC program is running, a file is being read or written, etc.
5. Parameters that allow a user to pass an external command line to the BI.
6. A table indicating which commands allow which keyword parameters (e.g. OPEN does not allow the AD keyword but does allow the L keyword).
7. The current value for all keywords (A,B,E,L,S,D,etc.).
8. The address of the pathname buffers within the BI.
9. A subroutine used by the BI to access the MLI.

10. Parameter lists used by the BI to access the MLI.
11. Vectors to the BI's buffer allocate and free subroutines.
12. The current HIMEM MSB.

In addition to the ProDOS vectors in the global pages, the Monitor ROM and Applesoft maintain additional vectors of general interest from $3F0 through $3FF. They are:

ADDR	USAGE
$3F0	LO/HI address of the routine which handles a BRK machine language instruction. Supported by the Autostart and Apple IIe and IIc ROMs. Normally contains the address of a Monitor ROM routine which prints the contents of the registers.
$3F2	LO/HI address of routine which will handle RESET for Autostart and Apple IIe ROM. Normally the BI restart address ($BE00) is stored here, but the user may change it if he wishes to handle RESET himself.
$3F4	Power-up byte. Contains a "funny complement" of the RESET address with an $A5. This scheme is used to determine if the machine was just powered up or if RESET was pressed. If a power-up occurred, the Autostart ROM or Apple IIe ROM ignores the address at $3F2 (since it has never been initialized), and attempts to boot a diskette. To prevent this from happening when you change $3F2 to handle your own RESETs, EOR (exclusive OR) the new value at $3F3 with an $A5 and store the result in the power-up byte.
$3F5	A JMP to a machine language routine which is to be called when the "&" feature is used in Applesoft. Initialized by ProDOS to point to the BI command scanner vector.
$3F8	A JMP to a machine language routine which is to be called when a control-Y is entered from the monitor.
$3FB	A JMP to a machine language routine which is to be called when a non-maskable interrupt (NMI) occurs.
$3FE	LO/HI address of ProDOS's IRQ maskable interrupt handler dispatcher. If you wish to handle an IRQ interrupt, install an interrupt handler into ProDOS—do not replace this vector.

WHAT HAPPENS DURING BOOTING

When an Apple is powered on, its memory is essentially devoid of any programs. In order to get ProDOS running, a diskette is "booted." The term "boot" refers to the process of bootstrap loading ProDOS into RAM. Bootstrap loading involves a series of steps which load successively bigger pieces of a program until all of the program is in memory and running. In the case of ProDOS, bootstrapping occurs in two major stages, corresponding to the loading of the ProDOS Kernel and the BASIC Interpreter. Within these major stages, there are minor stages which must be performed to complete the loading process. Figures 5.2 and 5.3 diagram the processes involved in loading the Kernel and the BI respectively from the diskette. A description of this process follows.

The first boot stage is the execution of the ROM on the disk controller card. This is called the **Boot ROM**, and it exists on either the diskette controller card or a hard disk controller card at

$Cs00 (where "s" is the slot number). Thus, when the Apple is first powered on, the Monitor ROM searches the slots for a disk controller card (starting with slot 7 and moving down in slot number) and, upon finding one, it branches to $Cs00 (usually $C600 if the controller is in slot 6). Control is also passed to this address should the user type PR#6 in BASIC or C600G or 6(ctrl)P in the monitor. The diskette controller Boot ROM is a machine language program of about 256 bytes in length. When executed, it "recalibrates" the diskette arm by pulling it back to track 0 (the "clacketty-clack" noise that is heard), and then reads sector 0 from track 0 into RAM memory at location $800. Once this sector has been read, the Boot ROM jumps (GOTO's) to $801 which is the second stage boot, the ProDOS Loader.

The **ProDOS Loader** occupies the first block on a ProDOS diskette (physical sectors 0 and 2). Since the Boot ROM has only loaded sector 0, the first task the ProDOS Loader must perform is to load the remaining sector of itself. It does this by calling the Boot ROM as a subroutine, loading it at $900. Having completed this, a portion of the Boot ROM is copied into a subroutine in the ProDOS Loader itself (this variable code is different for a diskette or a hard disk), and uses this to search the diskette's Volume Directory for a system file with the name "PRODOS". This file contains an image of the ProDOS Relocator, the BI Loader, and the ProDOS Kernel itself. If the file can be found, its contents are read into memory at $2000, and the ProDOS Loader jumps to the ProDOS Relocator at $2000.

The **ProDOS Relocator** prints a copyright and version number on the screen, and then begins to examine the machine in use to find out its model. This is done by testing the Monitor ROM for special model-dependent indicators and by checking for language card memory. The ProDOS Relocator assembles the data it has collected into a byte of flags indicating whether the machine is an Apple II, Apple II Plus, Apple IIe, Apple IIc, or an Apple III in Apple II emulation mode. It also indicates the amount of memory available. Once this has been established, the Kernel image is copied either to the bank switched memory (language card) if the machine has 64K or more, or to $9000 for a 48K Apple. If the machine has 128K, a /RAM drive is set up in the alternate 64K memory. The peripheral card configuration is also checked, and a table of occupied slots and interface card identifications is made.

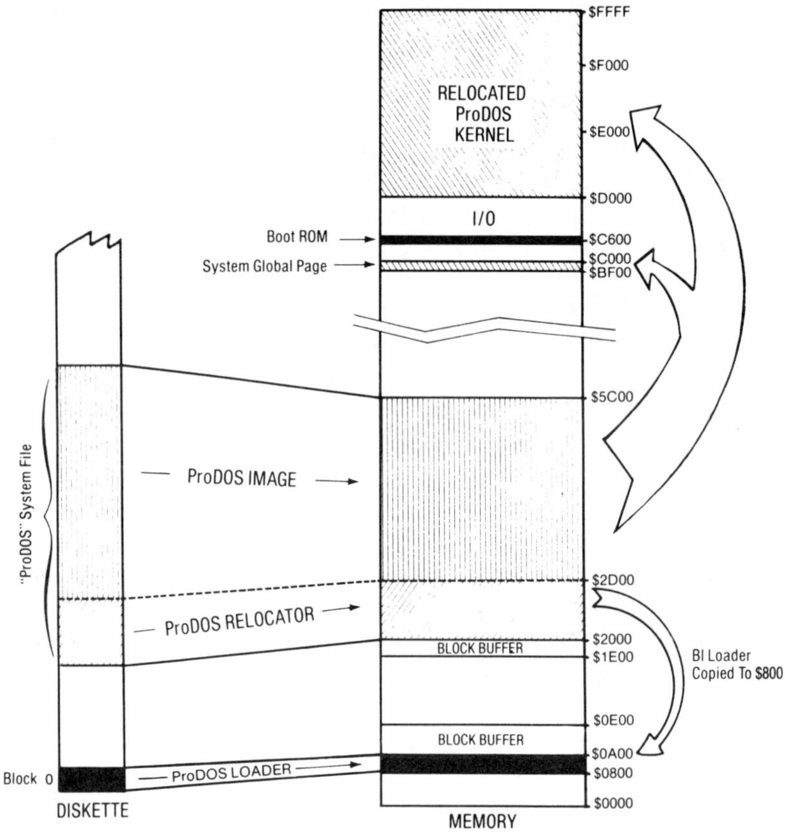

Figure 5.2 ProDOS Kernel Bootstrap Process

The initialization of the Kernel is completed by moving an image of the System Global Page to $BF00 and initializing it as necessary. The BI Loader image is then copied to $800 and control transfers there to begin booting the BI.

The **BI Loader** searches the Volume Directory for the first system file it can find whose name ends with ".SYSTEM". The file which is found will normally be BASIC.SYSTEM, but any other interpreter could be loaded in this way. If a file is found, its contents are loaded into memory at $2000 and control passes to the BI Relocator at $2000.

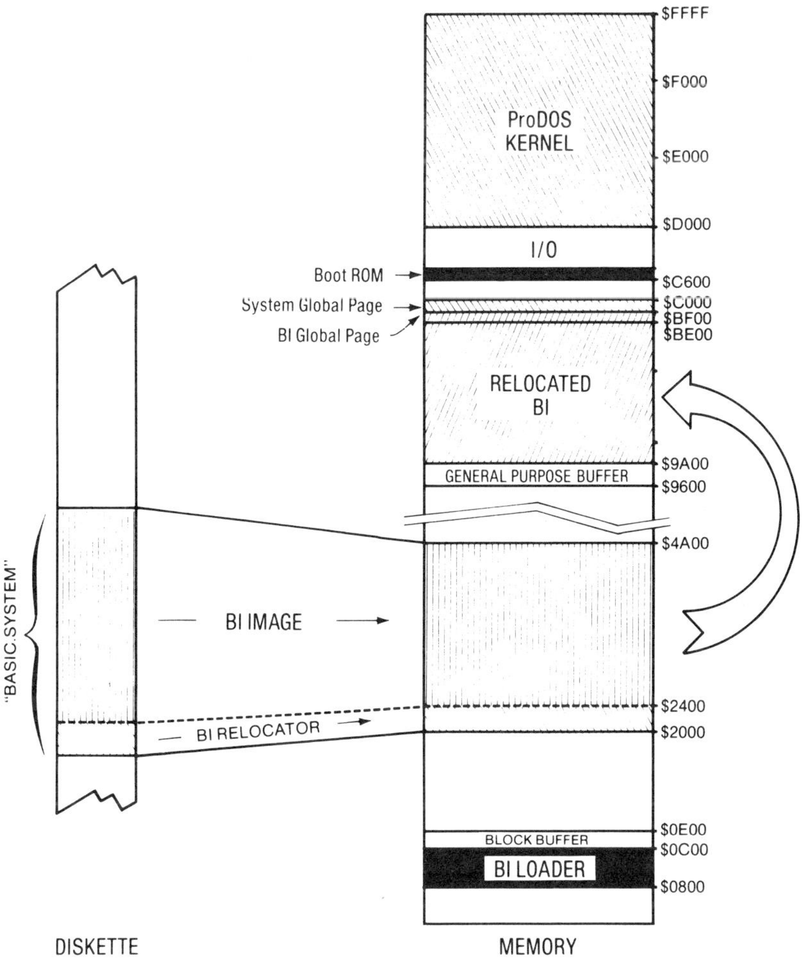

Figure 5.3 Basic Interpreter (BI) Bootstrap Process

The **BI Relocator** copies the BI image to high memory ($9A00), sets up the BI Global Page at $BE00, and marks the pages occupied by these as "in-use" in the System Global Page's memory bit map. The screen and keyboard vectors in zero page (CSWL/H and KSWL/H) are modified to cause immediate transfer of control to the relocator, and a jump to BASIC's coldstart entry is executed. As soon as Applesoft has completed initialization, it prints a prompt character "]". This causes control to transfer back into the BI Relocator. CSWL/H and KSWL/H are restored to their normal settings, and initialization of the BI Global Page is completed. If a

"STARTUP" file can be found in the Volume Directory, an initial command line of "-STARTUP" is dummied up and, after completing the vectors in page 3 ($3F0 etc.), control transfers to the BI through its vector at $BE00.

The various stages of the boot process are covered again in greater detail in the ProDOS Program Logic Supplement—see Chapter 8 for details.

CHAPTER 6

USING ProDOS FROM ASSEMBLY LANGUAGE

CAVEAT

This chapter is aimed at the advanced assembly language programmer who wishes to access the disk at any level. Access to the disk by BASIC programs is well documented in the ProDOS manual, *BASIC Programming With ProDOS*. The material presented in this chapter may be beyond the comprehension (at least for the present) of a programmer who has never used assembly language.

Access to a diskette from assembly language may be accomplished at four different levels:

Level 0	Direct access of the diskette controller
Level 1	Block access
Level 2	Machine Language Interface (MLI) access
Level 3	BI command access

At the lowest level is direct access of the diskette controller. Here, data is accessed byte by byte. This may be required to implement diskette protection schemes or to perform low level diagnostic or correction of I/O errors. The next level of access is by ProDOS blocks (two sectors per block). This is done using the appropriate ProDOS device driver; in this case, the diskette device driver. At a higher level still is the ProDOS Machine Language Interface (MLI). Here, data may be accessed on a file basis.

Finally, the highest level of access is through the ProDOS BASIC Interpreter. Here, entire ProDOS command lines may be executed to produce formatted directory listings and the like. A detailed description of the programming considerations at each of these levels follows.

DIRECT USE OF THE DISKETTE DRIVE

It is often desirable or necessary to access the Apple's disk drives directly from assembly language, without the use of ProDOS. Applications which might use direct disk access range from a user written operating system to ProDOS-independent utility programs.Direct access is acomplished using 16 addresses that provide eight on/off switches which directly control the hardware. For information on the disk hardware, please refer to APPENDIX D. The device address assignments are given in Table 6.1.

TABLE 6.1 ProDOS Hardware Addresses

	"OFF" SWITCHES		"ON" SWITCHES	
SWITCH	BASE ADDRESS	FUNCTION	BASE ADDRESS	FUNCTION
Q0	$C080	Phase 0 off	$C081	Phase 0 on
Q1	$C082	Phase 1 off	$C083	Phase 1 on
Q2	$C084	Phase 2 off	$C085	Phase 2 on
Q3	$C086	Phase 3 off	$C087	Phase 3 on
Q4	$C088	Drive off	$C089	Drive on
Q5	$C08A	Select drive 1	$C08B	Select drive 2
Q6	$C08C	Shift data register	$C08D	Load data register
Q7	$C08E	Read	$C08F	Write

The last two switches are difficult to explain in single phrase definitions because they interact with each other forming a 4-way switch. The four possible settings are given in Table 6.2.

TABLE 6.2 Four Way Q6/Q7 Switches

Q6	Q7	FUNCTION
Off	Off	Enable read sequencing.
Off	On	Shift data register every four cycles while writing.
On	Off	Check write protect and initialize sequencer for writing.
On	On	Load data register every four cycles while writing.

The addresses are slot dependent and the offsets are computed by multiplying the slot number by 16. In hexadecimal this works out nicely. Simply add the value $s0 (where s is the slot number) to the base address. To engage disk drive number 1 in slot number 6, for example, we would add $60 to $C08A (device address assignment for engaging drive 1) for a result of $C0EA. However, since it is generally desirable to write code that is not slot dependent, one would normally use $C08A,X (where the X-register contains the value $s0). Table 6.3 shows the range of addresses for each slot number.

TABLE 6.3 Address Ranges For Slots

SLOT NUMBER	ADDRESS RANGE
0	$C080—$C08F
1	$C090—$C09F
2	$C0A0—$C0AF
3	$C0B0—$C0BF
4	$C0C0—$C0CF
5	$C0D0—$C0DF
6	$C0E0—$C0EF
7	$C0F0—$C0FF

In general, the above addresses need only be accessed with any valid 6502 instruction. However, in the case of reading and writing bytes (last four addresses), care must be taken to insure that the data will be in an appropriate register. All of the following would engage drive number 1. (Assume slot number 6.)

```
BIT $CØEA
LDA $CØ8A,X      (where X-register contains $6Ø)
CMP $CØ8A,X      (where X-register contains $6Ø)
```

Below are typical examples demonstrating the use of the device address assignments. For more examples, see APPENDIX A. All examples assume that the label SLOT is set to 16 times the desired slot number (e.g. $60 for slot 6).

STEPPER PHASE OFF OR ON

Basically, each of the four phases (0-3) must be turned on and then off again. Done in ascending order moves the arm inward. In descending order, the arm moves outward. For optimum performance, the timing between accesses to these locations is critical, making this a nontrivial exercise. An example is provided in APPENDIX A demonstrating how to move the arm to a given location.

MOTOR OFF OR ON

```
LDX #SLOT        Put slot number times 16 in X-register.
LDA $CØ88,X      Turn motor off.

LDX #SLOT        Put slot number times 16 in X-register.
LDA $CØ89,X      Turn motor on (selected drive).
```

NOTE: A sufficient delay should be provided to allow the motor time to come up to speed before reading or writing to the disk. Either a specific delay or a routine that watches the data register can be used. See APPENDIX A for an example.

ENGAGE DRIVE 1 OR 2

```
        LDX #SLOT       Put slot number times 16 in X-register.
        LDA $C08A,X     Engage drive 1.

        LDX #SLOT       Put slot number times 16 in X-register.
        LDA $C08B,X     Engage drive 2.
```

READ A BYTE

```
        LDX #SLOT       Put slot number times 16 in X-register.
        LDA $C08E,X     Insure Read mode.

READ    LDA $C08C,X     Put contents of data register in Accumulator.
        BPL READ        Loop until the high bit is set.
```

NOTE: $C08E,X must be accessed to assure Read mode. The loop is necessary to assure that the accumulator will contain valid data. If the data register does not yet contain valid data, the high bit will be zero.

SENSE WRITE PROTECT

```
        LDX #SLOT       Put slot number times 16 in X-register.
        LDA $C08D,X
        LDA $C08E,X     Sense write protect.
        BMI ERROR       If high bit set, protected.
```

WRITE LOAD AND WRITE A BYTE

```
        LDX #SLOT       Put slot number times 16 in X-register.
        LDA DATA        Load Accumulator with byte to write.
        STA $C08D,X     Write load.
        ORA $C08C,X     Write byte.
```

NOTE: $C08F,X must already have been accessed to insure Write mode and a 100-microsecond delay should be invoked before writing.

Due to hardware constraints, normal data bytes must be written in 32-cycle loops. The example below writes the two bytes $D5 and $AA to the disk. It does this by an immediate load of the accumulator, followed by a subroutine call (WRITE9) that writes the byte in the accumulator. Timing is so critical that different routines may be necessary, depending on how the data is to be accessed, and code cannot cross memory page boundaries without an adjustment.

```
         LDA #$D5       Load byte to write.      (2 cycles)
         JSR WRITE9     Go write it.             (6)
         LDA #$AA       Load byte to write.      (2)
         JSR WRITE9     Go write it.             (6)
         ...
WRITE9   CLC            Provide different        (2)
WRITE7   PHA            delays to produce        (3)
         PLA            correct timing.          (4)
WRITE    STA $C08D,X    Store byte in register.  (5)
         ORA $C08C,X    Write byte.              (4)
         RTS            Return to caller.        (6)
```

CALLING A STORAGE DEVICE DRIVER (BLOCK ACCESS)

ProDOS is device independent in that it requires a device driver for all storage devices. ProDOS comes with two device drivers built in. One supports the standard Apple floppy disk drive (Disk II or equivalent). The other supports a RAM drive on the Apple IIc or an Apple IIe that has 128K of memory. ProDOS can also support the ProFile hard disk which has its device driver on ROM. It seems clear that there will be many kinds of storage devices available in the future, each with its own driver.

These device drivers are used as subroutines by the MLI and provide the means of accessing the appropriate device. Four basic functions are currently defined for a device driver. They are **STATUS**, **READ**, **WRITE**, and **FORMAT**. However, not all device drivers will provide all four functions. The Disk II Device Driver, for example, does not support FORMAT; because of space constraints, this function is provided in the program named FILER.

The READ BLOCK and WRITE BLOCK calls in the MLI provide the only means of using a device driver from ProDOS and is the preferred method. While it is not generally recommended, any device driver can be called directly. This could prove useful in particular applications that don't require the MLI. Great care should be taken when calling the device driver directly because doing so can easily destroy data on the particular storage device.

While the parameters to call a device driver are quite straightforward, there are several potential difficulties to consider. First, RAM based device drivers normally reside in bank-switched memory, and therefore must be carefully selected and deselected. Second, a request for an unsupported device function may produce undesirable results.

There are four inputs stored in six zero page locations that must contain the appropriate information when a call is made to a device driver. The first input is the **Command Code**, which indicates which operation is requested. As mentioned earlier, four operations are currently defined. The first of these is STATUS, which is used to determine if the device is ready to be accessed (either Read or Write). Although not all device drivers do so, it is suggested that the number of blocks the device supports be returned, in additon to the status. This should be done using the X (low byte) and Y (high byte) registers. The remaining operations are quite straightforward—READ for reading a block, WRITE for writing a block, and FORMAT to format or initialize the media.

The second input is the **Unit Number**, indicating in which slot and drive the desired device resides. Only two drives per slot are supported directly, but it is possible to interface a controller card that supports additional drives or volumes.

The third input is a 2-byte **Buffer Pointer** that indicates the location of a 512-byte area for data transfer. The MLI verifies that no memory conflicts exist, but most device drivers will not do so; therefore, some degree of care should be exercised in determining this input.

The fourth input is a 2-byte **Block Number** indicating which block is to be used for data transfer. The value should be in keeping with the number of blocks available on the desired device.

The four inputs necessary are listed in Table 6.4.

Although Apple has defined the manner in which device drivers are to be called, some variations will occur. Even the drivers provided by Apple vary slightly from one another. For this reason it is advisable to make calls to any device driver with great caution. The parameter list descriptions that follow detail the four kinds of calls that are available. Not all device drivers will support all four call types and a request to an unsupported call type could prove dangerous.

Table 6.4 Device Driver Parameters—General Format

LOCATION	DESCRIPTION	OPTIONS
$42	Command code	$00 = STATUS $01 = READ $02 = WRITE $03 = FORMAT
$43	Unit Number	DSSS0000 D = Drive number (0 = drive 1, 1 = drive 2); SSS = Slot number (0 to 7)
$44-45	I/O Buffer	Can be $0000 to $FFFF
$46-47	Block Number	Can be $0000 to $FFFF
	Return code	The processor CARRY flag is set upon return from the device driver if an error occurred. The ACCUMULATOR contains the return code. $00 = No errors $27 = I/O error $28 = No device connected $2B = Write protect error

CALLING THE DISK II DEVICE DRIVER

Access to standard Apple floppy disk drives (Disk II or equivalent) is performed using the Disk II Device Driver provided with ProDOS. As mentioned above, the Disk II Device Driver does not support the FORMAT call. If such a request is made, it will be interpreted as a WRITE call, and serious problems may result. Formatting floppy disks is performed by the separate utility program called **FILER**.

The I/O buffer location is not checked for validity by the Disk II Device Driver. The block number must be in the range $0-$117 or an error type $27 (I/O error) will result.

The Disk II Device Driver performs the same READ and WRITE functions as the RWTS routines of DOS 3.3, but these routines have been substantially modified to decrease disk access time. A comparison of RWTS to the Disk II Device Driver is contained in *Understanding the Apple IIe* by Jim Sather (1985, Quality Software).

DEVICE DRIVER PARAMETER LISTS BY COMMAND CODE

$00 STATUS request

FUNCTION This call returns the status of a particular device and is generally used to determine if a device is present, and if so, whether it is write protected. Additionally, some drivers will return the number of blocks supported by that device.

REQUIRED INPUTS

$42	Must be $00.
$43	Unit number of disk to be accessed. The bit assignment of a ProDOS unit number is as follows: DSSS0000, where D is the drive number (0 = drive 1, 1 = drive 2) and SSS is the slot number (1—7).
$44-45	Unused.
$46-47	Unused but sometimes checked for validity (use $0000).

RETURNED VALUES

Carry Flag	Clear	—No error occurred
	Set	—Error occurred (see Accumulator for type)
Accumulator	$00	—No errors
	$27	—I/O error or bad block number
	$28	—No device connected to unit
	$2B	—Disk is write protected
X-register	Blocks available (low byte)	
Y-register	Blocks available (high byte)	

$01 READ request

FUNCTION This call will read a 512-byte block and store it at the specified memory location. Most drivers will not check the memory location, so some care is suggested.

REQUIRED INPUTS

$42	Must be $01
$43	Unit number of disk to be accessed. The bit assignment of a ProDOS unit number is as follows: DSSS0000, where D is the drive number (0 = drive 1, 1 = drive 2), and SSS is the slot number (1—7).
$44-45	Address (LO/HI) of the caller's 512-byte buffer into which the block will be read. The buffer need not be page aligned.
$46-47	Block number (LO/HI) to read. Must be valid for the device being called.

RETURNED VALUES

Carry Flag	Clear	—No error ocurred
	Set	—Error occurred (see Accumulator for type)
Accumulator	$00	—No errors
	$27	—I/O error or bad block number
	$28	—No device connected to unit

$02 WRITE request

FUNCTION This call will write a 512-byte block from the specified memory location. Since all write operations could potentially destroy data, care is suggested.

REQUIRED INPUTS

$42	Must be $02
$43	Unit number of disk to be accessed. The bit assignment of a ProDOS unit number is as follows: DSSS0000, where D is the drive number (0 = drive 1, 1 = drive 2), and SSS is the slot number (1—7).
$44-45	Address (LO/HI) of the caller's 512-byte buffer into which the block will be read. The buffer need not be page aligned.
$46-47	Block number (LO/HI) to read. Must be valid for the device being called.

RETURNED VALUES

Carry Flag	Clear	—No error ocurred
	Set	—Error occurred (see Accumulator for type)
Accumulator	$00	—No errors
	$27	—I/O error or bad block number
	$28	—No device connected to unit
	$2B	—Disk is write protected.

$03 FORMAT request

FUNCTION This call will format the media present in the specified device. Since all data will be destroyed, extreme care is suggested.

REQUIRED INPUTS

$42	Must be $03
$43	Unit number of disk to be accessed. The bit assignment of a ProDOS unit number is as follows: DSSS0000, where D is the drive number (0 = drive 1, 1 = drive 2), and SSS is the slot number (1—7).

RETURNED VALUES

Carry Flag	Clear	—No error ocurred
	Set	—Error occurred (see Accumulator for type)
Accumulator	$00	—No errors
	$27	—I/O error or bad block number
	$28	—No device connected to unit
	$2B	—Disk is write protected
Return code	$00	—No errors
	$27	—I/O error
	$28	—No device connected
	$2B	—Write protected

CALLING THE MACHINE LANGUAGE INTERFACE

The **Machine Language Interface** (MLI) consists of a set of externally callable subroutines in the ProDOS Kernel. Over 20 different functions may be performed to access and manipulate files in a device independent manner (i.e. the programmer need not be concerned with whether the device is a diskette drive or a hard disk). To avoid duplication of code and to eliminate direct calls to unpublished entry points within ProDOS, it is recommended that all file access be performed using the standardized ProDOS Machine Language Interface.

All calls to the MLI are made through the System Global Page at $BF00. The first item in this page is a JMP (GOTO) to the MLI. Thus, to call the MLI, code the following:

```
JSR $BFØØ
DFB function_code
DW  addr_of_parms
```

where "function_code" should be replaced with a 1-byte hexadecimal code representing the function you want to perform, and "addr_of_parms" is the 2-byte address of a parameter list you have created in your program's memory which indicates such things as the file name being accessed, the record number to access, etc. Note that programming reentrant or "ROMable" code or routines that cannot have instructions mixed with data will be made more difficult by this convention. In these cases, it may be advisable to move the JSR $BF00, the three bytes following, and a RTS instruction to a RAM data area and call them there.

Upon return, the processor CARRY flag will be set if an error has occurred, and the return code will be placed in the A register. All other registers are saved and restored by the MLI. The valid function_codes are summarized in Table 6.5. It is interesting to note that most of the function calls are identical between ProDOS and the Apple III SOS operating system. The names used are the standardized labels for these functions established by Apple for SOS and ProDOS.

Table 6.5 MLI Functions

CODE	NAME	DESCRIPTION
$40	ALLOC_INTERRUPT	Install interrupt handler
$41	DEALLOC_INTERRUPT	Remove interrupt handler
$65	QUIT	Exit from one Interpreter and dispatch another
$80	READ_BLOCK	Read disk block by unit number
$81	WRITE_BLOCK	Write disk block by unit number
$82	GET_TIME	Read calendar/clock peripheral card and set system date/time
$C0	CREATE	Create a new file or directory
$C1	DESTROY	Delete a file or directory
$C2	RENAME	Rename a file or directory
$C3	SET_FILE_INFO	Change a file's attributes
$C4	GET_FILE_INFO	Return a file's attributes
$C5	ONLINE	Return names of one or all online volumes
$C6	SET_PREFIX	Change default pathname prefix
$C7	GET_PREFIX	Return default pathname prefix
$C8	OPEN	Open a file
$C9	NEWLINE	Set end-of-line character for line-by-line reads
$CA	READ	Read one or more bytes from an open file
$CB	WRITE	Write one or more bytes to an open file
$CC	CLOSE	Close one or more open files, flushing buffers
$CD	FLUSH	Flush all write buffers for one or more files
$CE	SET_MARK	Change File Position within an open file
$CF	GET_MARK	Return File Position within an open file
$D0	SET_EOF	Change end-of-file position of an open file
$D1	GET_EOF	Return end-of-file position of an open file
$D2	SET_BUF	Change File Buffer's address for an open file
$D3	GET_BUF	Return File Buffer's address for an open file

The general form for a parameter list is as follows:

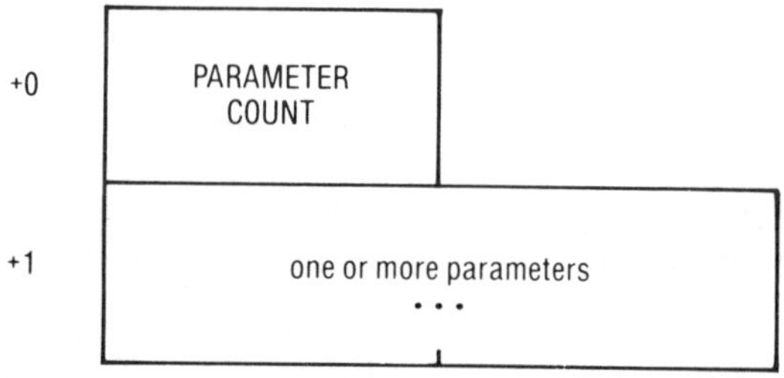

The PARAMETER_COUNT is a 1-byte count of the number of parameters which follow. It is used by the MLI to validity check the parameter list to make sure that the address following the caller's JSR to the MLI really points to a valid parameter list.

BE PREPARED! YOURE ENTERING THE DEPTHS OF ProDOS.

MLI PARAMETER LISTS BY FUNCTION CODE

$40 ALLOC_INTERRUPT: INSTALL INTERRUPT HANDLER

FUNCTION This function allows the user to install his own interrupt handling routine into the ProDOS table. The user's handler resides in memory outside ProDOS, and only its entry point address is stored in the System Global Page table by this MLI call. Up to four such routines may be installed at any time. When a maskable interrupt (IRQ) occurs, ProDOS calls each handler in the order in which they were installed to allow the interrupt to be serviced. (See Chapter 7 for more information about writing interrupt handlers.)

PARAMETER LIST FORMAT

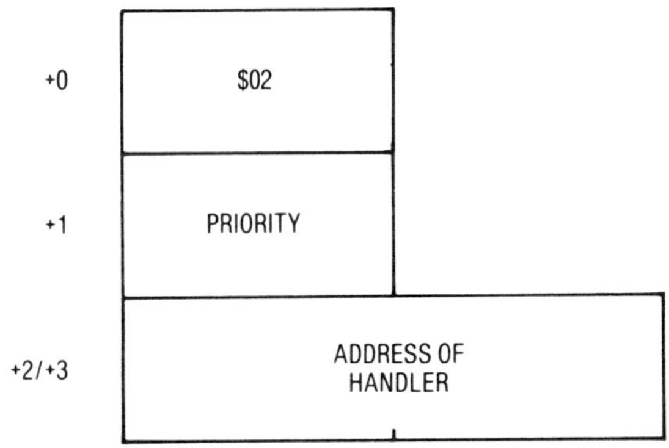

REQUIRED INPUTS

+0 Parameter count (2 parameters in list).
+2/+3 Address (LO/HI format) of user-written interrupt handling routine.

RETURNED VALUES

+1 Priority assigned to this handler by ProDOS: 1, 2, 3 or 4. This is the handler's position in the calling sequence. It is assigned the highest priority (earliest position) available.

Return Code
- $00 —No errors
- $04 —Parameter count is not $02
- $25 —Interrupt handler table full (4 are installed)
- $53 —Invalid parameter in list (address is zero)

$41 DEALLOC_INTERRUPT: REMOVE INTERRUPT HANDLER

FUNCTION This function removes a previously installed interrupt handling routine's address from the ProDOS table.

PARAMETER LIST FORMAT

Offset	Field
+0	$01
+1	PRIORITY

REQUIRED INPUTS

- +0 Parameter count (1 parameter in list).
- +1 Priority of handler to be removed (1, 2, 3, or 4) as returned by MLI call $40 when it was installed.

RETURNED VALUES

Return Code
- $00 —No errors
- $04 —Parameter count is not $01
- $53 —Invalid parameter in list (PRIORITY is not 1, 2, 3, or 4)

$65 QUIT: EXIT FROM ONE INTERPRETER, DISPATCH ANOTHER

FUNCTION This function causes the MLI to move three pages of code from $D100 in the alternate 4K of the Language card to $1000 and branch to it. This code frees any memory allocated by the interpreter in thc Systcm Memory Bit Map in the System Global Page, and then prompts the user for the name of a new Interpreter (System Program) to be executed. It then loads the new Interpreter and executes it. For more information on this call and on writing an Interpreter, see Chapter 7.

PARAMETER LIST FORMAT

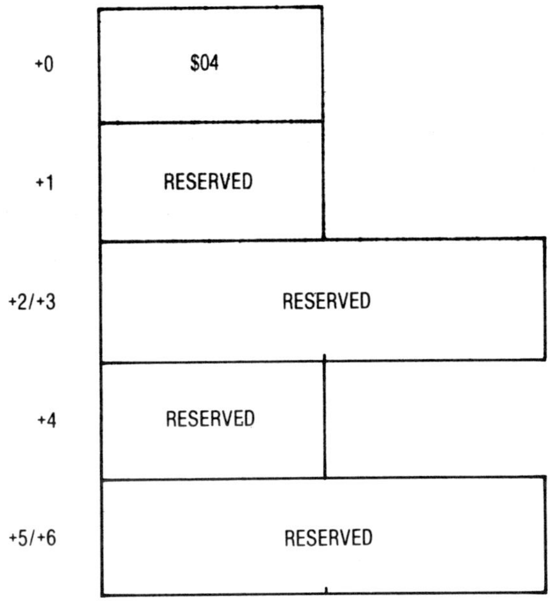

REQUIRED INPUTS

+0 Parameter count (4 parameters in list).

+1—+6 All other fields in the parameter list are reserved for future use. They must be present and they must be initialized to zeroes.

RETURNED VALUES

Return Code $04 —Parameter count is not $04

$80 READ_BLOCK: READ DISK BLOCK BY UNIT NUMBER

FUNCTION This function calls the device handler for a given unit to read a 512-byte disk block. Calling this function is essentially the same as calling the device driver directly with the following additional actions: the buffer memory is validity checked for prior use; interrupts are disabled prior to the call to the driver; the unit number is validity checked and mapped into the appropriate device driver's address; the bank switched memory (language card) is enabled prior to the call and restored to its previous condition when the call completes. For these reasons, it is recommended that all block I/O be performed through the READ_BLOCK and WRITE_BLOCK MLI calls rather than calling the drivers directly. Direct calls are only recommended when the application will not be using the ProDOS Kernel and only the driver itself is available in memory.

PARAMETER LIST FORMAT

Offset	Contents
+0	$03
+1	UNIT NUMBER
+2/+3	ADDRESS OF DATA BUFFER
+4/+5	BLOCK NUMBER

REQUIRED INPUTS

+0	Parameter count (3 parameters in list).
+1	Unit number of disk to be accessed. The bit assignment of a ProDOS unit number is as follows: DSSS0000, where D is the drive number (0 = drive 1, 1 = drive 2) and SSS is the slot number (1 through 7).
+2/+3	Address (LO/HI) of the caller's 512-byte buffer into which the block will be read. The buffer need not be page aligned.
+4/+5	Block number (LO/HI) to read. This may range from \$0000 to \$0117 for a diskette. The validity of this number is checked by the driver itself.

RETURNED VALUES

Return Code	\$00	—No errors
	\$04	—Parameter count is not \$03
	\$27	—I/O error or bad block number
	\$28	—No device connected to unit
	\$56	—Bad buffer (already in use by ProDOS)

$81 WRITE_BLOCK: WRITE DISK BLOCK BY UNIT NUMBER

FUNCTION This function calls the device handler for a given unit to write a 512-byte disk block. Calling this function is essentially the same as calling the device driver directly with the following additional actions: the buffer memory is validity checked for prior use; interrupts are disabled prior to the call to the driver; the unit number is validity checked and mapped into the appropriate device driver's address; the bank switched memory (language card) is enabled prior to the call and restored to its previous condition when the call completes. For these reasons, it is recommended that all block I/O be performed through the READ_BLOCK and WRITE_BLOCK MLI calls rather than calling the drivers directly. Direct calls are only recommended when the application will not be using the ProDOS Kernel and only the driver itself is available in memory.

PARAMETER LIST FORMAT

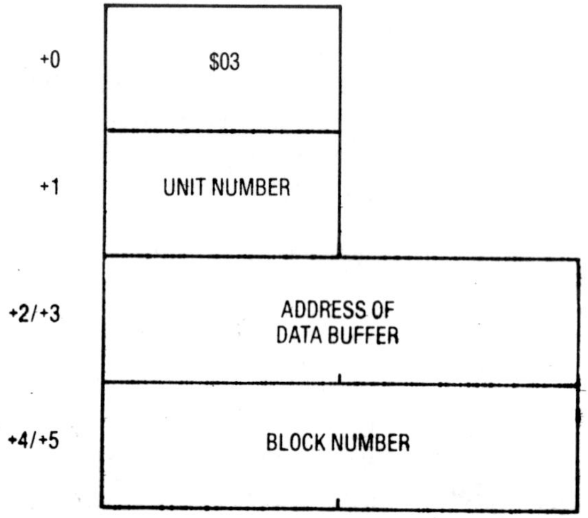

REQUIRED INPUTS

+0 Parameter count (3 parameters in list).

+1 Unit number of disk to be accessed. The bit assignment of a ProDOS unit number is as follows: DSSS0000, where D is the drive number (0 = drive 1, 1 = drive 2) and SSS is the slot number (1 through 7).

+2/+3 Address (LO/HI) of the caller's 512-byte buffer from which the block will be written. The buffer need not be page aligned.

+4/+5 Block number (LO/HI) to write. This may range from $0000 to $0117 for a diskette. The validity of this number is checked by the driver itself.

RETURNED VALUES

Return Code
$00 —No errors
$04 —Parameter count is not $03
$27 —I/O error or bad block number
$28 —No device connected to unit
$2B —Disk is write protected
$56 —Bad buffer (already in use by ProDOS)

$82 GET_TIME: READ CALENDAR/CLOCK PERIPHERAL CARD

FUNCTION This function accesses any calendar/clock card which might be in the system and sets the system date and time in the System Global Page. If no calendar/clock handler has been installed (DATETIME vector in the System Global Page), the call is ignored.

PARAMETER LIST

None (parameter list address following JSR is $0000)

REQUIRED INPUTS

None

RETURNED VALUES

$BF90/$BF91	System Global Page date field is filled in. Its format is (LO/HI): YYYYYYYM MMMDDDDD where YYYYYYY is the year (offset from 1900), MMMM is the month (1 through 12), and DDDDD is the day.
$BF92/$BF93	System Global Page time field is filled in. Its format is (LO/HI): HHHHHHHH MMMMMMMM where HHHHHHHH is the hour since midnight and MMMMMMMM is the minute (0 through 59).
Return Code	$00 —No errors

$C0 CREATE: CREATE A NEW FILE OR DIRECTORY

FUNCTION This function creates a new file (either a data file or a directory file). One 512-byte block of disk space is allocated to the new file. The file may not already exist. If it is desirable to recreate an old file, issue the DESTROY call first. If the pathname given indicates that the file's directory entry will be in a subdirectory and there are no free directory entries there, the subdirectory will be extended by one block. The Volume Directory may not be extended. If the new file is a directory file, a directory header is created and written to the key block.

PARAMETER LIST FORMAT

Offset	Field
+0	$07
+1/+2	ADDRESS OF PATHNAME
+3	ACCESS BITS
+4	FILE TYPE
+5/+6	AUXILIARY FILE TYPE
+7	STORAGE TYPE
+8/+9	CREATION DATE
+A/+B	CREATION TIME

REQUIRED INPUTS

+0 Parameter count (7 parameters in list).

+1/+2 Address (LO/HI) of pathname buffer for file to be created. The pathname buffer consists of a 1-byte length followed by 1 to 63 characters of name. If the first character is a "/", the name is considered to be fully qualified. If not, the current default prefix is added to the name by ProDOS when the file is created.

+3 Access privileges associated with this file. The access bits are:

DNBXXXWR

(high bit to low bit) where...

- D (bit 7) if 1 allows the file to be DESTROYed.
- N (bit 6) if 1 allows the file to be RENAMEd.
- B (bit 5) if 1 indicates file needs backing up.
- X (bits 4, 3, and 2) are reserved for future use.
- W (bit 1) if 1 allows the file to be written.
- R (bit 0) if 1 allows the file to be read.

Full access is $C3. A file is "locked" in the BASIC interpreter sense if the D, N, W and R bits are all zeroes. It is unlocked if they are all ones. The B bit is forced to one when the file is created. WARNING: It is possible to set the "X" reserved bits to ones with this call since no validity check is made by the MLI on CREATE (a check is made for SET_FILE_INFO, however).

+4 Type of data stored in the file. Commonly supported file types are:

$01	BAD	File containing bad blocks.
$04	TXT	File containing ASCII text (BASIC data file).
$06	BIN	File containing a binary memory image or machine language program.
$0F	DIR	File is a directory.
$19	ADB	AppleWorks data base file

$1A	AWP	AppleWorks word processing file
$1B	ASF	AppleWorks spread sheet file
$F0	CMD	ProDOS added command file.
$F1-$F8		User defined file types.
$FC	BAS	File contains an Applesoft program.
$FD	VAR	File contains Applesoft variables (STORE/ RESTORE).
$FE	REL	File contains a relocatable object module (EDASM).
$FF	SYS	File contains a ProDOS system program.

Other less commonly used file types are defined in APPENDIX E. Assignment of a file type is a convention which serves to inform the program which accesses a file what data format it should expect to find there. You are not prevented from storing binary data in a TXT file or ASCII text in a BIN file, but this runs counter to convention and is discouraged.

+5/+6 Auxiliary data pertaining to the file. Its usage is defined according to its file type above. The current uses of this field by the BI are:

TXT	contains the default record length (LO/HI).
BIN	contains the address (LO/HI) at which to load the image.
BAS	contains the address (LO/HI) of the BASIC program image.
VAR	contains the address (LO/HI) of the BASIC variables image.
SYS	contains $2000 (LO/HI), the load address for system files.

+7 Storage type or type of file organization. If this byte contains $0D, the file is a linked subdirectory file. If it is $01, it is a standard seedling file (at the time of its creation). Other values are reserved for future use. If a value of $00, $02, or $03 is given, $01 is assumed. All values other than $00-$03 or $0D will result in an error.

+8/+9 Date of creation. If this field is set to zero, the MLI uses the current system date (if any). If this field is non-zero, it is the creation date in the (LO/HI) form YYYYYYYM MMMDDDDD where YYYYYYY is the year past 1900, MMMM is the month (1-12) and DDDDD is the day of the month.

+A/+B Time of creation. If this field is set to zero, the MLI uses the current system time (if any). If this field is non-zero, it is the creation time in the (LO/HI) form HHHHHHHH MMMMMMMM where HHHHHHHH is the hour past midnight and MMMMMMMM is the minute within the hour.

RETURNED VALUES

Return Code
$00 —No errors
$04 —Parameter count is not $07
$27 —I/O error
$2B —Disk is write protected
$40 —Pathname has invalid syntax
$44 —Path to file's subdirectory is bad
$45 —Volume directory not found
$47 —Duplicate file name already in use
$48 —Disk full
$49 —Volume directory full
$4B —Bad storage type (use only $0D or $01)
$53 —Invalid parameter or address pointer
$5A —Damaged disk freespace bit map

$C1 DESTROY: DELETE A FILE OR DIRECTORY

FUNCTION This function deletes a file or empty subdirectory. Open files may not be deleted. The Volume Directory may not be deleted. A subdirectory is considered "locked" if it contains any files at all, and may not be DESTROYed until all its files and subdirectories are DESTROYed.

PARAMETER LIST FORMAT

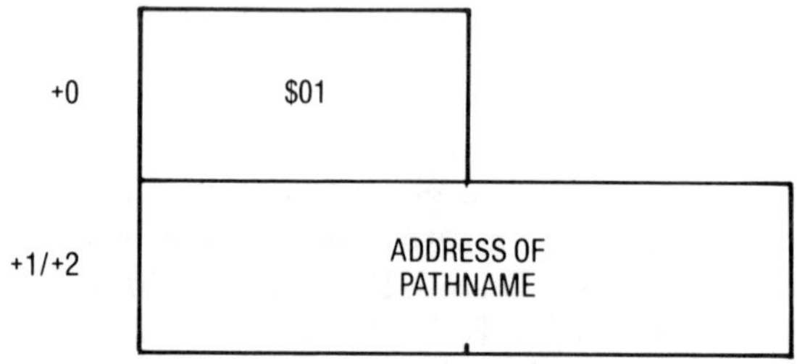

REQUIRED INPUTS

+0 Parameter count (1 parameter in list).

+1/+2 Address (LO/HI) of pathname buffer for file to be deleted. The pathname buffer consists of a 1-byte length followed by 1 to 63 characters of name. If the first character is a "/", the name is considered to be fully qualified. If not, the current default prefix is added to the name by ProDOS.

RETURNED VALUES

Return Code
$00 —No errors
$04 —Parameter count is not $01
$27 —I/O error
$2B —Disk is write protected
$40 —Pathname has invalid syntax
$44 —Path to file's subdirectory is bad
$45 —Volume directory not found
$46 —File not found in specified directory

$4A — Incompatible file format
$4B — Bad storage type
$4E — Access refused: DESTROY bit not enabled or non-empty subdirectory
$50 — Access refused: File is currently open
$5A — Damaged disk freespace bit map

$C2 RENAME: RENAME A FILE OR DIRECTORY

FUNCTION This function renames a file or subdirectory. Only the final name in the path specification may be renamed. This function will not rename multiple directories in a pathname specification (e.g. /project/myfile may not be renamed to /task/yourfile since this involves renaming something other than the final name in the pathname). RENAME will not create new subdirectories or move a file's entry from one directory to another (e.g. you may not rename /project/myfile to /project/another/myfile since this involves moving the file's entry to subdirectory "another"). A volume may be renamed if no files are currently opened for it. A file or subdirectory may be renamed if it is not open, or if it is a read-only file (WRITE access disabled). The new file name may not be the same as another in the same directory.

PARAMETER LIST FORMAT

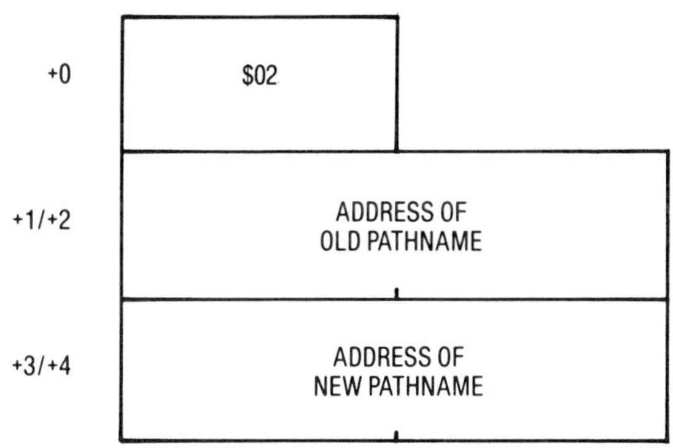

REQUIRED INPUTS

+0	Parameter count (2 parameters in list).
+1/+2	Address (LO/HI) of pathname buffer for file to be renamed. The pathname buffer consists of a 1-byte length followed by 1 to 63 characters of name. If the first character is a "/", the name is considered to be fully qualified. If not, the current default prefix is added to the name by ProDOS.
+3/+4	Address (LO/HI) of pathname buffer for the new name. The qualifying levels of the name, if any, should match those of the old pathname given at +1/+2. Only the last name should be different. The format of the new pathname buffer is identical to that of the old pathname buffer given above. The current default prefix, if any, will be added to a non-fully qualified pathname.

RETURNED VALUES

Return Code
- $00 —No errors
- $04 —Parameter count is not $02
- $27 —I/O error
- $2B —Disk is write protected
- $40 —Pathname has invalid syntax
- $44 —Path to file's subdirectory is bad
- $45 —Volume directory not found
- $46 —File not found in specified directory
- $47 —New name duplicates one already in directory
- $4A —Incompatible file format
- $4B —Bad storage type
- $4E —Access refused: RENAME bit not enabled
- $50 —Access refused: File is currently open
- $57 —Two volumes are online with the same volume name

$C3 SET_FILE_INFO: CHANGE FILE'S ATTRIBUTES

FUNCTION This function changes the attributes (e.g. file type, storage type, etc.) which are stored in the directory entry which describes a file. The file may be open or closed. SET_FILE_INFO will not act upon a Volume Directory (an error of $40 will result). Before issuing this function call, it is recommended that GET_FILE_INFO ($C4) be used to determine the current parameter settings for the file. (Note that the parameter lists for the two calls have a compatible format.)

PARAMETER LIST FORMAT

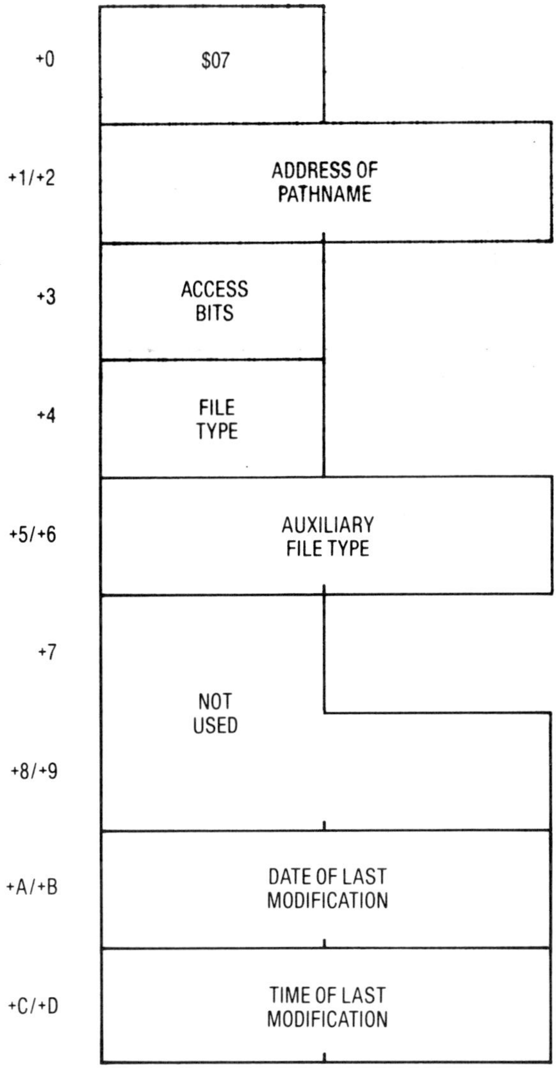

REQUIRED INPUTS

+0 Parameter count (7 parameters in list).

+1/+2 Address (LO/HI) of pathname buffer for file. The pathname buffer consists of a 1-byte length followed by 1 to 63 characters of name. If the first character is a "/", the name is considered to be fully qualified. If not, the current default prefix is added to the name by ProDOS.

+3 New access privileges to be associated with this file. The access bits are:

DNBXXXWR

(high bit to low bit) where...

D (bit 7) if 1 allows the file to be DESTROYed.
N (bit 6) if 1 allows the file to be RENAMEd.
B (bit 5) if 1 indicates file needs backing up.
X (bits 4, 3, and 2) are reserved for future use.
W (bit 1) if 1 allows the file to be written.
R (bit 0) if 1 allows the file to be read.

Full access is $C3. A file is "locked" in the BASIC interpreter sense if the D, N, W and R bits are all zeroes. It is unlocked if they are all ones. Note that a "locked" file is not protected against SET_FILE_INFO (how else would one unlock it?). If an attempt is made to use the "X" reserved bits, an error will occur. They should be set to zeroes.

+4 Type of data stored in the file. Commonly supported file types are:

$01	BAD	File containing bad blocks.
$04	TXT	File containing ASCII text (BASIC data file).
$06	BIN	File containing a binary memory image or machine language program.
$0F	DIR	File is a directory.
$19	ADB	AppleWorks data base file
$1A	AWP	AppleWorks word processing file
$1B	ASF	AppleWorks spread sheet file
$F0	CMD	ProDOS added command file.

$F1-$F8		User defined file types.
$FC	BAS	File contains an Applesoft program.
$FD	VAR	File contains Applesoft variables (STORE/ RESTORE).
$FE	REL	File contains a relocatable object module (EDASM).
$FF	SYS	File contains a ProDOS system program.

Other less commonly used file types are defined in APPENDIX E. Assignment of a file type is a convention which serves to inform the program which accesses a file what data format it should expect to find there. You are not prevented from storing binary data in a TXT file or ASCII text in a BIN file, but this runs counter to convention and is discouraged.

+5/+6 Auxiliary data pertaining to the file. Its usage is defined according to its file type above. The current uses of this field by the BI are:

TXT	contains the default record length (LO/HI).
BIN	contains the address (LO/HI) at which to load the image.
BAS	contains the address (LO/HI) of the BASIC program image.
VAR	contains the address (LO/HI) of the BASIC variables image.
SYS	contains $2000 (LO/HI), the load address for system files.

+7 Ignored. May be set to zero.

+8/+9 Ignored. May be set to zero.

+A/+B Date of last modification. If this field is set to zero, the MLI uses the current system date (if any). If this field is non-zero, it is the modification date in the (LO/HI) form

YYYYYYYM MMMDDDDD where YYYYYYY is the year past 1900, MMMM is the month (1-12) and DDDDD is the day of the month.

+C/+D Time of last modification. If this field is set to zero, the MLI uses the current system time (if any). If this field is non-zero, it is the modification time in the (LO/HI) form HHHHHHHH MMMMMMMM where HHHHHHHH is the hour past midnight and MMMMMMMM is the minute within the hour.

RETURNED VALUES

Return Code
- \$00 — No errors
- \$04 — Parameter count is not \$07
- \$27 — I/O error
- \$2B — Disk is write protected
- \$40 — Pathname has invalid syntax
- \$44 — Path to file's subdirectory is bad
- \$45 — Volume directory not found
- \$46 — File not found in specified directory
- \$4A — Incompatible file format
- \$4B — Bad storage type
- \$4E — Access refused: Reserved access bits were used
- \$53 — Parameter value out of range
- \$5A — Damaged disk freespace bit map

\$C4 GET_FILE_INFO: RETURN FILE'S ATTRIBUTES

FUNCTION This function reads the attributes (e.g. file type, storage type, etc.), which describe the file and are stored in the directory entry, and returns them in the parameter list provided by the caller. The file may be open or closed. If information about a Volume Directory is requested, the size of the volume in blocks and the blocks in use count are also returned.

PARAMETER LIST FORMAT

Offset	Field
+0	$0A
+1/+2	ADDRESS OF PATHNAME
+3	ACCESS BITS
+4	FILE TYPE
+5/+6	AUXILIARY FILE TYPE
+7	STORAGE TYPE
+8/+9	BLOCKS USED
+A/+B	DATE OF LAST MODIFICATION
+C/+D	TIME OF LAST MODIFICATION
+E/+F	CREATION DATE
+10/+11	CREATION TIME

REQUIRED INPUTS

+0 Parameter count ($A parameters in list).
+1/+2 Address (LO/HI) of pathname buffer for file. The pathname buffer consists of a 1-byte length followed by 1 to 63 characters of name. If the first character is a "/", the name is considered to be fully qualified. If not, the current default prefix is added to the name by ProDOS.

RETURNED VALUES

+3 Access privileges associated with this file. The access bits are:

DNBXXXWR

(high bit to low bit) where...

D (bit 7) if 1 allows the file to be DESTORYed.
N (bit 6) if 1 allows the file to be RENAMEd.
B (bit 5) if 1 indicates file needs backing up.
X (bits 4, 3, and 2) are reserved for future use.
W (bit 1) if 1 allows the file to be written.
R (bit 0) if 1 allows the file to be read.

Full access is $C3. A file is "locked" in the BASIC interpreter sense if the D, N, W and R bits are all zeroes. It is unlocked if they are all ones.

+4 Type of data stored in the file. Commonly supported file types are:

$01	BAD	File containing bad blocks.
$04	TXT	File containing ASCII text (BASIC data file).
$06	BIN	File containing a binary memory image or machine language program.
$0F	DIR	File is a directory.
$19	ADB	AppleWorks data base file
$1A	AWP	AppleWorks word processing file
$1B	ASF	AppleWorks spread sheet file
$F0	CMD	ProDOS added command file.
$F1-$F8		User defined file types.

$FC	BAS	File contains an Applesoft program.
$FD	VAR	File contains Applesoft variables (STORE/ RESTORE).
$FE	REL	File contains a relocatable object module (EDASM).
$FF	SYS	File contains a ProDOS system program.

Other less commonly used file types are defined in APPENDIX E. Assignment of a file type is a convention which serves to inform the program which accesses a file what data format it should expect to find there. You are not prevented from storing binary data in a TXT file or ASCII text in a BIN file, but this runs counter to convention and is discouraged.

+5/+6 Auxiliary data pertaining to the file. Its usage is defined according to its file type above. The current uses of this field by the BI are:

TXT	contains the default record length (LO/HI).
BIN	contains the address (LO/HI) at which to load the image.
BAS	contains the address (LO/HI) of the BASIC program image.
VAR	contains the address (LO/HI) of the BASIC variables image.
SYS	contains $2000 (LO/HI), the load address for system files.

If the GET_FILE_INFO request is for the Volume Directory, this field contains the size of this volume in blocks.

+7 Storage type or type of file organization. Currently supported storage types are:

$0D	Linked directory file
$01	Seedling file (no index blocks)
$02	Sapling file (one index level)
$03	Tree file (two index levels)

	Other values are reserved for future use.
+8/+9	Number of 512-byte disk blocks in use by file including index blocks and data blocks. If the GET_FILE_INFO call is made on the volume itself (Volume Directory), this field contains the total number of disk blocks in use on the volume (including system overhead).
+A/+B	Date of last modification. If this field is non-zero, it is the date of the last modification in the (LO/HI) form YYYYYYYM MMMDDDDD where YYYYYYY is the year past 1900, MMMM is the month (1-12) and DDDDD is the day of the month.
+C/+D	Time of last modification. If this field is non-zero, it is the time of the last modification in the (LO/HI) form HHHHHHHH MMMMMMMM where HHHHHHHH is the hour past midnight and MMMMMMMM is the minute within the hour.
+E/+F	Date of file's creation. If this field is non-zero, it is the creation date in the (LO/HI) form YYYYYYYMMMMDDDDD where YYYYYYY is the year past 1900, MMMM is the month (1-12) and DDDDD is the day of the month.
+10/+11	Time of file's creation. If this field is non-zero, it is the creation time in the (LO/HI) form HHHHHHHH MMMMMMMM where HHHHHHHH is the hour past midnight and MMMMMMMM is the minute within the hour.
Return Code	$00 —No errors $04 —Parameter count is not $0A $27 —I/O error $40 —Pathname has invalid syntax $44 —Path to file's subdirectory is bad $45 —Volume directory not found $46 —File not found in specified directory

$4A —Incompatible file format
$4B —Bad storage type
$53 —Parameter value out of range
$5A —Damaged disk freespace bit map

$C5 ONLINE: RETURN NAMES OF ONE OR ALL ONLINE VOLUMES

FUNCTION This function examines all mounted disk volumes and returns their names in the buffer provided by the caller. If a single volume is to be identified, the caller must provide a specific unit number (slot and drive).

PARAMETER LIST FORMAT

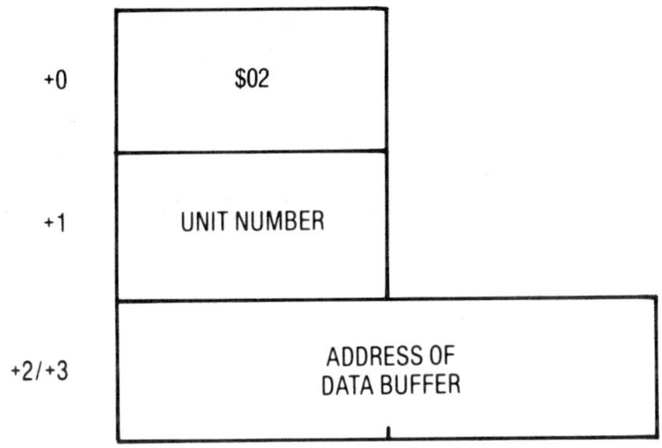

REQUIRED INPUTS

+0 Parameter count (2 parameters in list).

+1 Unit number of specific device to be examined. If all online volumes are to be identified, set this field to zero. The bit assignment for a specific unit number is: DSSS0000, where D is the drive number (0=drive 1, 1=drive 2) and SSS is the slot number (1 through 7).

+2/+3 Address (LO/HI) of a buffer to contain the volume names returned by ProDOS. If a specific unit is to be examined, a 16-byte buffer must be provided. If the call is non-specific (UNIT = 0), then the buffer must be 256 bytes to allow for up to 16 online volumes.

RETURNED VALUES

Buffer — If the return code in the accumulator is zero, the caller's buffer will contain zero or more volume name entries of format described below. The volume names will be given in the order in which ProDOS searches for a volume, i.e. the boot volume first, followed by slot numbers lower than the boot slot, wrapping around to higher slots last.

ONLINE VOLUME ENTRY

byte 0	DSSSLLLL: where D is the drive number (0=drive 1, 1=drive 2), SSS is the slot number (1 through 7), and LLLL is the length of the name which follows. If LLLL is zero, an error occurred in examining this volume. The return code is in the first byte of the name field. If byte 0 is zero, then there are no more volume entries in the buffer.
bytes 1-15	Volume name or 1-byte error code. No slash precedes the name.

Return Code
- $00 —No errors
- $04 —Parameter count is not $02
- $55 —Volume Control Block full (too many open files)
- $56 —Bad buffer address (check system memory bit map)

The following error codes may appear for a specific unit in byte 1 of a buffer entry. If so, the return code above will be $00.

- $27 —I/O error on this unit
- $28 —Device not connected (e.g. no drive 2)
- $2E —Diskette switched while file was open
- $45 —Volume directory not found
- $52 —Not a ProDOS disk volume
- $57 —Duplicate volume—Byte 3 of buffer entry contains the unit number of the duplicate

$C6 SET_PREFIX: CHANGE DEFAULT PATHNAME PREFIX

FUNCTION This function changes the default prefix which is attached to any pathnames passed to the MLI which are not fully qualified (do not start with a slash). The MLI follows the prefix given, locating each directory at each level of the prefix to make sure that they exist on a mounted volume.

PARAMETER LIST FORMAT

Offset	Contents
+0	$01
+1/+2	ADDRESS OF PATHNAME

REQUIRED INPUTS

+0 Parameter count (1 parameter in list).

+1/+2 Address (LO/HI) of pathname buffer for the new prefix. The pathname buffer consists of one byte of length followed by 1 to 63 characters of name. If the first character is a "/", the name is considered to be fully qualified. If not, the old default prefix is added to the new one to form a completely qualified default prefix (for a total length of no more than 64 characters). The last name in the prefix must be that of a directory file. The prefix may be eliminated by specifying a null (0 length) prefix. An ending slash is assumed if it is omitted.

RETURNED VALUES

Return Code
$00 —No errors
$04 —Parameter count is not $01
$40 —Pathname has invalid syntax or prefix too long
$44 —Path to final subdirectory is bad
$45 —Volume directory not found
$46 —Final subdirectory file not found
$4A —Incompatible file format
$4B —Bad storage type
$5A —Damaged disk freespace bit map

$C7 GET_PREFIX: RETURN DEFAULT PATHNAME PREFIX

FUNCTION This function returns the default prefix, if any, to the caller's buffer.

PARAMETER LIST FORMAT

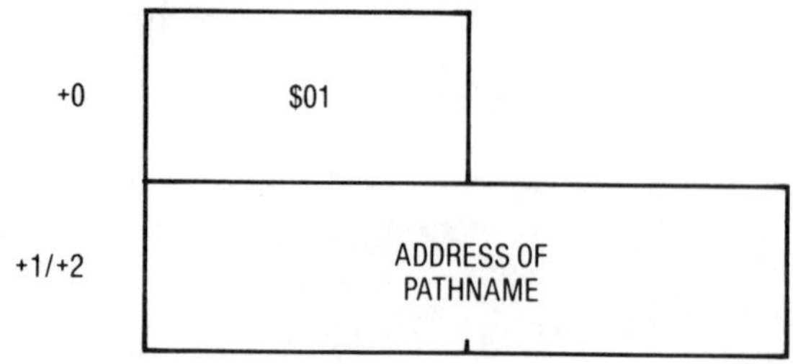

REQUIRED INPUTS

+0	Parameter count (1 parameter in list).
+1/+2	Address (LO/HI) of pathname buffer into which the MLI will copy the default prefix. The buffer must be at least 64 bytes long.

RETURNED VALUES

Buffer	The buffer will contain the current MLI default prefix. The prefix consists of one byte of length followed by up to 63 characters of prefix. If the length is zero, the prefix is null. Otherwise, the prefix starts and ends with a slash.
Return Code	\$00 —No errors \$04 —Parameter count is not \$01 \$56 —Bad buffer address (check system memory bit map)

$C8 OPEN: OPEN A FILE

FUNCTION This function locates a file on a volume and sets up internal control blocks (a File Control Block—FCB, and a Volume Control Block—VCB) to allow the user to read or write it. A reference number (from 1 to 8) is assigned by the MLI to the open file for future identification. (The reference number uniquely identifies the FCB which is being used with the file.) The current position for reading or writing is set to zero (start of the file). At most, eight files may be open at one time. More than one OPEN may be issued to the same file if the file's access is WRITE disabled (read-only file).

Once a file is opened, it should always be closed (using the MLI CLOSE call). This is to permit the MLI to release the reference number for use by other OPENs. In addition, the MLI keeps a count of the number of files which are open on a volume. If the diskette is switched while files are open, error return codes are produced.

A directory file may also be opened (for READs only). When accessing a directory, do not make assumptions about the length of an entry or the number of entries per block—use the fields in the directory header which are provided for this purpose. This will help to insure that your program will work for future releases of ProDOS. A directory file may be read only, not written.

PARAMETER LIST FORMAT

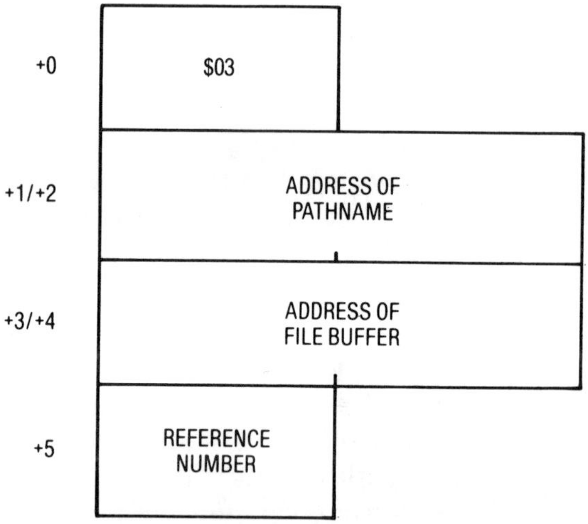

REQUIRED INPUTS

+0 Parameter count (3 parameters in list).

+1/+2 Address (LO/HI) of pathname buffer for file. The pathname buffer consists of one byte of length followed by 1 to 63 characters of name. If the first character is a "/", the name is considered to be fully qualified. If not, the current default prefix is added to the name by ProDOS.

+3/+4 Address (LO/HI) of a 1024-byte file buffer, provided by the caller in his memory, to be used by the MLI while the file is open. The buffer must begin on an even page boundary (LO portion of address must be zero). The MLI uses the buffer to hold the current data block and the current index block respectively. Its contents need not be intitialized by the caller. It should not be tampered with by the caller while the file remains open.

$BF94 The LEVEL byte in the System Global Page may be set to indicate the level of this OPEN. If a subsequent CLOSE is issued with a REF NUM of zero, then all files of a given level or higher will be closed. This feature is handy in that it allows group CLOSEs on user-defined classes of files. Normally, LEVEL is set to zero.

RETURNED VALUES

+5 A reference number assigned to this open file by the MLI (from $01 to $08). The caller should make a note of this number and use it in all future references to this open file. A reference number is used to identify open files instead of the pathname since it is possible to maintain multiple "opens" on the same read-only file.

Return Code
- $00 — No errors
- $04 — Parameter count is not $03
- $27 — I/O error
- $40 — Pathname has invalid syntax
- $42 — Eight files are already open
- $44 — Path to file's subdirectory is bad
- $45 — Volume directory not found
- $46 — File not found in specified directory
- $4B — Bad storage type
- $50 — File already open (WRITE enabled)
- $53 — Parameter value out of range (REF NUM)
- $56 — Bad buffer address (check system memory bit map)
- $5A — Damaged disk freespace bit map

$C9 NEWLINE: SET END OF LINE CHARACTER

FUNCTION A file may be read as either a continuous stream of bytes or as a collection of lines, terminated by "newline" characters (such as a RETURN character). When a file is first opened, the former assumption is made. To enable the line by line mode, the NEWLINE function may be invoked, specifying the end of line character to be used. All future READ operations on the specified open file will be terminated either when a newline character is detected, or when the read length is exhausted (or at end of file).

PARAMETER LIST FORMAT

Offset	Contents
+0	$03
+1	REFERENCE NUMBER
+2	AND MASK
+3	NEWLINE CHARACTER

REQUIRED INPUTS

+0 Parameter count (3 parameters in list).

+1 Reference number for an open file as returned by OPEN.

+2 AND mask. The value given here is logically ANDed with the contents of each byte read before a comparison is made with the NEWLINE character given in +3. If the AND mask is zero, then the line by line mode is disabled and the continuous byte stream mode is enabled. If a mask of $FF is given, the NEWLINE character must exactly match what is read. Other values for the AND mask allow "don't care" bits. For example, $7F allows the MSB to be either on or off without affecting the comparison (e.g. $0D or $8D will both be treated as newline if $0D is the NEWLINE character and the AND mask is $7F).

+3 The actual value of the NEWLINE character. Normally, when line by line mode is used, this is should be set to $0D. Note that if the AND mask is $00, this character is ignored (even if it is also $00; if $00 is to be the newline character, set the AND mask to $FF).

RETURNED VALUES

Return Code $00 —No errors
$04 —Parameter count is not $03
$43 —Invalid reference number

$CA READ: READ ONE OR MORE BYTES FROM AN OPEN FILE

FUNCTION This function reads a number of bytes, starting at the current file position in an open file. The number of bytes read depends upon the length requested by the caller, whether or not a newline character has been set (see the $C9 function call), and whether the end of file is reached during the read. The current file position is updated to point to the byte following the last byte read.

In general, read operations will be much more efficient if the amount of data transferred exceeds a block (512 bytes). Special "direct read" code exists within the MLI to prevent "double buffering" and allow direct reads to the caller's buffer without going through the I/O buffer attached to the file. This fast access is only used when whole blocks may be read at a time. Use of the NEWLINE feature automatically disables "direct reads." (NOTE: It is this "direct read" feature which makes ProDOS I/O faster than Apple DOS.)

Note that, once a file is opened, no check is made by the MLI that the user has not switched diskette volumes in the drive. If this occurs, it is possible to read random portions of the new diskette volume! If the programmer is issuing a READ after a period of disk inactivity, it is recommended that a ONLINE call ($C5) be issued to make sure that the same diskette is still in the drive.

PARAMETER LIST FORMAT

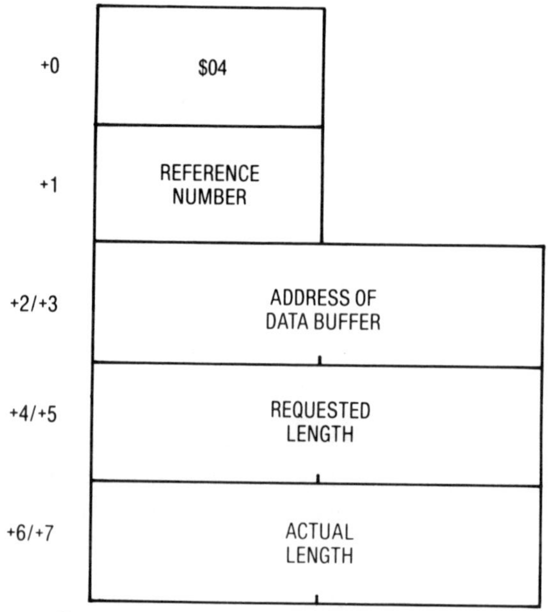

REQUIRED INPUTS

+0 Parameter count (4 parameters in list).

+1 Reference number for an open file as returned by OPEN.

+2/+3 Address (LO/HI) of a sufficiently large buffer provided by the caller into which the data will be read. This buffer should not be confused with the "file buffer" passed to OPEN which is separate, and should not be used by the caller's program.

+4/+5 Maximum number (LO/HI) of bytes of data to read. This is usually the size of the data buffer. If lines are being read, make sure this value is as large as the longest line, including the end of line character itself.

RETURNED VALUES

+6/+7 Actual number (LO/HI) of bytes placed in the caller's data buffer by the MLI. This value will differ from the requested length in +4/+5 if a newline character was found, if the end of the file was reached, or if an error occurred during the read operation. If a newline character terminated the read, this length will include the newline character itself. If the read began at the end of file position, this field is set to zero, and the end of file return code ($4C) is placed in the A register.

Return Code
- $00 —No errors
- $04 —Parameter count is not $04
- $27 —I/O error
- $43 —Invalid reference number
- $4C —At end of file, nothing was read
- $4E —Access refused: Read bit not enabled
- $56 —Bad buffer address (check System memory bit map)
- $5A —Damaged disk freespace bit map

$CB WRITE: WRITE ONE OR MORE BYTES TO AN OPEN FILE

FUNCTION This function writes a number of bytes to disk, starting at the current file position in an open file. You may not write to a directory. The current file position is updated to point to the byte following the last byte written. The end of file mark is moved if necessary, and new data and/or index blocks are allocated to the file as necessary. In the interest of efficiency, the data may or may not be written to disk at this time. As much as one block's worth (512 bytes) may remain in the file buffer to be written later when the block is filled, the file is closed or flushed, or when the file position is changed. For this reason, it is important to close all files before powering off the machine.

Note that, once a file is opened, no check is made by the MLI that the user has not switched diskette volumes in the drive. If this occurs, it is possible to write on random portions of the new diskette volume! If the programmer is issuing a WRITE after a period of disk inactivity, it is recommended that a RETURN ONLINE VOLUMES call ($C5) be issued to make sure that the same diskette is still in the drive.

Note that there is no "direct write" feature similar to the "direct read" feature described under the READ MLI call.

PARAMETER LIST FORMAT

Offset	Field
+0	$04
+1	REFERENCE NUMBER
+2/+3	ADDRESS OF DATA BUFFER
+4/+5	REQUESTED LENGTH
+6/+7	ACTUAL LENGTH

REQUIRED INPUTS

+0	Parameter count (4 parameters in list).
+1	Reference number for an open file as returned by OPEN.
+2/+3	Address (LO/HI) of the data to be written to disk. This buffer should not be confused with the "file buffer" passed to OPEN which is separate, and should not be used by the caller's program.
+4/+5	Number (LO/HI) of bytes of data to write from the data buffer.

RETURNED VALUES

+6/+7	Actual number of bytes written. Unless an error occurs during the operation, this field should match the requested length in +4/+5.
Return Code	\$00 —No errors
	\$04 —Parameter count is not \$04
	\$27 —I/O error
	\$2B —Disk is write protected
	\$43 —Invalid reference number
	\$48 —Disk full
	\$4E —Access refused: WRITE bit not enabled
	\$56 —Bad buffer address (check System memory bit map)
	\$5A —Damaged disk freespace bit map

$CC CLOSE: CLOSE OPEN FILE(S), FLUSHING BUFFERS

FUNCTION For a specific open file, this function flushes any data which has not yet actually gone to disk from the file buffer, releases the file buffer to the caller for reuse, sets the BACKUP bit in the ACCESS flags for the file, updates the directory entry for the file with block count, etc., and frees the reference number and File Control Block (FCB) for use with a later OPEN. Each OPEN must have a corresponding CLOSE. If a non-specific call is made (REFNUM = 0), all open files at the current LEVEL ($BF94) or higher are closed.

PARAMETER LIST FORMAT

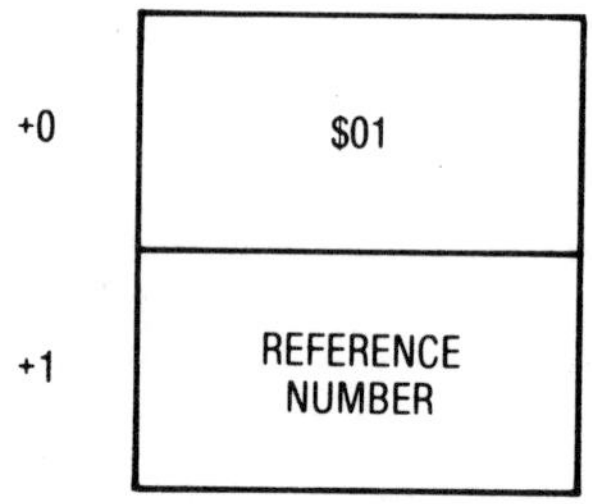

REQUIRED INPUTS

+0	Parameter count (1 parameter in list).
+1	Reference number for an open file as returned by OPEN or $00 if all files at the current level or higher are to be closed. If a multiple file request is made and an error occurs on one file, this does not prevent the MLI from attempting to complete the close operation for any other files. If multiple errors occur, only the last error return code is passed back to the caller.
$BF94	Current file LEVEL in the System Global Page. If set to $00 before this call, all open files are closed.

RETURNED VALUES

Return Code
- $00 —No errors
- $04 —Parameter count is not $01
- $27 —I/O error
- $2B —Disk is write protected
- $43 —Invalid reference number
- $5A —Damaged disk freespace bit map

$CD FLUSH: FLUSH ALL WRITE BUFFERS FOR FILES

FUNCTION For a specific open file, this function flushes any data which has not yet actually gone to disk from the file buffer, updates the directory entry for the file, and sets the BACKUP bit in the ACCESS flags for the file (if data was written).

If no write operations have occurred, then the FLUSH call is ignored. If a non-specific call is made (REFNUM = 0), all open files at the current LEVEL ($BF94) or higher are flushed. The flush call is useful when it is desirable to force write data out to disk before a long period of inactivity in case of power loss or other disasters.

PARAMETER LIST FORMAT

Offset	Contents
+0	$01
+1	REFERENCE NUMBER

REQUIRED INPUTS

+0	Parameter count (1 parameter in list).
+1	Reference number for an open file as returned by OPEN, or $00 if all files at the current level or higher are to be flushed. If a multiple file request is made and an error occurs on one file, this does not prevent the MLI from attempting to complete the flush operation for any other files. If multiple errors occur, only the last error return code is passed back to the caller.
$BF94	Current file LEVEL in the System Global Page. If set to $00 before this call, all open files are flushed.

RETURNED VALUES

Return Code	$00 —No errors
	$04 —Parameter count is not $01
	$27 —I/O error
	$2B —Disk is write protected
	$43 —Invalid reference number
	$5A —Damaged disk freespace bit map

$CE SET_MARK: CHANGE FILE POSITION WITHIN AN OPEN FILE

FUNCTION When a file is first opened, the MLI establishes a "file position" at which reading or writing will occur at the beginning of the file (zero). As data is read or written, the file position is moved to allow sequential access to the file. This file position describes the relative byte offset to the next byte in the file to be accessed. If random access to a file is desired, the caller may use this function to change the position to another location in the file before issuing a READ or WRITE call. If the file position is moved to an area of the file where no data exists (i.e. an area which has never been written), new data and/or index blocks will be allocated when the next WRITE call is made. This function may be used in conjunction with the GET_EOF call ($D1) to append data to the end of a file.

PARAMETER LIST FORMAT

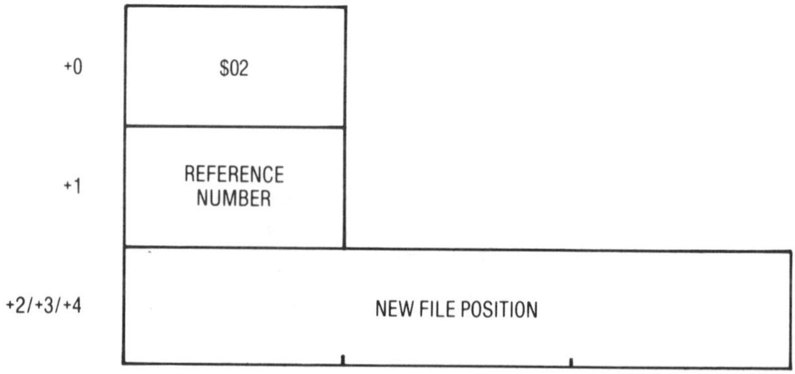

REQUIRED INPUTS

+0 Parameter count (2 parameters in list).

+1 Reference number for an open file as returned by OPEN.

+2/+3/+4 The new file position to be set. This is a 3-byte number (least significant byte first, most significant byte last) representing the byte offset into the file. The position of the first byte in a file is zero. The position may not exceed the current end of file position.

RETURNED VALUES

Return Code	\$00 — No errors
	\$04 — Parameter count is not \$02
	\$43 — Invalid reference number
	\$4D — File position beyond end of file
	\$5A — Damaged disk freespace bit map

\$CF GET_MARK: RETURN FILE POSITION WITHIN AN OPEN FILE

FUNCTION When a file is first opened, the MLI establishes a "file position" at which reading or writing will occur at the beginning of the file (zero). As data is read or written, the file position is moved to allow sequential access to the file. This file position describes the relative byte offset to the next byte in the file to be accessed. This function will return the current value of the file position.

PARAMETER LIST FORMAT

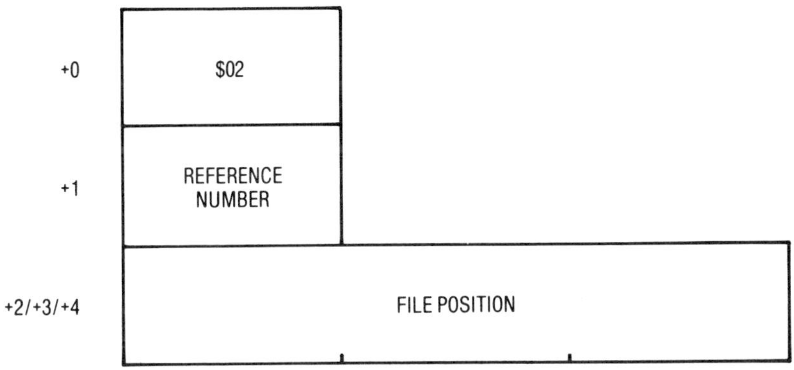

REQUIRED INPUTS

+0	Parameter count (2 parameters in list).
+1	Reference number for an open file as returned by OPEN.

RETURNED VALUES

+2/+3/+4	The current file position value. This is a 3-byte number (least significant byte first, most significant byte last) representing the byte offset into the file of the next byte to be read or written. The position of the first byte in a file is zero.
Return Code	\$00 —No errors
	\$04 —Parameter count is not \$02
	\$43 —Invalid reference number

\$D0 SET_EOF: CHANGE END OF FILE POSITION OF AN OPEN FILE

FUNCTION This function changes the end of file mark (or file size). It is not normally necessary to change the end of file mark since the WRITE function will automatically extend the EOF mark as new data is written to the end of the file. This function is useful, however, to truncate a file or to allow random positioning within a very large sparse file. If the new end of file position passed by the caller is less than the old one, the file is truncated and excess data and index blocks are freed for reuse by the system. If it exceeds or equals the old value, no new blocks will be allocated until they are needed in a WRITE operation. If the new end of file would leave the current file position outside the limits of the file, it is forced back to the new end of file position. The EOF mark of a directory file may not be changed with SET.EOF. Note that the file size does not necessarily represent the amount of disk space the file requires, since the file may be sparse (see Chapter 4).

PARAMETER LIST FORMAT

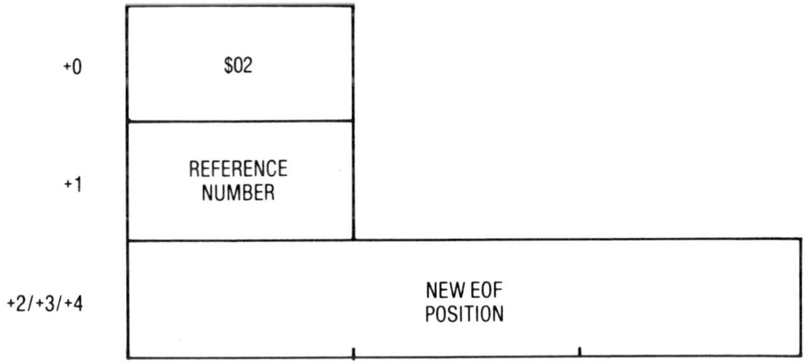

REQUIRED INPUTS

+0	Parameter count (2 parameters in list).
+1	Reference number for an open file as returned by OPEN.
+2/+3/+4	The new end of file position. This is a 3-byte number (least significant byte first, most significant byte last) representing the byte offset into the file of the last byte plus one. The position of the first byte in the file is zero (the EOF of an empty file).

RETURNED VALUES

Return Code	$00 —No errors
	$04 —Parameter count is not $02
	$27 —I/O error
	$43 —Invalid reference number
	$4D —Position is too large for volume
	$4E —Access refused: WRITE bit not enabled
	$5A —Damaged disk freespace bit map

$D1 GET_EOF: RETURN END OF FILE POSITION OF AN OPEN FILE

FUNCTION This function returns the value of the end of file mark for an open file. GET_EOF may be used to determine the size of a sequential file or to find the end of a file so that data may be appended to it. GET_EOF for a directory file will return the number of blocks used multiplied by 512 bytes. Note that the file size does not necessarily represent the amount of disk space the file requires, since the file may be sparse (see Chapter 4).

PARAMETER LIST FORMAT

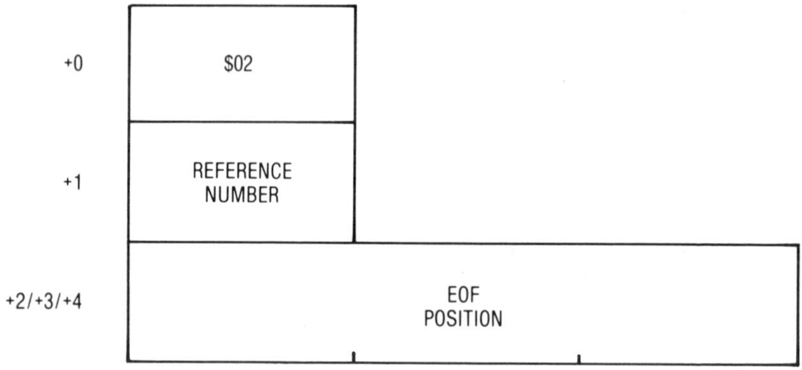

REQUIRED INPUTS

+0 Parameter count (2 parameters in list).
+1 Reference number for an open file as returned by OPEN.

RETURNED VALUES

+2/+3/+4 The current end of file position. This is a 3-byte number (least significant byte first, most significant byte last) representing the byte offset into the file of the last byte plus one. The position of the first byte in the file is zero (the EOF of an empty file).

Return Code $00 —No errors
$04 —Parameter count is not $02
$43 —Invalid reference number

$D2 SET_BUF: CHANGE OPEN FILE'S BUFFER ADDRESS

FUNCTION This function allows the caller to move an open file's file buffer to another location in memory. Since READ and WRITE references are by Reference Number, the MLI must memorize the location of the file buffer at OPEN time. If the buffer must be moved, this call allows the programmer to inform the MLI and allow it to move the contents of the buffer to the new location. The system memory bit map is updated to reflect the change.

PARAMETER LIST FORMAT

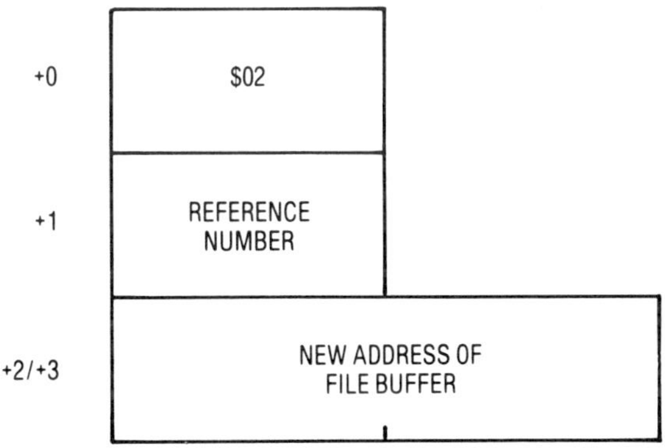

REQUIRED INPUTS

+0 Parameter count (2 parameters in list).

+1 Reference number for an open file as returned by OPEN.

+2/+3 The address (LO/HI) of a new 1024-byte location in which the MLI may maintain the open file's buffer. It must be on an even page boundary (LO byte of address is zero) and not be allocated by the MLI to any open file. The contents of the current file buffer are transferred to this new area, and the old buffer is marked released in the System Global Page memory bit map.

RETURNED VALUES

Return Code $00 —No errors
$04 —Parameter count is not $02
$43 —Invalid reference number
$56 —Buffer already in use by MLI

$D3 GET_BUF: RETURN OPEN FILE'S BUFFER ADDRESS

FUNCTION This function returns the address of the file buffer associated with an open file to the caller.

PARAMETER LIST FORMAT

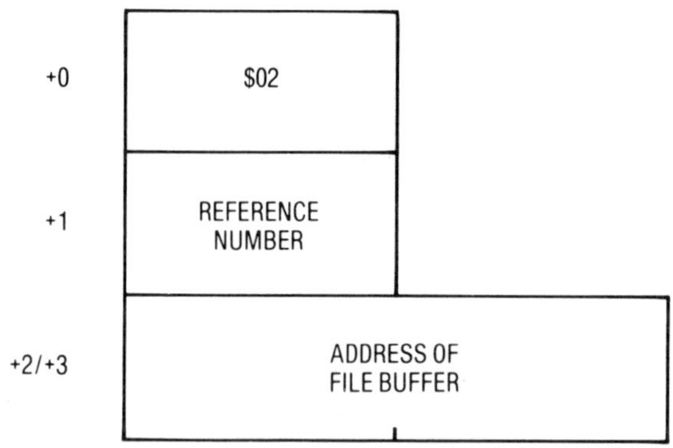

REQUIRED INPUTS

+0 Parameter count (2 parameters in list).
+1 Reference number for an open file as returned by OPEN.

RETURNED VALUES

+2/+3 The address (LO/HI) of the 1024-byte file buffer in use by the MLI for this file.
Return Code $00 —No errors
$04 —Parameter count is not $02
$43 —Invalid reference number

MLI ERROR CODES

$00 No error occurred. Operation completed successfully.

$01 Invalid MLI function code number.

$04 Incorrect parameter count in parameter list for the function code used.

$25 The ProDOS interrupt handler vector table is full. There are already four addresses stored there.

$27 A device driver reported an Input/Output error on the media. This could be anything from the diskette drive door being open to a real error on the surface of the diskette.

$28 No device is connected for the unit number given. This can happen if no identifiable controller ROM was present in the indicated slot.

$2B An attempt was made to write to the disk, but it was write protected. Remove the tape over the write-protect notch if you wish to write on this diskette.

$2E In the process of performing an ONLINE call, the MLI discovered that a diskette for which there were open files had been removed from its drive and replaced by another volume. Since no check is made when writing to an open file, it is possible that some blocks on the new volume have been damaged.

$40 The pathname has invalid syntax. Check to make sure the first byte is a count of the number of characters that follow. Also, be sure that each sub-level index begins with an alphabetic character and that each level is separated from the next by a slash (/).

$42 Eight files are open and there is no more room in the MLI's File Control Block (FCB) table for another open file. If you didn't expect any files to be open, set the LEVEL to zero and issue a global CLOSE.

$43 The reference number passed in the parameter list does not denote an open file. Make sure that the OPEN call was successful before issuing other calls by reference number.

$44 The pathname supplied could not be followed to the final directory. One or more of the subordinate directories in the path did not exist.

$45 The volume indicated by the pathname is not currently mounted on any drive.

$46 The file indicated by the last name in the pathname was not found in the final directory.

$47 A CREATE or RENAME was attempted and the file named already exists. To perform the operation would create a duplicate entry in the directory.

$48 An attempt was made to find one or more free disk blocks (to extend a directory, add a new data block for a file, etc.), but the Volume Bit Map indicates that the diskette is now full.

$49 An attempt was made to CREATE another file in the Volume Directory, but there are no free entries. Unlike subdirectories, the Volume Directory is of a fixed size (51 entries) and cannot be extended.

$4A An earlier version of the ProDOS MLI is being used to read a file which was created with a later version. The older MLI cannot handle this file properly. Use a newer version of ProDOS. This error can also occur if the final subdirectory header has an improper format. The byte at +$14 in the subdirectory key block (reserved bytes) must contain 5 and only 5 one bits (it is usually $75).

$4B The storage type of a file is not one of the storage types currently supported by this version of ProDOS. Currently, only Seedlings ($01), Saplings ($02), Trees ($03) and Directories ($0D) are supported.

$4C A READ operation was attempted and the current file position is at the End of File mark. No data was transferred.

$4D An attempt was made to move the file position past the End of File mark. If this position is desired, first move the EOF mark.

$4E An error occurred having to do with the ACCESS bits for a file. Usually this means you attempted to WRITE to a write protected file, or you attempted to DESTROY or RENAME a locked file. You can also get this error if any of the reserved bits are ones for the ACCESS byte of a SET_FILE_INFO call.

$50 An attempt was made to OPEN, RENAME, or DESTROY a previously OPENed file. Multiple OPENs are only allowed if the file's WRITE ACCESS bit is off (write disabled).

$51 When searching a directory, it was determined that the count of active file entries in the directory header was larger than the number of entries actually encountered. The directory is damaged and some file entries may be lost.

$52 The disk volume which was accessed is not a ProDOS disk. The criteria for determining whether a volume is a ProDOS formatted volume are: the first two bytes of the Volume Directory key block must be zero (previous block pointer); and the byte at offset 4 into the Volume Directory key block must be $E or $F (storage type).

$53 One or more of the values in the parameter list is not within its acceptable range. For example, an interrupt handler address of $0000 was passed to ALLOC_INTERRUPT.

$55 At most, only eight "mounted" volumes may be known to ProDOS at one time. Usually this is no problem since only eight files may be open at a time. However, if a single file is open on each of eight different volumes and an ONLINE call is made requesting the volume name mounted on a ninth device, this error will result.

$56 The address of the I/O file buffer passed to OPEN or SET_BUF is invalid. The buffer overlaps a previously assigned buffer, memory below $200, or ProDOS itself. The buffer must be in the caller's memory, and all four of its pages must be marked free in the System Global Page memory bit map.

$57 In the process of mounting volumes and recording their names in the Volume Control Block (VCB) table, the MLI discovered two volumes with the same name. Since all file references must be made by volume name and not necessarily by slot and drive, this condition is not permitted.

$5A The Volume Bit Map describing the freespace on the volume is damaged. A one bit was found, indicating a free block, for a block outside the legal extent of the volume (for a block number beyond the end of the volume).

PASSING COMMAND LINES TO THE BASIC INTERPRETER

For machine language programs running under the ProDOS **BASIC Interpreter** (BI), an interface is provided to allow execution of command lines created by a program, as if they had been entered from the keyboard. This is the highest level and perhaps the easiest to use ProDOS interface. Through it, a machine language program may easily produce CATALOG listings, DELETE or RENAME files, etc.

To call the BI command handler, place the command string in the monitor GETLN line input buffer at $200. The line may be up to 255 characters in length, and must be followed by a carriage return character ($8D). The most significant bit of each character should be set, and all alphabetics should be in upper case. Once this has been done, call $BE03 in the BI's Global Page (JSR $BE03).

If an error occurs, the BI error code will be placed in the accumulator. Possible codes are listed in Table 6.6

Table 6.6 BASIC Interpreter Error Codes

CODE	MESSAGE
$00	No error
$01	Not used
$02	RANGE ERROR
$03	NO DEVICE CONNECTED
$04	WRITE PROTECTED
$05	END OF DATA
$06	PATH NOT FOUND
$07	Not used
$08	I/O ERROR
$09	DISK FULL
$0A	FILE LOCKED
$0B	INVALID PARAMETER
$0C	NO BUFFERS AVAILABLE
$0D	FILE TYPE MISMATCH
$0E	PROGRAM TOO LARGE
$0F	NOT DIRECT COMMAND
$10	SYNTAX ERROR
$11	DIRECTORY FULL
$12	FILE NOT OPEN
$13	DUPLICATE FILE NAME
$14	FILE BUSY
$15	FILE(S) STILL OPEN

If you wish to print an error message, you need not have a table of messages similar to the above. Instead, place the error number in the A register and call $BE0C (JSR $BE0C).

Keep in mind that, unless the machine language program was called by a BASIC program, only direct commands may be issued (as if from the keyboard). BASIC file commands such as OPEN,

READ, WRITE, APPEND, and POSITION will result in a NOT DIRECT COMMAND error. Under Apple DOS, commands could be printed with a control-D from an assembly language program, exactly as with BASIC programs. Under ProDOS, this method no longer works. This is because the intercepts used for the "control-D interface" are no longer in the screen output vector, but are now in the Applesoft trace facility, which, of course, isn't active when your machine language program is running.

COMMON ALGORITHMS

Given below are several pieces of code which may be used when working with ProDOS.

IS ProDOS ACTIVE?

The following series of instructions should be used prior to attempting to call the ProDOS MLI.

```
        LDA $BF00       GET MLI VECTOR JMP
        CMP #$4C        IS IT A JUMP?
        BNE NOPRODS     NO, PRODOS NOT ACTIVE
```

WHAT KIND OF MACHINE IS THIS?

This code will test to determine what type of Apple is running the program.

```
        LDA #$08
        BIT $BF98       TEST MACHID FROM GLOBAL PAGE
        BEQ OLDSYS      OLDER SYSTEM
        BPL UNKN        FUTURE SYSTEM - UNKNOWN
        BVC APIIC       IT'S AN APPLE IIC
        BVS UNKN        OTHERWISE, UNKNOWN
OLDSYS  BMI EOR3        EITHER A IIE or a III
        BVC APII        IT'S AN APPLE II
        BVS APIIP       IT'S AN APPLE II+
EOR3    BVS APIII       IT'S AN APPLE III
        ...             OTHERWISE ITS AN APPLE IIE
```

HOW MUCH MEMORY IS IN THIS MACHINE?

This code will determine whether the Apple has 48K, 64K or 128K of RAM.

```
LDA $BF98       GET MACHID FROM GLOBAL PAGE
ASL A           MOVE BITS TO TEST POSITION
ASL A
BPL SMLMEM      48K
ASL A
BVS MEM128      128K
...             OTHERWISE 64K
```

GIVEN A PAGE NUMBER, SEE IF IT IS FREE

This code examines ProDOS's memory bit map to see if a page is marked free. If so, the page is marked as allocated.

```
BITMAP  EQU $BF58         SEE PAGE 8-6

        LDA #PAGE         GET PAGE NUMBER (MSB OF ADDR)
        JSR LOCATE        LOCATE ITS BIT IN BITMAP
        AND BITMAP,Y      IS IT ALLOCATED?
        BNE INUSE         YES, CAN'T TOUCH IT
        TXA               PUT BIT PATTERN IN ACCUM
        ORA BITMAP,Y      MARK THIS PAGE AS IN USE
        STA BITMAP,Y      UPDATE MAP
        ...               WE'VE GOT IT NOW

LOCATE  PHA               SAVE PAGE NUMBER
        AND #$Ø7          ISOLATE BIT POSITION
        TAY               THIS IS INDEX INTO MASK TABLE
        LDX BITMASK,Y     PUT PROPER BIT PATTERN IN X
        PLA               RESTORE PAGE NUMBER
        LSR A             DIVIDE PAGE BY 8
        LSR A
        LSR A
        TAY               Y-REG IS OFFSET INTO BITMAP
        TXA               PUT BIT PATTERN IN ACCUM
        RTS               DONE

BITMASK DFB $8Ø,$4Ø,$2Ø,$1Ø BIT MASK PATTERNS
        DFB $Ø8,$Ø4,$Ø2,$Ø1
```

IS A BASIC PROGRAM RUNNING?

This code will allow your machine language program to determine whether it was called by a BASIC program.

```
LDA $BE42        CHECK BI'S STATE
BEQ NOTRUN       IN IMMEDIATE MODE
...              ELSE, BASIC PROGRAM RUNNING
```

SETTING UP YOUR OWN RESET VECTOR

The code below will set up a user-defined RESET handler.

```
        LDA #>RESRTN     SET UP LSB
        STA $3F2
        LDA #<RESRTN     SET UP MSB
        STA $3F3
        EOR #$A5         MAKE POWER-UP BYTE
        STA $3F4
        ...              RESET VECTOR READY
RESRTN  ...              RESET HANDLER ROUTINE
```

ACTIVATE A PRINTER OR OTHER PERIPHERAL

To activate a printer or other peripheral driver under the ProDOS BASIC Interpreter, do **not** modify the vectors in zero page (CSWL/CSWH or KSWL/KSWH). Doing so will "disconnect" the interpreter and prevent it from intercepting command lines. Instead, store the address of the peripheral driver in BI Global Page in the VECTOUT ($BE30) or VECTIN ($BE32) words. The following code will start up a printer in Slot 1.

```
LDA $BE30        SAVE ORIGINAL CONTENTS OF VECTOUT
STA OLDVEC       IN MY MEMORY SO I CAN TURN THE
LDA $BE31        PRINTER OFF WHEN I'M THRU
STA OLDVEC+1
LDA #$00         PLACE $C100 IN VECTOUT
STA $BE30
LDA #$C1
STA $BE31
...              BEGIN PRINTING VIA COUT
LDA OLDVEC
STA $BE30        RESTORE PREVIOUS OUTPUT VECTOR
LDA OLDVEC+1
STA $BE31
```

CHAPTER 7

CUSTOMIZING ProDOS

SYSTEM PROGRAMMING WITH ProDOS

Apple has provided a number of customizing interfaces to ProDOS which allow a programmer to tailor the operation of the system to his specific application needs. These interfaces are considered "safe" and acceptable when working with ProDOS.

Before discussing specific system programming considerations, it is important to understand how ProDOS uses memory and what areas are reserved for its use versus those available for applications programs. Referring to Figure 7.1, the following areas of memory are officially "owned" by the ProDOS Kernel: $D000-$FFFF in the language card (primary $D000-$DFFF bank); $BF00-$BFFF; Zero page locations $3A-$4F; and part of the second 4K bank of the language card (starting at $D100). The rest of this 4K bank is reserved for the QUIT code driver and future uses. The ProDOS Kernel also reserves portions of auxiliary memory (128K) for future use—namely, the same locations it uses in main memory, zero page locations $80-$FF, and locations $200-$3FF. Apple's future plans for these memory areas include networking and menu managers, so if you use them you do so at your own risk. In a 128K machine, ProDOS currently sets up an electronic "RAM drive" volume in the auxiliary memory. At present, this volume encompasses most of the auxiliary 64K. In the future, its size may be reduced to accommodate enhancements as mentioned above. You can use the auxiliary memory for your own applications if you disable the /RAM device driver (see instructions later in this chapter). If the BASIC Interpreter is used, an additional area of memory from $9600-$BEFF is allocated to its use. $3D0-$3FF is used as a system vector area as defined by the *Apple II Reference Manual for the IIe Only.*

Note that ProDOS routines, including the clock driver, make heavy use of $200-$2FF, the monitor GETLN input line buffer. If your programs use this area you should not depend upon it across ProDOS system calls. You should also be aware of the fact that the MLI cannot be called from memory in the auxiliary bank, and that memory outside the area between $200 and $BEFF in the main RAM bank may not be used for buffers passed to the MLI.

Pro DOS CAN BE TAILORED TO SUIT SPECIFIC NEEDS.

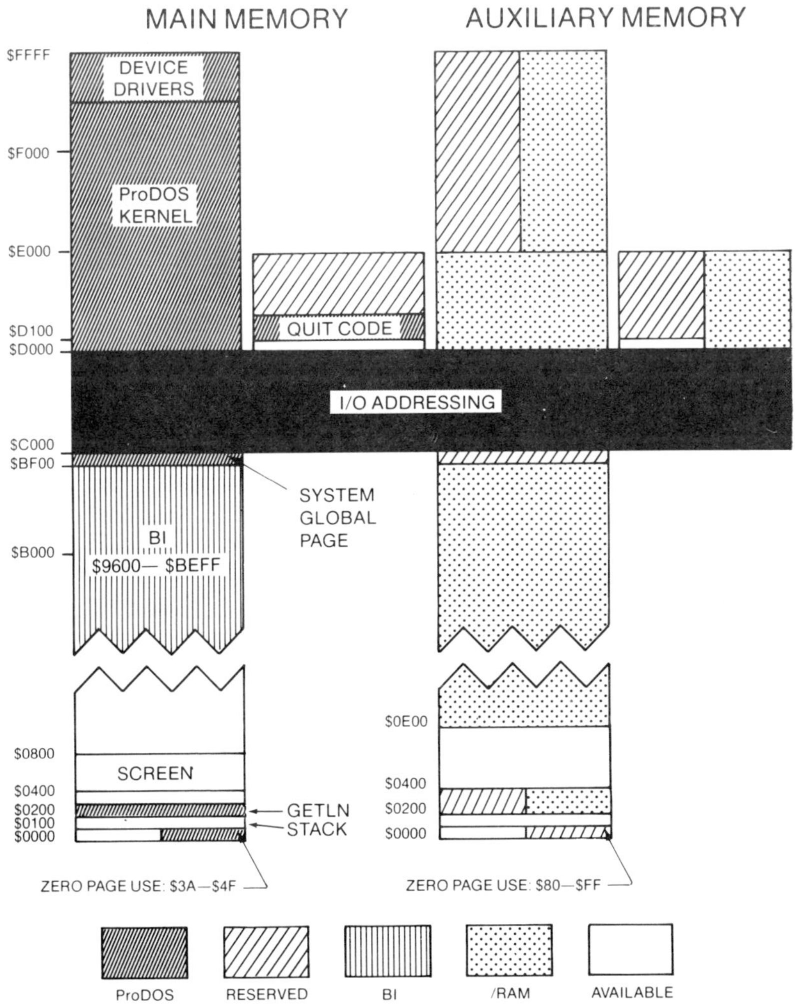

Figure 7.1 ProDOS Memory Usage

INSTALLING A PROGRAM BETWEEN THE BI AND ITS BUFFERS

Once in a while it is useful to find a "safe" place in memory to put a machine language program (a printer driver, or external command handler, perhaps) where BASIC and ProDOS will never walk over it. If the program is less than 200 bytes long, $300 is a good choice. For larger programs, it is usually better to "tuck" the program in between the ProDOS BASIC Interpreter and its file I/O buffers. The program need not be relocatable, since the BI will always be in the same place in memory, and the program can be placed at a fixed location just beneath it (see Figure 5.1). More than one program may be "tucked" in this area, but this may require one or more of them to be relocated, depending upon the order in which they are loaded.

To request space for a program, you must execute a call to the BI's buffer allocation subroutine using a vector in the BI Global Page. You may request a buffer of any size as long as it is an even multiple of pages (one page is 256 bytes). When called, the buffer allocation routine relocates any open file buffers as well as its General Purpose Buffer downward in memory, lowering Applesoft's HIMEM pointer as necessary, and returns the address of the first page in the new buffer. The new buffer will be placed directly below $9A00. Subsequent calls to the buffer allocation routine will cause allocations of buffers below earlier ones. The BI file buffers will always be lower in memory than any externally allocated buffers. When you are finished with all of the buffers you have allocated, you may free all of them with a single call. There is no provision for freeing individual buffers.

To allocate a buffer, invoke the following subroutine:

```
GBUFF    LDA #4          ALLOCATE 4 PAGES (1024 BYTES)
         JSR $BEF5       CALL GETBUFR
         BCS ERROR       DID AN ERROR OCCUR?
         STA BUFMSB      STORE BUFFER ADDRESS MSB
         LDA #0
         STA BUFLSB      STORE BUFFER ADDRESS LSB
         RTS             ALL DONE
```

To free all buffers you have allocated:

```
        FBUFFS   JSR $BEF8          CALL FREEBUFR
```

Note that you may allocate as many buffers as you wish using the GBUFF subroutine, but that a single call to FBUFFS frees all buffers.

ADDING YOUR OWN COMMANDS TO THE ProDOS BASIC INTERPRETER

There exists a well defined interface to allow you to write your own command handlers for the ProDOS BASIC Interpreter. Suppose, for example, that you wish to add a COPY command which will accept an input pathname, followed by a comma and an output pathname. You can write a handler for such a command in assembly language, install the handler between the BI and its buffers (see the previous section), and then inform the BI of its existence. Every time the BI receives a command line it doesn't recognize, it will pass it through to your handler before passing it to Applesoft. Note that this implies that your command's name must be different from any existing ProDOS command name. You may not replace or supersede an existing ProDOS command.

TEACH ProDOS YOUR OWN COMMANDS

To install your own command handler, place its entry point address in the vector in the BI Global Page at $BE07 and $BE08. These two bytes are the address portion of a Jump (JMP) instruction (EXTERNCMD) which normally points to a Return from Subroutine (RTS) instruction within the BI. It is not a good idea to assume that this address is pointing to an RTS since someone else's command handler could have been previously installed. To make sure you do not "disconnect" an earlier installed command handler and that yours is "daisy chained" to it, save the address you find in EXTERNCMD + 1 and branch to it from your handler if the command line passed is not your command.

Each time the BI scans a command line and cannot find the command name in its table of valid names, it will call your routine. Your program should compare the command in the command line with yours. The address of the command line is in VPATH1 ($BE6C/$BE6D) in the BI Global Page. The command line consists of a length byte followed by one or more ASCII characters with their most significant bit off. If the command is not yours, jump to the next handler (previous contents of $BE07/$BE08) with the carry set (SEC) to indicate the command is not yours. If the command is yours, there are two options. If the command's syntax is not compatible with other ProDOS commands (i.e. it has nonstandard operands or keywords), you may immediately begin performing the function indicated. When the program finishes, it should store a zero in PBITS in the BI Global Page ($BE54) to indicate no operands are to be parsed, and return (RTS) with the carry clear (CLC). In this case, do not JMP to the next handler as you would if the command was not yours. If, on the other hand, the command has standard ProDOS syntax, you can use the BI's syntax scanner to pick off the operands and optional keywords. To do this, once you have identified the command as yours, store the address of the beginning of your code which will process the command (after the syntax scan) in XTERNADDR ($BE50/$BE51) in the BI Global Page, store a $00 in XCNUM ($BE53) to indicate that this is an external command, and store the length of your command name (less one) in XLEN ($BE52) so that the BI will know where to start looking for operands. You should also set up PBITS (two bytes of flags) in the BI Global Page to describe the operands the BI is likely to find on your command. If you have a very simple command with only a pathname as an operand, you can set PBITS to $01,$00. If you want the BI to automatically provide the prefix of the current volume (default slot, drive) as well as allow the S and D keywords, set PBITS to $01,$04. Once you have set up XTERNADDR, XCNUM, XLEN, and PBITS, return (RTS) to the BI with the carry clear (CLC). When the command line has been successfully scanned, control will return to your handler at the location you indicated in XTERNADDR. If a SYNTAX ERROR occurs, control will not return. When your command handler completes its tasks, it may return to the BI with an RTS instruction (the carry here is insignificant). Your handler need not save or restore any registers.

An example of a command handler is given in APPENDIX A. This program installs a handler between the BI and its buffers, and connects it to ProDOS through the the EXTERNCMD vector. If the ProDOS user enters the command "TYPE" followed by a pathname, the command handler reads the indicated file and prints it on the screen.

DISABLE /RAM VOLUME FOR 128K MACHINES

If your application needs to use the additional 64K in the Extended 80-column Card (or the alternate 64K bank in the IIc) for its own purposes, rather than as an electronic disk drive (RAM drive), you should disable the /RAM device driver. You might want to do this if you plan to use the "double HIRES" graphics feature of the Apple IIe and IIc, for example.

The /RAM device driver is installed by the ProDOS Loader/Relocator when the Kernel is loaded. Part of it resides in the Kernel itself (from $FF00-$FF7F), and the remainder resides in auxiliary memory at $200-$3FF. Its address is placed in the list of device drivers for Slot 3, Drive 2 in the System Global Page.

One way to avoid conflicts between /RAM and your application is to BSAVE a dummy file such that its blocks will coincide with the area of memory you will be using. If you BSAVE an 8K file to /RAM (before any other operations on the /RAM volume), it will fall across $2000-$3FFF, the primary HIRES buffer. If you save a second 8K file it will fall across $4000-$5FFF, the secondary HIRES buffer. This is the easiest way to use "double HIRES" graphics while leaving the /RAM volume partially available for your use as an electronic disk drive.

If you want to totally disable the /RAM device driver, you must remove its entry from the System Global Page device driver vector list (DEVADR32). You must also remove the device number for Slot 3, Drive 2 from the online devices list (DEVLST), and reduce the device count (DEVCNT) by one. If you plan to reinstall the /RAM volume later, be sure to save the contents of DEVADR32 in a safe place so you can later restore it. Note that it is good programming practice to leave /RAM installed upon exiting your program so that other applications may use it. Reinstalling /RAM erases ("formats") the volume, so you should not reinstall it upon entry to an application which will be reading files passed via the /RAM volume by a previous application.

The following subroutine will remove the /RAM driver, allowing alternate uses of the auxiliary 64K:

```
         SKP 1
*        START BY CHECKING TO SEE IF /RAM COULD BE THERE
         SKP 1
REMOVE   LDA $BF98         CHECK MACHID
         AND #$30          ISOLATE MEMORY BITS
         CMP #$30          128K?
         BNE NORAM         NO - NO AUX MEMORY
         LDA $BF26
         CMP $BF16         IF SLOT 3, DRV 1 <> DRV 2 VECTOR..
         BNE GOTRAM        THEN IT'S INSTALLED
         LDA $BF27
         CMP $BF17
         BNE GOTRAM
NORAM    SEC ;             INDICATE NO /RAM INSTALLED
OKXIT    RTS
         SKP 1
*        SAVE OLD VECTOR AND REMOVE IT
         SKP 1
GOTRAM   LDA $BF26         SAVE OLD VECTOR CONTENTS
         STA OLDVEC
         LDA $BF27
         STA OLDVEC+1
         LDA $BF16         POINT IT AT "UNINSTALLED DEV"
         STA $BF26
         LDA $BF17
         STA $BF27
         SKP 1
```

```
*         SQUISH OUT DEVICE NUMBER FROM DEVLST
          SKP 1
          LDX $BF31          GET DEVCNT
DEVLP     LDA $BF32,X        PICK UP LAST DEVICE NUM
          AND #$70           ISOLATE SLOT
          CMP #$30           SLOT = 3?
          BEQ GOTSLT         YES, CONTINUE
          DEX
          BPL DEVLP          CONTINUE SEARCH BACKWARDS
          BMI NORAM          CAN'T FIND IT IN DEVLST
GOTSLT    LDA $BF32+1,X      GET NEXT NUMBER
          STA $BF32,X        AND MOVE THEM FORWARD
          INX
          CPX $BF31          REACHED LAST ENTRY?
          BNE GOTSLT         NO, LOOP
          DEC $BF31          REDUCE DEVCNT BY 1
          LDA #$00           ZERO LAST ENTRY IN TABLE
          STA $BF32,X
          CLC
          BCC OKXIT          BRANCH ALWAYS TAKEN
          SKP 1
OLDVEC    DW  0              OLD VECTOR SAVEAREA
```

To reinstall the /RAM driver, execute this subroutine:

```
          SKP 1
*         SEE IF SLOT 3 HAS A DRIVER ALREADY
          SKP 1
HIMEM     EQU $73            PTR TO BI'S GENERAL PURPOSE BUFFER
          SKP 1
INSTALL   LDX $BF31          GET DEVCNT
INSLP     LDA $BF32,X        GET A DEVNUM
          AND #$70           ISOLATE SLOT
          CMP #$30           SLOT 3?
          BEQ INSOUT         YES, SKIP IT
          DEX
          BPL INSLP          KEEP UP THE SEARCH
          SKP 1
*         RESTORE THE DEVNUM TO THE LIST
          SKP 1
          LDX $BF31          GET DEVCNT AGAIN
          CPX #$0D           DEVICE TABLE FULL?
          BNE INSLP2
ERROR     ...                YOUR ERROR ROUTINE

INSLP2    LDA $BF32-1,X      MOVE ALL ENTRIES DOWN
          STA $BF32,X        TO MAKE ROOM AT FRONT
          DEX                FOR A NEW ENTRY
          BNE INSLP2
          LDA #$B0
          STA $BF32          SLOT 3, DRIVE 2 AT TOP OF LIST
          INC $BF31          UPDATE DEVCNT
          SKP 1
```

```
*        NOW PUT BACK THE DEVICE DRIVER VECTOR
         SKP 1
         LDA OLDVEC       FROM PREVIOUSLY SAVED VECTOR
         STA $BF26
         LDA OLDVEC+1
         STA $BF27
         SKP 1
*        FINALLY, REFORMAT THE /RAM VOLUME
         SKP 1
         LDA $BF32
         STA $43          DEVNUM = SLOT 3, DRIVE 2
         LDA #3
         STA $42          CMD = FORMAT
         LDA HIMEM        512-BYTE BLOCK BUFFER
         STA $44          (PAGE ALIGNED)
         LDA HIMEM+1      WE CAN USE BI'S G.P. BUFFER
         STA $45          (IF BI IS AROUND)
         STA $C080        SELECT L.C. FOR DRIVER
         JSR RAMDRV       GO FORMAT THE VOLUME
         STA $C081        SELECT MOTHERBOARD ROMS
INSOUT   RTS ;            AND EXIT TO CALLER
RAMDRV   JMP ($BF26)      <<< JUMP TO /RAM DRIVER >>>
```

WRITING YOUR OWN INTERPRETER

A ProDOS "Interpreter" (also known as a "System Program") is a machine language program which stands between the user and the ProDOS MLI, providing a function. An interpreter may be executed by the smart RUN command ("–"), may be invoked at boot time, or may be executed upon leaving another ProDOS interpreter. Interpreters are stored in SYS files on a ProDOS volume, and are initially loaded at $2000, although they may include code to relocate themselves elsewhere once they begin execution. Examples of interpreters are BASIC.SYSTEM (the "BI"), FILER, CONVERT, and EDASM.SYSTEM. According to convention, an interpreter must be able to pass control to any other interpreter when it exits.

When writing your own interpreter, you must be aware of these considerations:

1. You must BSAVE your interpreter as a "SYS" type file from location $2000. If you want your code to execute elsewhere in the machine, you may include a front-end which relocates the rest of the program (this is what the BI does). Normally, the memory available to you in a 64K system includes $800-$BEFF. If you are running in a 48K machine, the ProDOS Kernel occupies memory from $9000-$BFFF so you are limited to $800-$8FFF for your program.

2. If you want your interpreter to be automatically executed as the first interpreter when ProDOS boots, you must name it "xxxx.SYSTEM", where xxxx can be any name. It must also be the first SYS file using that naming convention to be found in the Volume Directory of the boot diskette.
3. In order to insure correct operation of the interrupt handler in the ProDOS Kernel, set the stack register (S) to point to the top of the stack page ($FF) upon entry, and do not use more than the top three quarters of the stack. The interrupt handler assumes that the last item on your stack is stored at $1FF, when it makes its determination of whether or not to save part of the contents of the stack before invoking an interrupt driver routine.
4. As soon as your program begins execution, it should set up the POWERUP byte in page 3 and three areas in the System Global Page as follows.

```
$3F4:    POWERUP byte
$BF58:   BITMAP (system memory bit map)
$BFFC:   IBAKVER (minimum version of MLI acceptable)
$BFFD:   IVERSION (version number of your interpreter)
```

When your interpreter gets control, it should first set up the RESET vector at $3F2/$3F3 to point to its own RESET handler and fix the POWERUP byte at $3F4 accordingly. The POWERUP byte should be fixed even if you do not replace the RESET handler address (unless you want to reboot on RESET). To fix the POWERUP byte, exclusive OR the contents of $3F3 with #$A5 and store the result at $3F4.

A subroutine for checking the system memory bit map was given in Chapter 6. Use this to mark those areas of memory which your program will use. Do not mark areas which may be used for MLI buffers. By doing this, the MLI can keep a watchful eye on the execution of your program to prevent accidental overlay of your code with buffers. To determine what values to use for IBAKVER and IVERSION, examine memory in the version of ProDOS you are using for development and note the values at $BFFE (KBAKVER) and $BFFF (KVERSION). Assemble the values you find there as constants into your program, and use these to initialize IBAKVER and IVERSION.

5. If you wish to use 80 columns, first check the MACHID byte in the System Global Page to see if 80 columns are available and then call (JSR) $C300. To disable 80-column hardware, load a #$15 into the A register and call $C300. Avoid using the Apple IIe and IIc 80-column soft switches, because these will not work for third party 80-column cards or in an Apple II or Apple II Plus.
6. When your program is ready to exit, close all open files, reinstall the /RAM driver if you disconnected it previously, and execute the following code.

```
EXIT     DEC $3F4         FORCE REBOOT ON RESET
         JSR $BF00        CALL THE MLI
         DFB $65          QUIT CALL
         DW  PARMS
         SKP 1
PARMS    DFB 4            4 PARMS
         DFB 0            QUIT TYPE = 0
         DW  0            RESERVED
         DFB 0            RESERVED
         DW  0            RESERVED
```

The MLI will free any memory you have allocated in the system bit map. It will then prompt the user for a new prefix and pathname for the next interpreter, and will load it and execute it. The code which performs these tasks is at $D100-$D3FF in the secondary 4K block of the language card. It is moved by the MLI to $1000-$12FF before execution. You may create your own quit code by replacing the three pages of code image in the language card if you wish.

INSTALLING NEW PERIPHERAL DRIVERS

If you are writing a driver for a peripheral, such as a printer or disk drive, you should be aware of the conventions to which ProDOS adheres when examining and calling drivers.

If your driver is in ROM on the peripheral card itself, it should follow the Apple II standards for peripherals as follows.

FOR NON-DISK DEVICES

ADDRESS	VALUE
$Cs05	$38 (standard BI requirement)
$Cs07	$18 (standard BI requirement)
$Cs0B	$01 (generic signature of firmware cards)
$Cs0C	$ci (specific device signature)

The device signature is made up of two nibbles. "c" defines the class of devices as shown below. The second nibble, "i", is a specific device identifier assigned by Apple Computer, Inc.

"c" NIBBLE	CLASS
$0	reserved
$1	printer
$2	joystick or X-Y input device
$3	serial or parallel card
$4	modem
$5	sound or speech device
$6	clock
$7	mass storage device
$8	80-column card
$9	network or bus interface
$A	special purpose (other)
$B-$F	reserved

ProDOS makes the following special check for a clock:

ADDRESS	VALUE
$Cs00	$08 (unique device signature for the Thunderclock)
$Cs02	$28
$Cs04	$58
$Cs06	$70

FOR DISK DEVICES

ADDRESS	VALUE	
$Cs01	$20	(unique disk device signature)
$Cs03	$00	
$Cs05	$03	
$Cs07	$3C	
$CsFC/D		Disk capacity in blocks (non-DISK II)
$CsFE		Status bits (non-DISK II) 1... .... removable media .1.. .... interruptable device ..nn .... number of volumes on device .... 1... format allowed .... .1.. write allowed .... ..1. read allowed ....1 status read allowed ProFILE status bits = $47
$CsFF		$00 = DISK II $xx = LSB of Block device driver in ROM for non-DISK II ($Csxx). ProFILE hard disk $xx = $EA. $xx may not equal $FF.

If your driver is in RAM (below $C000), and you are invoking it using the BASIC Interpreter's commands PR# A$xxxx or IN# A$xxxx, the first byte of your code must be a CLD instruction ($D8); otherwise, the BI will not recognize your routine as a valid driver. If your routine is short, you can place it in the $300-$3EF range. If it is longer, you can call the BI's buffer allocation routine (previously covered in this chapter) to place it between the BI and its buffers.

INSTALLING AN INTERRUPT HANDLER

If you plan to use a peripheral card which supports interrupts, you may want to write an interrupt handler for that card. You should use the ProDOS first level interrupt handler in the Kernel so that other cards may also service their interrupts. To do this, use the MLI:ALLOC_INTERRUPT call to install your interrupt handler's entry address in the interrupt vector table within the ProDOS System Global Page. When writing an interrupt handler, follow these steps in the order indicated.

1. Make sure your interrupt handler is stored in main memory between $200 and $BEFF.
2. Call the MLI with the ALLOC_INTERRUPT ($40) call to cause your routine's entry point to be placed in the vector table.
3. Perform whatever I/O is necessary specific to your peripheral to enable its interrupt generating mechanism.

When your interrupt routine is called, the first instruction executed should be a CLD (to let ProDOS know that this is a valid externally written routine). You should then determine whether the interrupt which caused your routine to be invoked was indeed from your peripheral. If it was not, return to the Kernel with the carry flag set. If it was, service the interrupt, and upon completion, return to the Kernel with the carry flag clear. Your interrupt handler need not save or restore any registers, and it may use up to 16 bytes of stack space and zero page locations $FA through $FF (these are saved and restored by the Kernel). The Kernel assumes that the "bottom" of the stack is at $1FF when it determines what to save. Your application should always start the stack pointer at $FF. Note that the Motherboard ROM is deactivated in an interrupt handler routine (do not attempt to print via $FDED, for example).

If you wish to remove a previously installed interrupt routine, first disable the interrupt generation mechanism on your peripheral card to prevent further interrupts from occurring, then call the MLI:DEALLOC_INTERRUPT function to remove your handler from the list.

When writing an interrupt service routine, you should minimize the actual function performed "on the interrupt." If you are collecting data from a serial port which will later be written to disk, do not write the data while in the interrupt service routine, since this may adversely impact the performance of the program which was executing when the interrupt occurred, or it may cause you to "lose" subsequent interrupts while processing the first. Instead, use the interrupt routine to fill a "circular buffer" which is periodically dumped to disk by the interrupted program. An example of this technique and of writing interrupt handlers in general is given in the DUMBTERM program in APPENDIX A.

If you wish to call the MLI while in an interrupt routine, you should take steps to allow any interrupted MLI call to complete before using the MLI yourself (the MLI is not reentrant). Check the MLIACTV flag ($BF9B) in the System Global Page to see if the MLI is active. If the MLI is not active, you may issue MLI calls

HANDLING

immediately. If the MLI is active, save the contents of CMDADR ($BF9C) and replace it with an address within your service routine. Then return to the Kernel with the carry clear. When the MLI call completes, control will be passed to you instead of the original MLI caller. You should carefully save all registers, perform your processing as needed, restore the registers again, and jump to the saved contents of CMDADR to allow the original caller to continue. Note that you can be interrupted during your processing unless you disable interrupts. If you are not careful, a subsequent interrupt could cause your interrupt service routine to overwrite the saved contents of CMDADR with an address within your own program, causing an infinite loop! It might be a good idea to set a flag when saving CMDADR and clear it only when you have completed all processing. Your interrupt service routine can then check the flag and discard any interrupts which occur while you are finishing up processing of the first interrupt.

INTERRUPTS

DIRECT MODIFICATION OF ProDOS—A WORD OF WARNING

Making changes to your copy of ProDOS should only be undertaken when **absolutely** necessary. In the past, many third party software packages were sold for DOS, the earlier Apple II operating system, which patched or made wholesale changes. Because of the dependency these programs had on fixed locations within DOS and their importance to the collective software offering for the machine, programmers at Apple felt hampered in their efforts to improve DOS. Bugs in DOS could only be fixed with patches to existing code—no reassembly could be performed on the DOS code as this would cause critical locations to move "out from under" existing applications. With the introduction of ProDOS, Apple started out fresh. Earlier shortcomings in DOS have been corrected with ProDOS and numerous enhancements have been added. Hopefully, most packages written for ProDOS will not have to depend on changing the operating system's code itself. In any case, be forewarned: Apple will not hesitate to reassemble the ProDOS Kernel or the BASIC Interpreter or other ProDOS components if changes are desirable, and the stated policy is that programs which depend on locations or entry points which are not published by Apple will do so at their own risk.

Although ProDOS provides most of the functionality needed by the BASIC or assembly language programmer, at times a custom change *is* desirable. When making a change, weigh its value against the difficulty of reconstructing and reapplying it for later versions of ProDOS as they become available. Of course, if you never plan to upgrade your version of ProDOS this is not a concern. In addition, wholesale modification of ProDOS without a clear understanding of the full implications of each change can result in an unreliable system.

APPLYING PATCHES TO ProDOS

The usual procedure for making changes to ProDOS involves "patching" the object or machine language code in ProDOS. Once a desired change is identified, a few instructions are stored over other instructions within ProDOS to modify the program. There are three levels at which changes to ProDOS may be applied.

- New code may be written and added to ProDOS through a "standard" interface. If this is done, as in the case of an interrupt handler, for example, there need not be any ProDOS version dependencies involved. Examples of this type of modification have been given earlier in this chapter.
- A patch may be applied to a ProDOS system component, such as the Kernel or the BASIC Interpreter, directly in memory. If this is done, a later reboot will cause the change to "fall out" or be removed. This method is usually used to test a change before making it permanent.
- A patch may be made directly to the diskette containing the ProDOS system component that you wish to modify. Most ProDOS system components are in the file "PRODOS" (this file is named "P8" on the Apple IIGS system disk). Exceptions are the ProDOS Loader, which is on block 0 of all bootable ProDOS volumes, and the ProDOS BASIC Interpreter, which has a file of its own, "BASIC.SYSTEM". The PRODOS and BASIC.SYSTEM files are SYS type files that may be BLOADed, modified using the monitor, and BSAVED back to diskette. If a change is made to the ProDOS Loader, a sector editor or the ZAP program given in APPENDIX A must be used. When applying patches to the BASIC.SYSTEM or ProDOS files, you first determine its address when executing, and then use Table 7.1 to find where the patch is located in the load image of the file. For example, if you

wish to patch $9B7C in the BASIC Interpreter, you must patch $257C after BLOADing BASIC.SYSTEM. If you wish to change $D32A in Version 1.0.1 of the MLI, BLOAD PRODOS and change $302A. the commands you would type in for these two examples are:

```
BLOAD BASIC.SYSTEM,TSYS,A$2000
CALL-151
257C:[bytes to patch]
3D0G
BSAVE BASIC.SYSTEM,TSYS,A$2000
```

and

```
BLOAD PRODOS,TSYS,A$2000
CALL-151
302A:[byte to patch]
3D0G
BSAVE PRODOS,TSYS,A$2000
```

Table 7.1a Load and Execute Locations for ProDOS LOADER

Versions: All versions through 1.3
Disk Location: Block 0
Load and Execute location: $0800-$09F6
Uses Memory: $0800-$0CFF

Table 7.1b Load and Execute Locations for FILE = "PRODOS"

VERSION	LOAD ADDRESS	COMPONENT	EXECUTE ADDRESS
1.0.1,2	$2000-$293C	RELOCATOR	$2000-$293C
1.0.1,2	$2234-$239F	SYSTEM FILE LOADER	$0800-$096B
1.0.1,2	$23A0-$23AF	PAGE 3 IMAGE	$03F0-$03FF
1.0.1,2	$2401-$2447	80-COL CARD CHECKER	$0080-$00C6
1.0.1,2	$2A00-$2BFD	/RAM DRIVER	$0200-$03FD**
1.0.1,2	$2C00-$2C8C	/RAM CALLER	$FF00-$FF8C
1.0.1,2	$2D00-$4DFF	MLI	$D000-$F0FF
1.0.1,2	zeroed	MLI DATA	$F100-$F7FF
1.0.1,2	$4E00-$4EFF	MLI GLOBAL PAGE	$BF00-$BFFF
1.0.1,2	$5000-$507C	CLOCK CODE	$F142-$F1BE
1.0.1,2	$5080-$50FF	IRQ HANDLER	$FF80-$FFFF
1.0.1,2	$5200-$58FF	DISK II DEVICE DRVR	$F800-$FEFF
1.0.1,2	$5900-$5BFF	QUIT CODE	$1000-$12FA*
1.1.1	$2000-$293C	RELOCATOR	$2000-$293C
1.1.1	$226C-$23D7	SYSTEM FILE LOADER	$0800-$096B

1.1.1	$23D8-$2401	PAGE 3 IMAGE	$03D6-$03FF
1.1.1	$2451-$2498	80-COL CARD CHECKER	$0080-$00C7
1.1.1	$2A00-$2BFD	/RAM DRIVER	$0200-$03FD**
1.1.1	$2C00-$2C8C	/RAM CALLER	$FF00-$FF8C
1.1.1	$2D00-$4DFF	MLI	$DE00-$FEFF
1.1.1	zeroed	MLI DATA	$D700-$DDFF
1.1.1	$4E00-$4EFF	MLI GLOBAL PAGE	$BF00-$BFFF
1.1.1	$4F00-$4F7C	CLOCK CODE	$D742-$D7BE
1.1.1	$4F80-$4FFF	IRQ HANDLER	$FF80-$FFFF
1.1.1	$5000-$56FF	DISK II DEVICE DRVR	$D000-$D6FF
1.1.1	$5700-$59FF	QUIT CODE	$1000-$12FA*
1.2,1.3	$2000-$2B3C	RELOCATOR	$2000-$2B3C
1.2,1.3	$22DB-$24ED	SYSTEM FILE LOADER	$0800-$0A12
1.2,1.3	$24EE-$2517	PAGE 3 IMAGE	$03D6-$03FF
1.2,1.3	$256B-$25B0	80-COL CARD CHECKER	$0080-$00C5
1.2,1.3	$2C00-$2DFD	/RAM DRIVER	$0200-$03FD**
1.2,1.3	$2E00-$2E8F	/RAM CALLER	$FF00-$FF8F
1.2,1.3	$2F00-$4FFF	MLI	$DE00-$FEFF
1.2,1.3	zeroed	MLI DATA	$D700-$DDFF
1.2,1.3	$5000-$50FF	MLI GLOBAL PAGE	$BF00-$BFFF
1.2,1.3	$5100-$519A	CLOCK CODE	$D742-$D7BE
1.2,1.3	$519B-$51FF	IRQ HANDLER	$FF9B-$FFFF
1.2,1.3	$5200-$58FF	DISK II DEVICE DRVR	$D000-$D6FF
1.2,1.3	$5900-$5BFF	QUIT CODE	$1000-$12CA*
1.2,1.3	$5C00-$5C5E	IIGS CLOCK CODE	$D742-$D7A0

* STORED AT $D100, BANK2
** IN AUXILIARY MEMORY

Table 7.1c Load and Execute Locations for FILE = "BASIC"

VERSION	LOAD ADDRESS	COMPONENT	EXECUTE ADDRESS
1.0	$2000-$23FF	BI RELOCATOR	$2000-$2259
1.0	$2400-$46FF	BASIC INTERPRETER	$9A00-$BDFD
1.0	$4700-$47FF	BI GLOBAL PAGE	$BE00-$BEFF
1.1	$2000-$23FF	BI RELOCATOR	$2000-$22A2
1.1	$2400-$46FF	BASIC INTERPRETER	$9A00-$BDFD
1.1	$4700-$47FF	BI GLOBAL PAGE	$BE00-$BEFF

The following patches are designed for the original version of ProDOS (Version 1.0.1, 1 JAN 84) except where indicated. Do not make these changes to your original ProDOS System diskette. Copy PRODOS and/or BASIC.SYSTEM to another disk and apply the patches to the copied program.

CHANGING THE NAME OF THE STARTUP FILE

You can change the name of the STARTUP file which the BI executes at bootup by patching the first block of BASIC.SYSTEM as follows.

```
BLOAD BASIC.SYSTEM,TSYS,A$2000
CALL -151
21E5:05 48 45 4C 4C 4F
BSAVE BASIC.SYSTEM,TSYS,A$2000
```

Here we are changing the name from STARTUP to HELLO. The first byte indicates the number of characters in the name (5) and may be a maximum of 7 characters. Each ASCII byte should have its most significant bit off. The Startup file may be of any type which can be run using the "–" (Smart RUN) command.

PUT CURSOR ON COMMAND THAT CAUSED ProDOS ERROR

When you get a ProDOS error message such as "PATH NOT FOUND" or "FILE TYPE MISMATCH" because you typed the wrong file name or misspelled it slightly, it would be nice if ProDOS would return the cursor on the line with your faulty command so you could easily retype it. To make ProDOS do this from now on, apply the following patches.

```
BLOAD BASIC.SYSTEM,TSYS,A$2000
CALL -151
257C:4C C0 BB
45C0:A4 25 88 88 88 84 25 20 22 FC 4C 3F D4
BSAVE BASIC.SYSTEM,TSYS,A$2000
```

NOTE: The patches described on this page are for Version 1.0.1 of ProDOS and probably will not work with other versions.

HOW TO WRITE TO A DIRECTORY FILE

The ProDOS MLI will not allow explicit WRITEs to a directory file under any circumstances (it makes no difference whether the DIR file is "locked" or not). Under normal conditions, the only program which may modify a directory file is the MLI itself (when CREATEing a new file, updating the INFO in an old one, or DESTROYing one). If you wish to directly modify a directory entry with your own program, you should follow this procedure to circumvent the MLI.

1. Open the directory file using MLI:OPEN.
2. READ the block requiring update.
3. Execute the following code to find the block number.

```
LDA $C08B          SELECT RAM CARD
LDA $C08B
LDA REFNUM         PICK UP REF NUM OF FILE
CLC
SBC #0             MAKE IT AN OFFSET
LSR A              *32 FOR INDEX INTO FCB'S
ROR A
ROR A
ROR A
TAX
LDA $F310,X        GET CURRENT BLOCK NO.
STA BLKNUM
LDA $F311,X
STA BLKNUM+1
STA $C081          SELECT MOTHERBOARD ROMS
```

4. Use MLI:WRITE_BLOCK to write back the block.

Note that $F310 and $F311 may be version dependent locations.

NOTE: The patches described on this page are for Version 1.0.1 of ProDOS and probably will not work with other versions.

CREATING A NEW FILE TYPE

When you CREATE a file with the MLI, you may specify any file type you wish. If you wish to define a new file type for your application, pick a number between $F1 and $F8. When a CAT or CATALOG command is issued in the BASIC Interpreter, the file type listed will be "$Fn". If you want to use a three letter abbreviation instead, you must modify the table in the BI. The patch given below is highly version dependent and will only work for ProDOS Version 1.0.1 (1 January 1984).

The first thing to do is examine the table of file types in the BI at $B9DB. This table consists of 14 entries of one byte each, giving the ProDOS file type number for each of the supported types. You will have to replace one of the entries that you never use with your own file type. The entries need not be in numerical order. Immediately following the type table is a table of 3-byte entries giving the names which correspond to the numeric types. This table is in reverse order to the first and begins at $B9E9. As an example, suppose you wished to replace the last entry in the tables, $19 "ADB", with $F1 "ABC".

```
BLOAD BASIC.SYSTEM,TSYS,A$2000
CALL -151
43E8:F1
43E9:C1 C2 C3
BSAVE BASIC.SYSTEM,TSYS,A$2000
```

Notice that $B9E8 maps to $43E8 in the unrelocated image of BASIC.SYSTEM.

NOTE: The patches described on this page are for Version 1.0.1 of ProDOS and probably will not work with other versions.

RECOVERING DATA FROM A DAMAGED DISK

If one of the sectors which makes up a block is damaged, ProDOS will return with an I/O error. If in fact the error was in the second half of the block, the first half will be read into memory before the I/O error occurs. However, if the error is in the first half of the block, ProDOS will not attempt to read the second half. To recover the second, undamaged sector of the block, the following patch will force ProDOS to ignore any errors while reading the first half of a block. Errors while reading the second half will still behave normally.

```
BLOAD PRODOS, TSYS, A$2000
CALL -151
5228:00
BSAVE PRODOS, TSYS, A$2000
```

The above patch, while it will work properly with undamaged blocks, is not advisable in normal use as it will fail to indicate when errors have occurred.

USING ProDOS WITH 40-TRACK DRIVES

The device driver supplied with ProDOS supports only 35 tracks. The code can be modified easily to support third party disk drives with 40 tracks, but there are a couple of things to consider. The patch will apply to all drives (regardless of the number of tracks supported) connected to Disk II or compatible controller cards. This should cause no difficulties even if one 35-track and one 40-track drive are on the same controller card. Because you will also want to format 40-track disks, it will be necessary to modify FILER. The patch to FILER will apply to all disks that you format, and will produce an error if you attempt to format a disk on a drive supporting less than 40 tracks.

NOTE: The patches described on this page are for Version 1.0.1 of ProDOS and probably will not work with other versions.

This patch modifies the ProDOS Disk II Device Driver, which is part of the "PRODOS" file (or "P8" file), so that it allows 320 blocks per volume instead of the normal 280 blocks per volume.

```
UNLOCK PRODOS
BLOAD PRODOS,TSYS,A$2000
CALL -151
address:40
3D0G
BSAVE PRODOS,TSYS,A$2000
LOCK PRODOS
```

ProDOS version	"address"
1.0.1	520D
1.0.2	52CD
1.1.1	56E3
1.2	58E3
1.3	58E3

This patch modifies FILER* to format 40 tracks instead of 35. It will not work on a 35-track drive.

```
UNLOCK FILER
BLOAD FILER,TSYS,A$2000
CALL -151
addr:40
79F4:28
3D0G
BSAVE FILER,TSYS,A$2000
LOCK FILER
```

FILER release date	"addr"
1 JAN 84	4244
18 JUN 84	426A

*Unlike the patch to ProDOS, this patch need not be applied to the disk. You may wish simply to make the patch and execute the program. To do this, replace 3D0G with 2000G, and don't BSAVE FILER. This patch works on the versions of FILER released in 1984. It does not work with some pre-release versions.

FORCING ProDOS TO LOAD IN 48K

Versions 1.0.1 and 1.0.2 of ProDOS were designed so that they can run in a computer which has only 48K of memory. All later versions require 64K or more. If you locate ProDOS in main RAM, however, you cannot use the BASIC Interpreter (since it is assembled for a fixed location which conflicts with the alternate location of the Kernel), or EDASM.SYSTEM from the toolkit package. You can, however, use other programs, such as the EXERCISER or BUGBYTER. Forcing a 48K load is sometimes useful even in a larger machine if you want to trace execution into the ProDOS Kernel itself using BUGBYTER. Under ordinary circumstances, as soon as the bank switched memory is enabled, the ROM monitor disappears and BUGBYTER goes berserk! If the Kernel is in main RAM, however, this does not occur. To force a 48K load you must first place a ".SYSTEM" program (with type SYS) on the diskette to be booted (make a copy of BUGBYTER called BUGBYTER.SYSTEM). This must be the first file whose name ends with ".SYSTEM" in the Volume Directory. You can then apply the following patch and reboot.

```
BLOAD BUGBYTER
CREATE BUGBYTER.SYSTEM,TSYS
BSAVE BUGBYTER.SYSTEM,TSYS,A$2000,L7177
BLOAD PRODOS,TSYS,A$2000
CALL -151
23FC:A9 50
BSAVE PRODOS,TSYS,A$2000
```

Remember that the versions of ProDOS used must be 1.0.1 or 1.0.2. Note that the value of $50 above is the MACHID desired (Apple II Plus with 48K). You may add to that the bits necessary for an 80-column card or compatible clock if you like. You may wish to append your own program to the BUGBYTER.SYSTEM image before BSAVEing it so that it will be available to you once the 48K system is loaded. You can do this by inserting a BLOAD MYPGM,A$3D00 after the CREATE, and changing the length of the BSAVE to accommodate BUGBYTER and your program combined. When you boot the 48K diskette, your program will be loaded at $3D00, immediately following BUGBYTER.

ANYONE SEEN MY MOUSE?

CHAPTER 8

ProDOS GLOBAL PAGES

Readers of *Beneath Apple DOS* may remember that Chapter 8 of that book was devoted to a detailed analysis of DOS program logic. The contents of that chapter comprised one quarter of the book, and represented a complete description of more than 10K of machine language code. Two factors have led to the approach taken in *Beneath Apple ProDOS*. First, ProDOS code is expected to be much more volatile than that of DOS. If material similar to Chapter 8 in *Beneath Apple DOS* had been published here, it would have quickly become obsolete because of reassemblies of the operating system components by Apple. Throughout its lifetime, DOS was only completely reassembled once—when the change was made from 3.1 to 3.2 in 1979. Our book documented a form of DOS in which most of the instructions had not "moved" in nearly five years! In contrast, before *Beneath Apple ProDOS* was published, two different versions of ProDOS were already being distributed—1.0.1 and 1.0.2. Although the differences between them are very minor, insertions of instructions and data have caused the shifting of major sections of code. Similar changes are expected in the future.

A second factor in the decision to shorten Chapter 8 involved the physical size of ProDOS. The equivalent components of ProDOS, compared to the DOS code covered in our earlier book, occupy over 22K of memory. A complete treatment of this code would be a book in and of itself. Coupled with the increased complexity of ProDOS which has resulted in longer chapters overall, as well as the previously mentioned volatility of the code, we decided that an in-depth coverage of ProDOS program logic did not belong here.

However, recognizing the importance of this material to many of our readers, a special **supplement** has been prepared that provides a detailed description of every piece of code and data within the major ProDOS components. It is available directly from Quality Software. Updated editions of this supplement will be available on a periodic basis as Apple releases new versions of ProDOS. In addition, any errata and changes to the main body of *Beneath Apple ProDOS* will be found in future supplements, eliminating the need to buy future editions of this book. **Instructions for ordering the supplement are provided at the end of this chapter.**

BASIC INTERPRETER GLOBAL PAGE

This page of memory is rigidly defined by the ProDOS BI. Fields given here will not move in later versions of ProDOS and may be referenced by external, user-written programs. Future additions to the global page may be made in areas which are marked "Not used".

ADDRESS	LABEL	CONTENTS
BE00-BE02	BI.ENTRY	JMP to WARMDOS (BI warmstart vector).
BE03-BE05	DOSCMD	JMP to SYNTAX (BI command line parse and execute).
BE06-BE08	EXTRNCMD	JMP to user-installed external command parser.
BE09-BE0B	ERROUT	JMP to BI error handler.
BE0C-BE0E	PRINTERR	JMP to BI error message print routine. Place error number in A-register.
BE0F	ERRCODE	ProDOS error code (also at $DE, Applesoft ONERR code).
BE10-BE1F	OUTVEC	Default output vector in monitor and for each slot (1-7).
BE20-BE2F	INVEC	Default input vector in monitor for each slot (1-7).
BE30-BE31	VECTOUT	Current output vector.
BE32-BE33	VECTIN	Current input vector.
BE34-BE35	VDOSIO	BI's output intercept address.

BE36-BE37		BI's input intercept address.
BE38-BE3B	VSYSIO	BI's internal redirection by STATE.
BE3C	DEFSLT	Default slot.
BE3D	DEFDRV	Default drive.
BE3E	PREGA	A-register savearea.
BE3F	PREGX	X-register savearea.
BE40	PREGY	Y-register savearea.
BE41	DTRACE	Applesoft TRACE is enabled flag (MSB on).
BE42	STATE	Current intercept state. 0 = immediate command mode. >0 = deferred.
BE43	EXACTV	EXEC file active flag (MSB on).
BE44	IFILACTV	READ file active flag (MSB on).
BE45	OFILACTV	WRITE file active flag (MSB on).
BE46	PFXACTV	PREFIX read active flag (MSB on).
BE47	DIRFLG	File being READ is a DIR file (MSB on).
BE48	EDIRFLG	End of directory flag (no longer used).
BE49	STRINGS	String space count used to determine when to garbage collect.
BE4A	TBUFPTR	Buffered WRITE data length.
BE4B	INPTR	Command line assembly length.
BE4C	CHRLAST	Previous output character (for recursion check).
BE4D	OPENCNT	Number of files open (not counting EXEC).
BE4E	EXFILE	EXEC file being closed flag (MSB on).
BE4F	CATFLAG	Line type to format next in DIR file READ.
BE50-BE51	XTRNADDR	External command handler address.
BE52	XLEN	Length of command name (less one).
BE53	XCNUM	Number of command:

$00	=external	$0A	=OPEN	$14	=WRITE
$01	=IN#	$0B	=READ	$15	=APPEND
$02	=PR#	$0C	=SAVE	$16	=CREATE
$03	=CAT	$0D	=BLOAD	$17	=DELETE
$04	=FRE	$0E	=BSAVE	$18	=PREFIX
$05	=RUN	$0F	=CHAIN	$19	=RENAME
$06	=BRUN	$10	=CLOSE	$1A	=UNLOCK
$07	=EXEC	$11	=FLUSH	$1B	=VERIFY
$08	=LOAD	$12	=NOMON	$1C	=CATALOG
$09	=SAVE	$13	=STORE	$1D	=RESTORE
				$1E	=POSITION

BE54-BE55	PBITS		Permitted command operands bits:
		$8000	Prefix needed. Pathname optional.
		$4000	Slot number only (PR# or IN#).
		$2000	Deferred command.
		$1000	File name optional.
		$0800	If file does not exist, create it.
		$0400	T: file type permitted.
		$0200	Second file name required.
		$0100	First file name required.
		$0080	AD: address keyword permitted.
		$0040	B: byte offset permitted.
		$0020	E: ending address permitted.
		$0010	L: length permitted.
		$0008	@: line number permitted.
		$0004	S or D: slot/drive permitted.
		$0002	F: field permitted.
		$0001	R: record permitted. (V always permitted but ignored.)

BE56-BE57	FBITS	Operands found on command line. Same bit assignments as above.
BE58-BE59	VADDR	A keyword value.
BE5A-BE5C	VBYTE	B keyword value.
BE5D-BE5E	VENDA	E keyword value.
BE5F-BE60	VLNTH	L keyword value.
BE61	VSLOT	S keyword value.
BE62	VDRIV	D keyword value.
BE63-BE64	VFELD	F keyword value.
BE65-BE66	VRECD	R keyword value.
BE67	VVOLM	V keyword value (ignored).
BE68-BE69	VLINE	@ keyword value.
BE6A	VTYPE	T keyword value (in hex).
BE6B	VIOSLT	PR# or IN# slot number value.
BE6C-BE6D	VPATH1	Primary pathname buffer (address of length byte).
BE6E-BE6F	VPATH2	Secondary pathname buffer (address of length byte).
BE70-BE84	GOSYSTEM	Call the MLI using the parameter tables which follow.
BE85	SYSCALL	MLI call number for this call.
BE86-BE87	SYSPARM	Address of MLI parameter list for this call.
BE88-BE8A		Return from MLI call.
BE8B-BE9E	BADCALL	MLI error return: translate error code to BI error number.
BE9F	BISPARE1	Not used.
BEA0-BEAB	SCREATE	CREATE parameter list.
BEAC-BEAE	SSGPRFX	GET_PREFIX, SET_PREFIX, DESTROY parameter list.

BEAF-BEB3	SRENAME	RENAME parameter list.
BEB4-BEC5	SSGINFO	GET_FILE_INFO, SET_FILE_INFO parameter list.
BEC6-BECA	SONLINE	ONLINE, SET_MARK, GET_MARK, SET_EOF, GET_EOF, SET_BUF, GET_BUF, QUIT parameter list.
BECB-BED0	SOPEN	OPEN parameter list.
BED1-BED4	SNEWLN	SET_NEWLINE parameter list.
BED5-BEDC	SREAD	READ, WRITE parameter list.
BEDD-BEDE	SCLOSE	CLOSE, FLUSH parameter list.
BEDF-BEF4	CCCSPARE	"COPYRIGHT APPLE, 1983"
BEF5-BEF7	GETBUFR	GETBUFR buffer allocation subroutine vector.
BEF8-BEFA	FREEBUFR	FREEBUFR buffer free subroutine vector.
BEFB		Original HIMEM MSB.
BEFC-BEFF		Not used.

ProDOS SYSTEM GLOBAL PAGE—MLI Global Page

Portions of this page of memory are rigidly defined by the MLI and are unlikely to move in later versions of ProDOS. However, some portions are less stable and could change in future releases.

ADDRESS	LABEL	CONTENTS
		Jump Vectors
BF00-BF02	ENTRY	JMP to MLI.
BF03-BF05	JSPARE	Jump to system death code (via $BFF6).
BF06-BF08	DATETIME	Jump to Date/Time routine (RTS if no clock).
BF09-BF0B	SYSERR	JMP to system error handler.
BF0C-BF0E	SYSDEATH	JMP to system death handler.
BF0F	SERR	System error number.

Device Information

BF10-BF11	DEVADR01	Slot 0 reserved.
BF12-BF13	DEVADR11	Slot 1, drive 1 device driver address.
BF14-BF15	DEVADR21	Slot 2, drive 1 device driver address.
BF16-BF17	DEVADR31	Slot 3, drive 1 device driver address.
BF18-BF19	DEVADR41	Slot 4, drive 1 device driver address.
BF1A-BF1B	DEVADR51	Slot 5, drive 1 device driver address.
BF1C-BF1D	DEVADR61	Slot 6, drive 1 device driver address.
BF1E-BF1F	DEVADR71	Slot 7, drive 1 device driver address.
BF20-BF21	DEVADR02	Slot 0 reserved.
BF22-BF23	DEVADR12	Slot 1, drive 2 device driver address.
BF24-BF25	DEVADR22	Slot 2, drive 2 device driver address.
BF26-BF27	DEVADR32	/RAM device driver address (need extra 64K).
BF28-BF29	DEVADR42	Slot 4, drive 2 device driver address.
BF2A-BF2B	DEVADR52	Slot 5, drive 2 device driver address.
BF2C-BF2D	DEVADR62	Slot 6, drive 2 device driver address.
BF2E-BF2F	DEVADR72	Slot 7, drive 2 device driver address.
BF30	DEVNUM	Slot and drive (DSSS0000) of last device.
BF31	DEVCNT	Count (minus 1) of active devices.
BF32-BF3F	DEVLST	List of active devices (slot, drive and identification—DSSSIIII).
BF40-BF4F		Copyright notice.
BF50-BF55	IRQXITX	Switch in language card and call IRQ handler at $FFD8.
BF56-BF57	TEMP	Temporary storage for IRQ code.
BF58-BF6F	BITMAP	Bitmap of low 48K of memory.
BF70-BF71	BUFFER1	Open file 1 buffer address.
BF72-BF73	BUFFER2	Open file 2 buffer address.
BF74-BF75	BUFFER3	Open file 3 buffer address.
BF76-BF77	BUFFER4	Open file 4 buffer address.
BF78-BF79	BUFFER5	Open file 5 buffer address.
BF7A-BF7B	BUFFER6	Open file 6 buffer address.
BF7C-BF7D	BUFFER7	Open file 7 buffer address.
BF7E-BF7F	BUFFER8	Open file 8 buffer address.

Interrupt Information

BF80-BF81	INTRUPT1	Interrupt handler address (highest priority).
BF82-BF83	INTRUPT2	Interrupt handler address.
BF84-BF85	INTRUPT3	Interrupt handler address.
BF86-BF87	INTRUPT4	Interrupt handler address (lowest priority).
BF88	INTAREG	A-register savearea.
BF89	INTXREG	X-register savearea.
BF8A	INTYREG	Y-register savearea.

BF8B	INTSREG	S-register savearea.
BF8C	INTPREG	P-register savearea.
BF8D	INTBANKID	Bank ID byte (ROM, RAM1, or RAM2).
BF8E-BF8F	INTADDR	Interrupt return address.

General System Info

BF90-BF91	DATE	YYYYYYYM MMMDDDDD.		
BF92-BF93	TIME	...HHHHH ..MMMMMM.		
BF94	LEVEL	Current file level.		
BF95	BUBIT	Backup bit.		
BF96-BF97	SPARE1	Currently unused.		
BF98	MACHID	Machine ID byte.		
		00..	0...	II
		01..	0...	II+
		10..	0...	IIe
		11..	0...	III emulation
		00..	1...	Future expansion
		01..	1...	Future expansion
		10..	1...	IIc
		11..	1...	Future expansion
		..00	....	Unused
		..01	....	48K
		..10	....	64K
		..11	....	128K
		....	.X..	Reserved
		....	..0.	No 80-column card
		....	..1.	80-column card present
		....	...0	No compatible clock
		....	...1	Compatible clock present
BF99	SLTBYT	Slot ROM map (bit on indicates ROM present).		
BF9A	PFIXPTR	Prefix flag (0 indicates no active prefix).		
BF9B	MLIACTV	MLI active flag (1... .... indicates active).		
BF9C-BF9D	CMDADR	Last MLI call return address.		
BF9E	SAVEX	X-register savearea for MLI calls.		
BF9F	SAVEY	Y-register savearea for MLI calls.		

Language Card Bank Switching Routines

BFA0-BFCF		Language card entry and exit routines.
BFA0	EXIT	
BFAA	EXIT1	
BFB5	EXIT2	
BFB7	MLIENT1	

Interrupt Routines

BFD0-BFF3		Interrupt entry and exit routines.
BFD0	IRQXIT	
BFDF	IRQXIT1	
BFE2	IRQXIT2	
BFE7	ROMXIT	
BFEB	IRQENT	

Data

BFF4	BNKBYT1	Storage for byte at $E000.
BFF5	BNKBYT2	Storage for byte at $D000.
BFF6-BFFB		Switch on language card and call system death handler ($D1E4).

Version Information

BFFC	IBAKVER	Minimum version of Kernel needed for this interpreter.
BFFD	IVERSION	Version number of this interpreter.
BFFE	KBAKVER	Minimum version of Kernel compatible with this Kernel.
BFFF	KVERSION	Version number of this Kernel.

ORDERING THE SUPPLEMENT TO BENEATH APPLE ProDOS

Each owner of *Beneath Apple ProDOS* may order one or more of the Beneath Apple ProDOS Supplements. As explained on page 8-2, each Supplement is for a particular version of ProDOS, and describes in detail every piece of code and data within the major ProDOS components. Supplements can only be purchased directly from Quality Software. To order, mail the coupon on the next page directly to Quality Software at the address on the coupon, along with the price of the Supplements ordered plus shipping and handling charges.* Your payment can be a check or bank draft in US dollars, or your VISA or MasterCard number and expiration date. California residents must add the appropriate sales tax. VISA or MasterCard holders may telephone their orders.

***SHIPPING & HANDLING CHARGES**

United States, Canada, and Mexico	$ 2.50
All other countries (insured air mail)	$10.00

***SUPPLEMENT PRICES**

Supplement for ProDOS Versions 1.0.1 and 1.0.2	$10.00
Supplement for ProDOS Versions 1.1.1	$12.50
Supplement for ProDOS 8, Versions 1.2 and 1.3	$12.50
Two different Supplements ordered at same time	$20.00
All three Supplements ordered at same time	$27.00

QUALITY SOFTWARE
21000 Devonshire Street, #114
Chatsworth, CA 91311
(818) 709-1721

SUPPLEMENT COUPON

Please cut this page out of the book or make a copy of it and mail it to Quality Software.

Please send me:

______ Supplement for ProDOS Versions 1.0.1 and 1.0.2

______ Supplement for ProDOS Version 1.1.1

______ Supplement for ProDOS 8, Versions 1.2 and 1.3

Name ______________________________

Street Address ______________________________

City, State, Postal Code ______________________________

Country ______________________________

Supplement Price* __________

(CA residents) Sales Tax __________

Shipping and Handling* __________

TOTAL __________

Check # ____________

OR VISA/Mastercard # ____________________ Expires _______

**See previous page. Prices subject to change without notice (11/88).*

Valid Coupon

APPENDIX A

EXAMPLE PROGRAMS

This section is intended to supply the reader with utility programs which can be used to examine and repair diskettes, as well as typical programming applications for ProDOS. These programs are provided in their source form to serve as examples of the programming necessary to interface practical programs to ProDOS. The reader who does not know assembly language may also benefit from these programs by entering them from the monitor in their binary form and saving them to disk for later use. The use of diskettes is assumed, although most of the programs will work with a hard disk or can be easily modified for this purpose. It is recommended that, until the reader is completely familiar with the operation of these programs, he should use them on an "expendable" diskette. None of the programs can physically damage a diskette, but they can, if used improperly, destroy the data on a diskette, requiring it to be reinitialized.

Seven programs are provided:

DUMP **TRACK DUMP UTILITY**
This is an example of how to access the disk drive directly through its I/O select addresses. DUMP may be used to dump to memory any given track in its raw, prenibblized form. This can be useful both in understanding how disks are formatted, and in diagnosing clobbered diskettes. DUMP will only operate on a Disk II drive or its equivalent.

FORMAT **REFORMAT A RANGE OF TRACKS**
This program will initialize a single track or a range of tracks on a diskette. FORMAT is useful in restoring a track whose sectoring has been damaged without reinitializing the entire diskette. FORMAT will only operate on a Disk II drive or its equivalent.

ZAP **DISK UPDATE UTILITY**
This program is the backbone of any attempt to patch a disk directory back together. It is also useful in examining the structure of files stored on disk and in applying patches to files or ProDOS directly. ZAP allows its user to read, and optionally write, any block on a disk volume. As such, it serves as a good example of a program which issues direct block I/O calls to the MLI.

MAP **MAP FREESPACE ON A VOLUME**
MAP is written in BASIC and proves that direct block I/O can be done directly from a BASIC program as well as from assembly language. MAP reads the volume freespace bit map and displays a map of freespace versus blocks in use on the screen.

FIB **FIND INDEX BLOCKS UTILITY**
FIB may be used when a directory for a volume has been destroyed. It searches every block on a volume for what appear to be index blocks, printing the block number location of each index block it finds. Knowing the locations of the index blocks and employing ZAP, the user can patch together a new directory.

TYPE **TYPE COMMAND**
The TYPE command may be added to the ProDOS BI as a new command. It allows a user to type (display) the contents of a file to the screen or a printer. TYPE serves as an example of an external command handler.

DUMBTERM **DUMB TERMINAL PROGRAM**
DUMBTERM serves as an example of programming with interrupts. It implements a simple terminal emulator program, using a CCS 7710 serial interface card. Interrupts are used to fill a circular buffer, allowing higher baud rates to be used.

STORING THE PROGRAMS ON DISKETTE

The enterprising programmer may wish to key in the source code for each program into an assembler and assemble the programs onto disk. The Apple ProDOS Assembler was used to produce the listings presented here, and interested programmers should consult the documentation for that assembler for more information on the pseudo-opcodes used. For the non-assembly language programmer, the binary object code of each program may be entered from the monitor using the following procedure.

The assembly language listings consist of columns of information as follows.

- The address of some object code
- The object code which should be stored there
- The statement number
- The statement itself

For example,

```
2000:A9 02          36 FIB      LDA   #2          BLOCK = 2
```

indicates that the binary code "A902" should be stored at $2000 and that this is statement 36. To enter a program in the monitor, the reader must type in each address and its corresponding object code. The following is an example of how to enter the FIB program.

```
CALL -151        (enter the monitor)
2000:A9 02
2002:8D E9 20
2005:A9 00
2007:8D EA 20

  ...etc...

20EB:00 00
20ED:00 00
BSAVE FIB,A$2000,L$EF
```

Note that if a line (such as line 2 in FIB) has no object bytes associated with it, it may be ignored. Also, **never** type in a four digit hex number, such as the ones found in FIB on lines 22 through 27 or the "2044" on line 41—type only two digit object code numbers.

When the program is to be run:

```
BLOAD FIB
CALL -151
2000G
```

The BSAVE commands which must be used with the other programs are:

```
BSAVE DUMP,A$2000,L$100
BSAVE FORMAT,A$2000,L$51C
BSAVE ZAP,A$2000,L$47
BSAVE FIB,A$2000,L$EF
BSAVE DUMBTERM,A$2000,L$F7
BSAVE TYPE,A$2000,L$1B4
```

A diskette containing these seven programs is available at a reasonable cost directly from Quality Software, 21000 Devonshire Street, #114, Chatsworth, CA 91311 or telephone (818) 709-1721.

DUMP—TRACK DUMP UTILITY

The DUMP program will dump any track on a diskette in its raw, pre-nibbilized format, allowing the user to examine the sector address and data fields and the formatting of the track. This allows the inquisitive reader to examine his own diskettes to better understand the concepts presented in the preceeding chapters. DUMP may also be used to examine some protected disks to see how they differ from normal ones and to diagnose diskettes with clobbered sector address or data fields with the intention of recovering from disk I/O errors. The DUMP program serves as an example of direct use of the Disk II hardware from assembly language, with no use of ProDOS.

To use DUMP, first store the number of the track you wish dumped at location $2003, the device number you wish to use at location $2004 (the program defaults to slot 6, drive 1), and begin execution at $2000. DUMP will return to the monitor after displaying the first part of the track in hexadecimal on the screen. The entire track image is stored, starting at $4000. For example:

```
BLOAD DUMP   (Load the DUMP program)
CALL -151    (Get into the monitor from BASIC)
```

(Now insert the diskette to be DUMPed)

```
2003:11 N 2000G      (Store an 11 (track 17) in $2003,
                     N terminates the store command,
                     go to location $2000)
```

The output might look like this...

```
4000- D5 AA 96 AA AB AA BB AB   (Start of sector address)
4008- AA AB BA DE AA E8 C0 FF
4010- 9E FF FF FF FF FF D5 AA   (Start of sector data)
4018- AD AE B2 9D AC AE 96 96   (Sector data)
 ...etc...
```

Quite often, a sector with an I/O error has only one bit which is in error, either in the address or data fields. A particularly patient programmer in some circumstances can determine the location of the error and devise a means to correct it.

```
0000:                  *      DUMP -- TRACK DUMP UTILITY.
----- NEXT OBJECT FILE NAME IS DUMP.S.0
2000:         2000                ORG    $2000

2000:                  **********************************************************
2000:                  *                                                        *
2000:                  * DUMP:THIS PROGRAM WILL ALLOW USER TO DUMP AN ENTIRE    *
2000:                  *  TRACK IN ITS RAW FORM INTO MEMORY FOR EXAMINATION.    *
2000:                  *                                                        *
2000:                  * INPUT: $2003 = TRACK TO BE READ (DEFAULTS TO $00)      *
2000:                  *        $2004 = UNIT NUMBER (DEFAULTS TO $60)           *
2000:                  *                                                        *
2000:                  * OUTPUT:$4000 = ADDRESS OF TRACK IMAGE                  *
2000:                  *                                                        *
2000:                  * ENTRY POINT: $2000                                     *
2000:                  *                                                        *
2000:                  * PROGRAMMER: PIETER M LECHNER 5/29/84                   *
2000:                  *                                                        *
2000:                  **********************************************************

2000:                  *  ZPAGE DEFINITIONS

2000:         0000     PTR        EQU    $0           WORK POINTER
2000:         003C     A1L        EQU    $3C          MONITOR POINTER
2000:         003E     A2L        EQU    $3E          MONITOR POINTER

2000:                  *  OTHER ADDRESSES

2000:         4000     BUFFER     EQU    $4000        TRACK IMAGE AREA
2000:         FCA8     DELAY      EQU    $FCA8        MONITOR DELAY ROUTINE
2000:         FDB3     XAM        EQU    $FDB3        MONITOR HEX DUMP SUBRTN

2000:                  *  DISK I/O SELECTS

2000:         C080     DRVSM0     EQU    $C080        STEP MOTOR POSITIONS
2000:         C081     DRVSM1     EQU    $C081
2000:         C082     DRVSM2     EQU    $C082
2000:         C084     DRVSM4     EQU    $C084
2000:         C086     DRVSM6     EQU    $C086
2000:         C088     DRVOFF     EQU    $C088        TURN DRIVE OFF AFTER 6 REVS
2000:         C089     DRVON      EQU    $C089        TURN DRIVE ON
2000:         C08A     DRVSL1     EQU    $C08A        SELECT DRIVE 1
2000:         C08C     DRVRD      EQU    $C08C        READ DATA LATCH
2000:         C08E     DRVRDM     EQU    $C08E        SET READ MODE

2000:                  *  RECALIBRATE AND POSITION THE ARM TO THE DESIRED TRACK

2000:4C 0A 20          ENTRY      JMP    START        SKIP DATA

2003:00                TRACK      DFB    $00          TRACK TO DUMP
2004:60                UNITNUM    DFB    $60          UNIT NUMBER TO USE
2005:60                SLOT       DFB    $60          SLOT NUMBER TO USE
2006:00                DESTRK     DFB    $00          DESTINATION TRACK
2007:00                CURTRK     DFB    $00          CURRENT TRACK
2008:00                DELTA      DFB    $00          NUMBER OF TRACKS TO MOVE
2009:00                FLAG       DFB    $00          DIRECTION & ODD/EVEN FLAGS

200A:AD 04 20          START      LDA    UNITNUM      GET UNIT NUMBER
200D:48                           PHA                 SAVE FOR LATER
200E:29 70                        AND    #$70         GET SLOT ONLY
2010:8D 05 20                     STA    SLOT
2013:AA                           TAX                 PUT SLOT IN X REG
2014:68                           PLA
2015:10 01    2018                BPL    DRIVE1       SELECT DRIVE 1
2017:E8                           INX                 SELECT DRIVE 2
2018:BD 8A C0          DRIVE1     LDA    DRVSL1,X     SELECT APPROPRIATE DRIVE
201B:AE 05 20                     LDX    SLOT         GET SLOT
201E:BD 89 C0                     LDA    DRVON,X      TURN DRIVE ON
2021:BD 8E C0                     LDA    DRVRDM,X     INSURE READ MODE
```

```
2024:20 82 20               JSR    RECALC        MOVE ARM TO TRACK 0

2027:AD 03 20               LDA    TRACK         GET TRACK TO READ
202A:8D 06 20               STA    DESTRK
202D:20 9F 20               JSR    ARMOVE        GO THERE

2030:              *  PREPARE TO DUMP TRACK TO MEMORY

2030:A9 00                  LDA    #>BUFFER      POINT AT DATA
2032:85 00                  STA    PTR
2034:A9 40                  LDA    #<BUFFER
2036:85 01                  STA    PTR+1
2038:A0 00                  LDY    #0

203A:              *  START DUMPING AT THE BEGINNING OF A SECTOR ADDRESS
203A:              *  FIELD OR A SECTOR DATA FIELD

203A:AE 05 20               LDX    SLOT
203D:BD 8C C0      LOOP1    LDA    DRVRD,X       WAIT FOR NEXT BYTE
2040:10 FB    203D          BPL    LOOP1
2042:C9 FF                  CMP    #$FF          AUTOSYNC?
2044:D0 F7    203D          BNE    LOOP1         NO, DON'T START IN MIDDLE
2046:BD 8C C0      LOOP2    LDA    DRVRD,X       WAIT FOR NEXT BYTE
2049:10 FB    2046          BPL    LOOP2
204B:C9 FF                  CMP    #$FF          TWO AUTOSYNCS?
204D:D0 EE    203D          BNE    LOOP1         NOT YET
204F:BD 8C C0      LOOP3    LDA    DRVRD,X
2052:10 FB    204F          BPL    LOOP3
2054:C9 FF                  CMP    #$FF          STILL AUTOSYNCS?
2056:F0 F7    204F          BEQ    LOOP3         YES, WAIT FOR DATA BYTE
2058:D0 05    205F          BNE    LOOP4         ELSE, START STORING DATA

205A:              *  ONCE ALIGNED, BEGIN COPYING THE TRACK TO MEMORY.
205A:              *  COPY AT LEAST TWICE ITS LENGTH TO INSURE WE GET IT
205A:              *  ALL.

205A:BD 8C C0      LOOPD    LDA    DRVRD,X       WAIT FOR NEXT DATA BYTE
205D:10 FB    205A          BPL    LOOPD
205F:91 00         LOOP4    STA    (PTR),Y       STORE IN MEMORY
2061:E6 00                  INC    PTR           BUMP POINTER
2063:D0 F5    205A          BNE    LOOPD
2065:E6 01                  INC    PTR+1         DONE $4000 BYTES YET?
2067:10 F1    205A          BPL    LOOPD         NO, CONTINUE
2069:AE 05 20               LDX    SLOT
206C:BD 88 C0               LDA    DRVOFF,X      TURN DRIVE OFF

206F:              *  WHEN FINISHED, DUMP SOME OF TRACK IN HEX ON SCREEN

206F:A9 00                  LDA    #>BUFFER      DUMP 4000.40AF
2071:85 3C                  STA    A1L
2073:A9 40                  LDA    #<BUFFER
2075:85 3D                  STA    A1L+1
2077:A9 AF                  LDA    #>BUFFER+$AF
2079:85 3E                  STA    A2L
207B:A9 40                  LDA    #<BUFFER+$AF
207D:85 3F                  STA    A2L+1
207F:4C B3 FD               JMP    XAM           EXIT VIA HEX DISPLAY

2082:              *  RECALIBRATE ARM

2082:A9 30         RECALC   LDA    #$30          PRETENT TO BE ON TRACK 48
2084:8D 07 20               STA    CURTRK
2087:A9 00                  LDA    #$00          SELECT TRACK 00
2089:8D 06 20               STA    DESTRK
208C:20 9F 20               JSR    ARMOVE        GO THERE
208F:AE 05 20               LDX    SLOT          GET SLOT NUMBER
2092:BD 80 C0               LDA    DRVSM0,X      TURN ALL PHASES OFF
2095:BD 82 C0               LDA    DRVSM2,X
2098:BD 84 C0               LDA    DRVSM4,X
209B:BD 86 C0               LDA    DRVSM6,X
209E:60                     RTS                  RETURN TO CALLER
```

```
209F:                  * ARM MOVE ROUTINE

209F:A9 00               ARMOVE   LDA   #$00
20A1:8D 09 20                     STA   FLAG          INITIALIZE FLAG
20A4:AD 07 20                     LDA   CURTRK        GET CURRENT TRACK
20A7:38                           SEC
20A8:ED 06 20                     SBC   DESTRK        SUBTRACT DESTINATION TRACK
20AB:F0 36    20E3                BEQ   DONE          IF EQUAL THEN EXIT
20AD:B0 04    20B3                BCS   OK            POSITIVE RESULT? YES, GO ON
20AF:49 FF                        EOR   #$FF          MAKE RESULT POSITIVE
20B1:69 01                        ADC   #$01
20B3:8D 08 20            OK       STA   DELTA         SAVE RESULT
20B6:2E 09 20                     ROL   FLAG          SET IN/OUT FLAG
20B9:4E 07 20                     LSR   CURTRK        ON ODD OR EVEN TRACK?
20BC:2E 09 20                     ROL   FLAG          PUT RESULT IN FLAG
20BF:0E 09 20                     ASL   FLAG          ADJUST FOR TABLE OFFSET
20C2:AC 09 20                     LDY   FLAG          GET TABLE OFFSET
20C5:B9 F8 20            LOOP     LDA   TABLE,Y       GET PHASE TO TURN ON
20C8:20 E4 20                     JSR   PHASE
20CB:B9 F9 20                     LDA   TABLE+1,Y     GET NEXT PHASE TO TURN ON
20CE:20 E4 20                     JSR   PHASE
20D1:98                           TYA
20D2:49 02                        EOR   #$02          ADJUST OFFSET
20D4:A8                           TAY
20D5:CE 08 20                     DEC   DELTA         DECREMENT NUMBER OF TRACKS TO
20D8:AD 08 20                     LDA   DELTA
20DB:D0 E8    20C5                BNE   LOOP          IF NOT DONE, DO ANOTHER
20DD:AD 06 20                     LDA   DESTRK        UPDATE CURRENT TRACK WITH
20E0:8D 07 20                     STA   CURTRK        WHERE THE ARM IS NOW
20E3:60                  DONE     RTS                 DONE, RETURN TO CALLER

20E4:                  * TURN A PHASE ON, WAIT THEN TURN IT OFF

20E4:0D 05 20            PHASE    ORA   SLOT          ADD SLOT TO PHASE
20E7:AA                           TAX
20E8:BD 81 C0                     LDA   DRVSM1,X      TURN ON A PHASE
20EB:20 F2 20                     JSR   WAIT          WAIT FOR ARM TO SETTLE
20EE:BD 80 C0                     LDA   DRVSM0,X      TURN OFF PHASE
20F1:60                           RTS                 RETURN TO CALLER

20F2:                  * 20 MILLISECOND DELAY ROUTINE

20F2:A9 56               WAIT     LDA   #$56          WAIT ABOUT 20 MILLISECONDS
20F4:20 A8 FC                     JSR   DELAY
20F7:60                           RTS                 RETURN TO CALLER

20F8:                  * PHASE TABLE

20F8:02 04 06 00         TABLE    DFB   $02,$04,$06,$00
20FC:06 04 02 00                  DFB   $06,$04,$02,$00


   3C A1L            3E A2L          209F ARMOVE      4000 BUFFER
 2007 CURTRK       FCA8 DELAY        2008 DELTA       2006 DESTRK
 20E3 DONE         2018 DRIVE1       C088 DRVOFF      C089 DRVON
 C08C DRVRD        C08E DRVRDM       C08A DRVSL1      C080 DRVSM0
 C081 DRVSM1       C082 DRVSM2       C084 DRVSM4      C086 DRVSM6
?2000 ENTRY        2009 FLAG         203D LOOP1       2046 LOOP2
 204F LOOP3        20C5 LOOP         205F LOOP4       205A LOOPD
 20B3 OK           20E4 PHASE          00 PTR         2082 RECALC
 2005 SLOT         200A START        20F8 TABLE       2003 TRACK
 2004 UNITNUM      20F2 WAIT         FDB3 XAM
** SUCCESSFUL ASSEMBLY := NO ERRORS
```

FORMAT—REFORMAT A RANGE OF TRACKS

FORMAT can be used to selectively format a single track, a range of tracks or an entire diskette. While it is primarily meant to be educational, it can assist in repairing damaged diskettes. For example, if a single sector was damaged, it could be repaired by FORMATting the particular track on which it resides. To avoid losing data, all other sectors on the track should be read and copied to another diskette prior to reFORMATting. After FORMAT is run, they can be copied back to the repaired diskette and data can be written to the previously damaged sector.

Note that FORMAT has very limited error handling capabilities; in addition, it may not work well on drives that are out of adjustment (too fast or slow). The method used to do the formatting, that of building an image of the track in memory and then writing that image to the diskette, is similar to the method used by "nibble" copy programs.

To run FORMAT, store the starting track number at location \$2003, the ending track number at location \$2004, the volume number at location \$2005, and the device number at location \$2006, then begin execution at \$2000. FORMAT will return to the monitor upon completion. If a track cannot be formatted for some reason (eg. physical damage etc.), an error will be indicated. For example:

```
BLOAD FORMAT     (Load the FORMAT program)
CALL -151        (Get into the monitor from BASIC)
```

(Now insert the diskette to be FORMATted)

```
2003:11 11 FE 60 N 2000G     (Store an 11 (track 17) in $2003,
                             store an 11 in $2004, store an FE
                             (volume 254) in $2005, store a 60
                             (slot 6 drive 1) in $2006, N
                             terminates the store command, go to
                             location $2000)
```

The output might look like this:

```
FORMATTING TRACK 22
```

WARNING: FORMAT will destroy existing data on the diskette in the indicated drive without allowing the user an opportunity to abort the program. Be sure the diskette in the drive is the one you wish to FORMAT.

```
0000:               *      FORMAT -- FORMAT RANGE OF TRACKS.
----- NEXT OBJECT FILE NAME IS FORMAT.0
2000:        2000                ORG   $2000

2000:               ***********************************************************
2000:               *                                                         *
2000:               * FORMAT: THIS PROGRAM WILL INITIALIZE A RANGE OF         *
2000:               *         TRACKS WITH ANY VOLUME NUMBER DESIRED.          *
2000:               *                                                         *
2000:               * INPUT: $2003 = FIRST TRACK TO BE INITIALIZED            *
2000:               *                DEFAULT ($00)                            *
2000:               *        $2004 = LAST TRACK TO BE INITILIZED              *
2000:               *                DEFAULT ($22)                            *
2000:               *        $2005 = VOLUME NUMBER                            *
2000:               *                DEFAULT ($FE)                            *
2000:               *        $2006 = UNIT NUMBER                              *
2000:               *                DEFAULT ($60)                            *
2000:               *                                                         *
2000:               * ENTRY POINT: $2000                                      *
2000:               *                                                         *
2000:               * PROGRAMMER: PIETER LECHNER 5/19/84                      *
2000:               *                                                         *
2000:               ***********************************************************

2000:               *  ZPAGE DEFINITIONS

2000:        0000   PTR       EQU   $0            WORK POINTER
2000:        003C   A1        EQU   $3C           MONITOR POINTERS
2000:        003E   A2        EQU   $3E                |
2000:        0042   A4        EQU   $42                v

2000:               *  MONITOR ROUTINES

2000:        FC10   BS        EQU   $FC10         BACKSPACE
2000:        FC58   HOME      EQU   $FC58         CLEAR SCREEN
2000:        FCA8   DELAY     EQU   $FCA8         DELAY ROUTINE
2000:        FCB4   NXTA4     EQU   $FCB4         INCREMENT POINTERS (A4/A1)
2000:        FCBA   NXTA1     EQU   $FCBA         INCREMENT POINTER (A1)
2000:        FDED   COUT      EQU   $FDED         CHARACTER OUTPUT
2000:        FDDA   PRBYTE    EQU   $FDDA         HEX OUTPUT
2000:        FE2C   MOVE      EQU   $FE2C         MOVE ROUTINE
```

```
2000:                *  DISK I/O SELECTS

2000:        C080    DRVSM0    EQU   $C080        STEP MOTOR POSITIONS
2000:        C081    DRVSM1    EQU   $C081
2000:        C082    DRVSM2    EQU   $C082
2000:        C084    DRVSM4    EQU   $C084
2000:        C086    DRVSM6    EQU   $C086
2000:        C088    DRVOFF    EQU   $C088        TURN DRIVE OFF
2000:        C089    DRVON     EQU   $C089        TURN DRIVE ON
2000:        C08A    DRVSL1    EQU   $C08A        SELECT DRIVE 1
2000:        C08B    DRVSL2    EQU   $C08B        SELECT DRIVE 2
2000:        C08C    DRVRD     EQU   $C08C        READ DATA LATCH
2000:        C08D    DRVWR     EQU   $C08D        WRITE DATA LATCH
2000:        C08E    DRVRDM    EQU   $C08E        SET READ MODE
2000:        C08F    DRVWRM    EQU   $C08F        SET WRITE MODE

2000:                *  FORMAT PROGRAM

2000:4C 07 20        FORMAT    JMP   ENTRY        SKIP OVER DATA

2003:00              STRK      DFB   $00          STARTING TRACK
2004:22              ETRK      DFB   $22          ENDING TRACK
2005:FE              VOLNUM    DFB   $FE          VOLUME NUMBER
2006:60              UNITNUM   DFB   $60          UNIT NUMBER

2007:                *  RECALIBRATE ARM TO THE DESIRED TRACK

2007:20 F7 22        ENTRY     JSR   SCREEN       CLEAR SCREEN/DISPLAY MESSAGE
200A:AD 06 20                  LDA   UNITNUM      GET UNIT NUMBER
200D:48                        PHA                SAVE FOR LATER
200E:29 70                     AND   #$70         GET SLOT ONLY
2010:8D D6 24                  STA   SLOT
2013:AA                        TAX                PUT SLOT IN X REG
2014:68                        PLA                CHECK WHICH DRIVE TO USE
2015:10 01    2018             BPL   DRIVE1       SELECT DRIVE 1
2017:E8                        INX                SELECT DRIVE 2
2018:BD 8A C0        DRIVE1    LDA   DRVSL1,X     SELECT APPROPRIATE DRIVE
201B:AE D6 24                  LDX   SLOT         GET SLOT
201E:BD 89 C0                  LDA   DRVON,X      TURN DRIVE ON
2021:BD 8E C0                  LDA   DRVRDM,X     INSURE READ MODE
2024:BD 8C C0                  LDA   DRVRD,X

2027:20 79 22                  JSR   RECALC       RECALIBRATE ARM
202A:AD 03 20                  LDA   STRK         GET STARTING TRACK
202D:8D D9 24                  STA   DESTRK
2030:20 96 22                  JSR   ARMOVE       GO THERE

2033:                *  BUILD TRACK IMAGE IN MEMORY

2033:20 3B 21                  JSR   FILLDATA     FILL DATA AREA WITH $96'S
2036:AD 03 20                  LDA   STRK
2039:8D D7 24                  STA   TRACK        INITIALIZE TRACK NUMBER
203C:A9 05                     LDA   #$05
203E:8D CE 24                  STA   RETRYCNT     INITIALIZE RETRY COUNT
2041:A9 CB                     LDA   #>END
2043:8D D2 24                  STA   CUREND
2046:A9 24                     LDA   #<END        SAVE CURRENT LENGTH
2048:8D D3 24                  STA   CUREND+1     OF SECTOR IMAGE
204B:38              LOOPA     SEC
204C:AD D2 24                  LDA   CUREND       COMPUTE LENGTH OF
204F:E9 40                     SBC   #>IMAGE      CURRENT SECTOR IMAGE
2051:8D D0 24                  STA   LENGTH
2054:AD D3 24                  LDA   CUREND+1
2057:E9 23                     SBC   #<IMAGE
2059:8D D1 24                  STA   LENGTH+1
205C:EE D0 24                  INC   LENGTH
205F:20 62 21                  JSR   FINDSTART    COMPUTE START OF TRACK IMAGE
2062:20 83 21                  JSR   BLDGAP1      BUILD GAP1 (128 BYTES)
2065:20 9F 21                  JSR   BLDTRK       BUILD TRACK IMAGE IN MEMORY
2068:20 C9 21        ANOTHER   JSR   FIXTRK       UPDATE ADDRESS INFO
```

```
206B:                   * INITIALIZE TRACK

206B:20 06 23                   JSR    PRTRK          PRINT TRACK NUMBER
206E:20 B5 20                   JSR    WRITE          WRITE A TRACK
2071:B0 1F    2092              BCS    ERROR1         WRITE PROTECT ERROR
2073:20 31 21                   JSR    VERIFY         VERIFY THE TRACK
2076:90 20    2098              BCC    NEXT           IF OK DO ANOTHER
2078:38                         SEC                   ELSE ADJUST GAP SIZE
2079:AD D2 24                   LDA    CUREND
207C:E9 02                      SBC    #$02
207E:8D D2 24                   STA    CUREND
2081:AD D3 24                   LDA    CUREND+1
2084:E9 00                      SBC    #$00
2086:8D D3 24                   STA    CUREND+1
2089:CE CE 24                   DEC    RETRYCNT       DECREMENT RETRY COUNT
208C:10 BD    204B              BPL    LOOPA          IF OK TRY AGAIN

208E:                   * ERROR OCCURED

208E:A9 02                      LDA    #$02
2090:D0 02    2094              BNE    ERR2
2092:A9 01              ERROR1  LDA    #$01
2094:20 13 23           ERR2    JSR    ERRHDL         PRINT ERROR MESSAGE
2097:60                         RTS                   EXIT PROGRAM

2098:EE D7 24           NEXT    INC    TRACK          INCREMENT TRACK NUMBER
209B:AD D7 24                   LDA    TRACK
209E:CD 04 20                   CMP    ETRK           COMPARE WITH LAST TRACK TO DO
20A1:F0 02    20A5              BEQ    LASTONE        IF EQUAL DO LAST ONE
20A3:B0 09    20AE              BCS    FINISH         IF DONE THEN EXIT PROGRAM
20A5:8D D9 24           LASTONE STA    DESTRK
20A8:20 96 22                   JSR    ARMOVE         GO TO DESIRED TRACK
20AB:4C 68 20                   JMP    ANOTHER        GO BACK AND DO ANOTHER

20AE:                   * WHEN DONE, EXIT

20AE:AE D6 24           FINISH  LDX    SLOT           GET SLOT
20B1:BD 88 C0                   LDA    DRVOFF,X       TURN DRIVE OFF
20B4:60                         RTS                   EXIT PROGRAM

20B5:                   * WRITE MEMORY TO DISK

20B5:A9 00              WRITE   LDA    #$00
20B7:85 00                      STA    PTR
20B9:AD D5 24                   LDA    START+1        POINT AT START OF DATA
20BC:85 01                      STA    PTR+1
20BE:AC D4 24                   LDY    START
20C1:AE D6 24                   LDX    SLOT
20C4:38                         SEC                   ASSUME ERROR
20C5:BD 8D C0                   LDA    DRVWR,X
20C8:BD 8E C0                   LDA    DRVRDM,X       CHECK WRITE PROTECT STATUS
20CB:30 30    20FD              BMI    WPERR
20CD:A9 FF                      LDA    #$FF
20CF:9D 8F C0                   STA    DRVWRM,X       WRITE 1 $FF
20D2:DD 8C C0                   CMP    DRVRD,X
20D5:EA                         NOP
20D6:4C E0 20                   JMP    LOOP1
20D9:49 80              ASYNC   EOR    #$80           TURN HIGH BIT ON
20DB:EA                         NOP
20DC:EA                         NOP
20DD:4C E9 20                   JMP    WRIT           DELAY EXTRA 8 CYCLES
20E0:48                 LOOP1   PHA
20E1:68                         PLA
20E2:B1 00              LOOP2   LDA    (PTR),Y        GET BYTE TO WRITE
20E4:C9 80                      CMP    #$80           IS IT "SYNC" BYTE
20E6:90 F1    20D9              BCC    ASYNC          YES, THEN MAKE ADJUSTMENT
20E8:EA                         NOP
20E9:9D 8D C0           WRIT    STA    DRVWR,X        WRITE A BYTE
20EC:DD 8C C0                   CMP    DRVRD,X
20EF:C8                         INY                   INCREMENT OFFSET
```

```
20F0:D0 EE    20E0                 BNE   LOOP1
20F2:E6 01                         INC   PTR+1          INCREMENT POINTER
20F4:10 EC    20E2                 BPL   LOOP2
20F6:BD 8E C0                      LDA   DRVRDM,X
20F9:BD 8C C0                      LDA   DRVRD,X        PUT IN READ MODE
20FC:18                            CLC
20FD:60                 WPERR      RTS

20FE:                   *  PREPARE TO DUMP TRACK TO MEMORY

20FE:A9 00              DUMP       LDA   #$00           POINT AT DATA
2100:85 00                         STA   PTR
2102:A9 40                         LDA   #$40
2104:85 01                         STA   PTR+1
2106:A0 00                         LDY   #0

2108:                   *  START DUMPING AS SOON AS TWO SYNC BYTES FOUND

2108:AE D6 24                      LDX   SLOT
210B:BD 8C C0           LOOP3      LDA   DRVRD,X        WAIT FOR NEXT BYTE
210E:10 FB    210B                 BPL   LOOP3
2110:C9 FF                         CMP   #$FF           AUTOSYNC?
2112:D0 F7    210B                 BNE   LOOP3          NO, DON'T START YET
2114:BD 8C C0           LOOP4      LDA   DRVRD,X        WAIT FOR NEXT BYTE
2117:10 FB    2114                 BPL   LOOP4
2119:C9 FF                         CMP   #$FF           TWO AUTOSYNCS?
211B:D0 EE    210B                 BNE   LOOP3          NOT YET

211D:                   *  ONCE ALIGNED, BEGIN COPYING THE TRACK TO MEMORY.
211D:                   *  COPY ENOUGH TO INSURE WE GET IT ALL

211D:BD 8C C0           LOOPD      LDA   DRVRD,X        WAIT FOR NEXT DATA BYTE
2120:10 FB    211D                 BPL   LOOPD
2122:91 00              LOOP5      STA   (PTR),Y        STORE IN MEMORY
2124:E6 00                         INC   PTR            BUMP POINTER
2126:D0 F5    211D                 BNE   LOOPD
2128:E6 01                         INC   PTR+1          DONE $2000 BYTES YET?
212A:A5 01                         LDA   PTR+1
212C:C9 60                         CMP   #$60           NO, CONTINUE
212E:D0 ED    211D                 BNE   LOOPD
2130:60                            RTS

2131:                   *  READ SECTOR ZERO TO VERIFY FORMATTING

2131:20 FE 20           VERIFY     JSR   DUMP           DUMP TRACK TO MEMORY
2134:20 F1 21                      JSR   SETUP
2137:20 39 22                      JSR   COMPARE        CHECK WHAT WE JUST WROTE
213A:60                            RTS

213B:                   *  FILL DATA AREA WITH $96'S

213B:18                 FILLDATA   CLC
213C:A9 57                         LDA   #>DATA
213E:85 3C                         STA   A1             SET A1 TO DATA START
2140:69 56                         ADC   #>DATALTH
2142:85 3E                         STA   A2             SET A1 TO DATA END
2144:A9 23                         LDA   #<DATA
2146:85 3D                         STA   A1+1
2148:69 01                         ADC   #<DATALTH
214A:85 3F                         STA   A2+1
214C:A9 96                         LDA   #$96
214E:8D CF 24                      STA   BYTE           INDICATE FILL BYTE
2151:20 55 21                      JSR   FILL           CALL FILL ROUTINE
2154:60                            RTS
```

```
2155:                 * FILL MEMORY WITH A CONSTANT

2155:A0 00            FILL      LDY   #$00          INITIALIZE OFFSET
2157:AD CF 24         LOOP      LDA   BYTE          GET BYTE TO USE
215A:91 3C                      STA   (A1),Y        STORE A BYTE
215C:20 BA FC                   JSR   NXTA1         CALL MONITOR INCREMENT
215F:90 F6    2157              BCC   LOOP          LOOP UNTIL DONE
2161:60                         RTS

2162:                 * COMPUTE START OF TRACK IMAGE

2162:A0 03            FINDSTART LDY   #$03
2164:AD D0 24                   LDA   LENGTH        MULTIPLY LENGTH BY 16
2167:0A               MORE      ASL   A
2168:2E D1 24                   ROL   LENGTH+1
216B:88                         DEY
216C:10 F9    2167              BPL   MORE
216E:8D D0 24                   STA   LENGTH

2171:38                         SEC                 SUBTRACT IT FROM $7F80
2172:A9 80                      LDA   #$80          TO FIND START
2174:ED D0 24                   SBC   LENGTH
2177:8D D4 24                   STA   START
217A:A9 7F                      LDA   #$7F
217C:ED D1 24                   SBC   LENGTH+1
217F:8D D5 24                   STA   START+1
2182:60                         RTS

2183:                 * BUILD GAP1 AT START OF TRACK IMAGE

2183:18               BLDGAP1   CLC
2184:AD D4 24                   LDA   START
2187:85 3C                      STA   A1            SET A1 TO START
2189:69 80                      ADC   #$80
218B:85 3E                      STA   A2            SET A2 TO START + $80
218D:AD D5 24                   LDA   START+1
2190:85 3D                      STA   A1+1
2192:69 00                      ADC   #$00
2194:85 3F                      STA   A2+1
2196:A9 7F                      LDA   #$7F          USE $7F FOR SYNC BYTE
2198:8D CF 24                   STA   BYTE
219B:20 55 21                   JSR   FILL          CALL FILL ROUTINE
219E:60                         RTS

219F:                 * BUILD TRACK IMAGE USING SECTOR IMAGE

219F:AD D2 24         BLDTRK    LDA   CUREND
21A2:85 3E                      STA   A2            SET A2 TO SECTOR IMAGE END
21A4:AD D3 24                   LDA   CUREND+1
21A7:85 3F                      STA   A2+1
21A9:A5 3C                      LDA   A1            SET A4 TO CURRENT POSITION
21AB:85 42                      STA   A4            IN TRACK IMAGE
21AD:A5 3D                      LDA   A1+1
21AF:85 43                      STA   A4+1
21B1:A9 0F                      LDA   #$0F          SET COUNT TO 16
21B3:8D CC 24                   STA   COUNT
21B6:A0 00                      LDY   #$00          CLEAR Y FOR MOVE ROUTINE
21B8:A9 40            MORE2     LDA   #>IMAGE
21BA:85 3C                      STA   A1            SET A1 TO SECTOR IMAGE START
21BC:A9 23                      LDA   #<IMAGE
21BE:85 3D                      STA   A1+1
21C0:20 2C FE                   JSR   MOVE          MOVE SECTOR IMAGE TO TRACK IMAGE
21C3:CE CC 24                   DEC   COUNT         DECREMENT COUNT
21C6:10 F0    21B8              BPL   MORE2         LOOP UNTIL WE HAVE 16 SECTORS
21C8:60                         RTS
```

```
21C9:                 * FIX ADDRESS INFORMATION IN TRACK IMAGE

21C9:A9 00            FIXTRK    LDA   #$00
21CB:8D D8 24                   STA   SECTOR         START WITH SECTOR ZERO
21CE:AD D4 24                   LDA   START
21D1:85 3C                      STA   A1             SET A1 TO TRACK IMAGE START
21D3:AD D5 24                   LDA   START+1
21D6:85 3D                      STA   A1+1
21D8:A9 00                      LDA   #$00
21DA:85 3E                      STA   A2             SET A2 TO $8000
21DC:A9 80                      LDA   #$80
21DE:85 3F                      STA   A2+1
21E0:20 22 22         AGAIN     JSR   POSITION       POSITION TO ADDRESS INFO
21E3:20 4C 22                   JSR   CMPADD         UPDATE ADDRESS INFO
21E6:EE D8 24                   INC   SECTOR         NEXT SECTOR
21E9:AD D8 24                   LDA   SECTOR
21EC:C9 10                      CMP   #$10           DONE ALL 16 YET?
21EE:D0 F0     21E0             BNE   AGAIN          IF NOT DO ANOTHER
21F0:60                         RTS

21F1:                 * SET POINTERS FOR VERIFY ROUTINE
21F1:                 * ON EXIT: A1 > 1ST ADDRESS FIELD IN TRACK IMAGE
21F1:                 *          A4 > 1ST ADDRESS FIELD IN LIVE DATA FROM DISK

21F1:A9 00            SETUP     LDA   #$00
21F3:85 3C                      STA   A1             SET A1 TO $4000
21F5:A9 40                      LDA   #$40
21F7:85 3D                      STA   A1+1
21F9:A9 00                      LDA   #$00
21FB:85 3E                      STA   A2             SET A2 TO $6000
21FD:A9 60                      LDA   #$60
21FF:85 3F                      STA   A2+1
2201:20 22 22                   JSR   POSITION       LOCATE 1ST ADDRESS FIELD
2204:A5 3C                      LDA   A1
2206:85 42                      STA   A4             SET A4 TO POSITION FOUND
2208:A5 3D                      LDA   A1+1
220A:85 43                      STA   A4+1
220C:AD D4 24                   LDA   START
220F:85 3C                      STA   A1             SET A1 TO START OF TRACK IMAGE
2211:AD D5 24                   LDA   START+1
2214:85 3D                      STA   A1+1
2216:A9 FE                      LDA   #$FE
2218:85 3E                      STA   A2             SET A2 TO $7FFE
221A:A9 7F                      LDA   #$7F
221C:85 3F                      STA   A2+1
221E:20 22 22                   JSR   POSITION       LOCATE 1ST ADDRESS FIELD
2221:60                         RTS

2222:                 * LOCATE AN ADDRESS FIELD

2222:A0 00            POSITION  LDY   #$00           INITIALIZE OFFSET
2224:A2 02            POS2      LDX   #$02           INITIALIZE COUNT
2226:20 BA FC         POS3      JSR   NXTA1          INCREMENT POINTER
2229:B0 0D     2238             BCS   DONE           IF PAST DATA THEN EXIT
222B:B1 3C                      LDA   (A1),Y         GET A BYTE
222D:DD DD 24                   CMP   TABLE,X        CHECK IT IN TABLE
2230:D0 F2     2224             BNE   POS2           NOT THERE, THEN TRY AGAIN
2232:CA                         DEX                  FOUND ONE, COUNT IT
2233:10 F1     2226             BPL   POS3           GO UNTIL WE HAVE THREE
2235:20 BA FC                   JSR   NXTA1          POINT ONE PAST
2238:60               DONE      RTS

2239:                 * COMPARE TWO AREAS OF MEMORY

2239:A0 00            COMPARE   LDY   #$00           INITIALIZE OFFSET
223B:B1 3C            LOOPC     LDA   (A1),Y         GET A BYTE (TRACK IMAGE)
223D:09 80                      ORA   #$80           TURN 7F'S TO FF'S
223F:D1 42                      CMP   (A4),Y         COMPARE WITH DISK IMAGE
2241:D0 07     224A             BNE   MISMATCH       EXIT ON MISMATCH
2243:20 B4 FC                   JSR   NXTA4          INCREMENT BOTH POINTERS
2246:90 F3     223B             BCC   LOOPC          LOOP UNTIL DONE
```

```
2248:18                         CLC                  INDICATE SUCCESS
2249:60                         RTS
224A:38                MISMATCH SEC                  INDICATE ERROR
224B:60                         RTS

224C:                  * COMPUTE ADDRESS FIELD INFORMATION AND STORE IN TRACK IMAGE

224C:AD 05 20          CMPADD   LDA   VOLNUM         GET VOLUME NUMBER
224F:20 6B 22                   JSR   COMPUTE        COMPUTE AND STORE IT
2252:AD D7 24                   LDA   TRACK          GET CURRENT TRACK
2255:20 6B 22                   JSR   COMPUTE        COMPUTE AND STORE IT
2258:AD D8 24                   LDA   SECTOR         GET CURRENT SECTOR
225B:20 6B 22                   JSR   COMPUTE
225E:AD 05 20                   LDA   VOLNUM
2261:4D D7 24                   EOR   TRACK
2264:4D D8 24                   EOR   SECTOR         GET CHECKSUM
2267:20 6B 22                   JSR   COMPUTE
226A:60                         RTS

226B:                  * NIBBLIZE A BYTE

226B:48                COMPUTE  PHA                  SAVE A-REGISTER
226C:4A                         LSR   A              0ABCDEFG  H
226D:09 AA                      ORA   #$AA           1A1C1E1G
226F:91 3C                      STA   (A1),Y         STORE IT
2271:68                         PLA                  ABCDEFGH
2272:09 AA                      ORA   #$AA           1B1D1F1H
2274:C8                         INY
2275:91 3C                      STA   (A1),Y         STORE IT
2277:C8                         INY
2278:60                         RTS

2279:                  *  RECALIBRATE DISK ARM

2279:A9 30             RECALC   LDA   #$30           PRETEND TO BE ON TRACK 48
227B:8D DA 24                   STA   CURTRK
227E:A9 00                      LDA   #$00           SELECT TRACK 00
2280:8D D9 24                   STA   DESTRK
2283:20 96 22                   JSR   ARMOVE         GO THERE
2286:AE D6 24                   LDX   SLOT           GET SLOT NUMBER
2289:BD 80 C0                   LDA   DRVSM0,X       TURN ALL PHASES OFF
228C:BD 82 C0                   LDA   DRVSM2,X
228F:BD 84 C0                   LDA   DRVSM4,X
2292:BD 86 C0                   LDA   DRVSM6,X
2295:60                         RTS                  RETURN TO CALLER

2296:                  *  ARM MOVE ROUTINE

2296:A9 00             ARMOVE   LDA   #$00
2298:8D DC 24                   STA   FLAG           INITIALIZE FLAG
229B:AD DA 24                   LDA   CURTRK         GET CURRENT TRACK
229E:38                         SEC
229F:ED D9 24                   SBC   DESTRK         SUBTRACT DESTINATION TRACK
22A2:F0 36    22DA              BEQ   DONE2          IF EQUAL THEN EXIT
22A4:B0 04    22AA              BCS   OK             POSITIVE RESULT? YES, GO ON
22A6:49 FF                      EOR   #$FF           MAKE RESULT POSITIVE
22A8:69 01                      ADC   #$01
22AA:8D DB 24          OK       STA   DELTA          SAVE RESULT
22AD:2E DC 24                   ROL   FLAG           SET IN/OUT FLAG
22B0:4E DA 24                   LSR   CURTRK         ON ODD OR EVEN TRACK?
22B3:2E DC 24                   ROL   FLAG           PUT RESULT IN FLAG
22B6:0E DC 24                   ASL   FLAG           ADJUST FOR TABLE OFFSET
22B9:AC DC 24                   LDY   FLAG           GET TABLE OFFSET
22BC:B9 EF 22          LOOP6    LDA   PTABLE,Y       GET PHASE TO TURN ON
22BF:20 DB 22                   JSR   PHASE
22C2:B9 F0 22                   LDA   PTABLE+1,Y     GET NEXT PHASE TO TURN ON
22C5:20 DB 22                   JSR   PHASE
22C8:98                         TYA
22C9:49 02                      EOR   #$02           ADJUST OFFSET
22CB:A8                         TAY
```

```
22CC:CE DB 24                   DEC   DELTA         DECREMENT NUMBER OF TRACKS
22CF:AD DB 24                   LDA   DELTA
22D2:D0 E8    22BC              BNE   LOOP6         IF NOT DONE, DO ANOTHER
22D4:AD D9 24                   LDA   DESTRK        UPDATE CURRENT TRACK WITH
22D7:8D DA 24                   STA   CURTRK        WHERE THE ARM IS NOW
22DA:60             DONE2       RTS                 DONE, RETURN TO CALLER

22DB:               *  TURN A PHASE ON, WAIT THEN TURN IT OFF

22DB:0D D6 24       PHASE       ORA   SLOT          ADD SLOT TO PHASE
22DE:AA                         TAX
22DF:BD 81 C0                   LDA   DRVSM1,X      TURN ON A PHASE
22E2:20 E9 22                   JSR   WAIT          WAIT FOR ARM TO SETTLE
22E5:BD 80 C0                   LDA   DRVSM0,X      TURN OFF PHASE
22E8:60                         RTS                 RETURN TO CALLER

22E9:               *  20 MILLISECOND DELAY ROUTINE

22E9:A9 56          WAIT        LDA   #$56          WAIT ABOUT 20 MILLISECONDS
22EB:20 A8 FC                   JSR   DELAY
22EE:60                         RTS                 RETURN TO CALLER

22EF:               *  PHASE TABLE

22EF:02 04 06 00    PTABLE      DFB   $02,$04,$06,$00
22F3:06 04 02 00                DFB   $06,$04,$02,$00

22F7:               * CLEAR SCREEN AND DISPLAY MESSAGE

22F7:20 58 FC       SCREEN      JSR   HOME          CLEAR SCREEN
22FA:A9 E0                      LDA   #>MESSAGE
22FC:85 00                      STA   PTR           POINT AT MESSAGE
22FE:A9 24                      LDA   #<MESSAGE
2300:85 01                      STA   PTR+1
2302:20 33 23                   JSR   PRINT         PRINT IT
2305:60                         RTS

2306:               * PRINT TRACK NUMBER

2306:AD D7 24       PRTRK       LDA   TRACK         GET TRACK NUMBER
2309:20 DA FD                   JSR   PRBYTE        PRINT IT
230C:20 10 FC                   JSR   BS
230F:20 10 FC                   JSR   BS            MOVE CURSOR BACK
2312:60                         RTS

2313:               * ERROR HANDLER

2313:C9 01          ERRHDL      CMP   #$01          IS IT ERROR #1
2315:D0 0A    2321              BNE   SECOND        NO, THEN ASSUME #2
2317:A9 F3                      LDA   #>MESSAGE1
2319:85 00                      STA   PTR           POINT AT MESSAGE 1
231B:A9 24                      LDA   #<MESSAGE1
231D:85 01                      STA   PTR+1
231F:D0 08    2329              BNE   PRINTIT       ALWAYS TAKEN
2321:A9 09          SECOND      LDA   #>MESSAGE2
2323:85 00                      STA   PTR           POINT AT MESSAGE 2
2325:A9 25                      LDA   #<MESSAGE2
2327:85 01                      STA   PTR+1
2329:20 33 23       PRINTIT     JSR   PRINT         PRINT IT
232C:AE D6 24                   LDX   SLOT          GET SLOT
232F:BD 88 C0                   LDA   DRVOFF,X      TURN DRIVE OFF
2332:60                         RTS                 EXIT PROGRAM
```

```
2333:                  * PRINT ROUTINE

2333:A0 00             PRINT     LDY   #$00             INITIALIZE OFFSET
2335:B1 00             CHAR      LDA   (PTR),Y          GET CHARACTER
2337:F0 06    233F               BEQ   TERMINATE        IF ZERO THEN EXIT
2339:20 ED FD                    JSR   COUT             PRINT CHARACTER
233C:C8                          INY
233D:D0 F6    2335               BNE   CHAR             DO ANOTHER
233F:60                TERMINATE RTS

2340:                  *  DATA AREA

2340:         2340     IMAGE     EQU   *

2340:D5 AA 96          HEADER1   DFB   $D5,$AA,$96

2343:         2343     ADDRESS   EQU   *
2343:AA AA             VOL       DFB   $AA,$AA
2345:AA AA             TRK       DFB   $AA,$AA
2347:AA AA             SEC       DFB   $AA,$AA
2349:AA AA             CHK       DFB   $AA,$AA

234B:DE AA EB          TRAILER1  DFB   $DE,$AA,$EB

234E:7F 7F 7F          GAP2      DFB   $7F,$7F,$7F
2351:7F 7F 7F                    DFB   $7F,$7F,$7F

2354:D5 AA AD          HEADER2   DFB   $D5,$AA,$AD

2357:         0056     DATA      DS    $56
23AD:         0100               DS    $100
24AD:         0001               DS    $01
24AE:         24AD     DATAEND   EQU   *-1
24AE:         0156     DATALTH   EQU   DATAEND-DATA

24AE:DE AA EB          TRAILER2  DFB   $DE,$AA,$EB

24B1:7F 7F 7F          GAP3      DFB   $7F,$7F,$7F
24B4:7F 7F 7F                    DFB   $7F,$7F,$7F
24B7:7F 7F 7F                    DFB   $7F,$7F,$7F
24BA:7F 7F 7F                    DFB   $7F,$7F,$7F
24BD:7F 7F 7F                    DFB   $7F,$7F,$7F
24C0:7F 7F 7F                    DFB   $7F,$7F,$7F
24C3:7F 7F 7F                    DFB   $7F,$7F,$7F
24C6:7F 7F 7F                    DFB   $7F,$7F,$7F
24C9:7F 7F 7F                    DFB   $7F,$7F,$7F
24CC:         24CB     END       EQU   *-1
24CC:         018C     LEN       EQU   END-IMAGE+1

24CC:00 00             COUNT     DFB   $00,$00
24CE:00                RETRYCNT  DFB   $00
24CF:00                BYTE      DFB   $00
24D0:00 00             LENGTH    DFB   $00,$00
24D2:00 00             CUREND    DFB   $00,$00
24D4:00 00             START     DFB   $00,$00
24D6:60                SLOT      DFB   $60
24D7:00                TRACK     DFB   $00
24D8:00                SECTOR    DFB   $00
24D9:00                DESTRK    DFB   $00              DESTINATION TRACK
24DA:00                CURTRK    DFB   $00              CURRENT TRACK
24DB:00                DELTA     DFB   $00              NUMBER OF TRACKS TO MOVE
24DC:00                FLAG      DFB   $00              DIRECTION & ODD/EVEN FLAGS
24DD:96 AA D5          TABLE     DFB   $96,$AA,$D5

24E0:                            MSB   ON
24E0:C6 CF D2 CD       MESSAGE   ASC   'FORMATTING      TRACK
24F2:00                          DFB   $00
24F3:8D                MESSAGE1  DFB   $8D
24F4:D7 D2 C9 D4                 ASC   'WRITE           PROTECT ERROR'
2507:87 00                       DFB   $87,$00
```

```
2509:8D               MESSAGE2  DFB   $8D
250A:D5 CE C1 C2                ASC   'UNABLE        TO FORMAT'
251A:87 00                      DFB   $87,$00
251C:                           MSB   OFF
```

ZAP—DISK UPDATE UTILITY

The next step up the ladder from DUMP and FORMAT is accessing data on the diskette at the block level. The ZAP program allows its user to specify a block number to be read into memory. The user can then make changes to the image of the block in memory, and subsequently use ZAP to write the modified image back over the block on disk. ZAP is particularly useful when it is necessary to patch up a damaged directory. Its use in this regard will be covered in more detail when FIB is explained.

To use ZAP, store the number of the block you wish to access at $2007 and $2008. Store the least significant byte of the number in $2007 and the most significant byte in $2008. For example, the key block of the Volume Directory may be read by entering 2007:02 00. $2009 should be initialized with either $80 to indicate that a sector is to be read into memory, or $81 to ask that memory be written out to the block on the disk. You may also specify the disk drive to be used (slot 6, drive 1 is assumed) by storing a hex value of $s0 at $2004, where "s" is the slot to be used. If you wish to access drive 2 for a given slot, turn on the most significant bit in $2004 (e.g. slot 6, drive 2 would be 2004:E0). An example to illustrate the use of ZAP follows.

```
CALL -151    (Get into the monitor)
BLOAD ZAP    (Load the ZAP program)
```

(Now insert the diskette to be ZAPped)

```
2007:02 00 80 N 2000G   (Store a 2 (key block of the Volume
                        directory) in $2007/8 and $80 (read
                        block) at $2009. N ends the store command
                        and 2000G runs ZAP.)
```

The output might look like this...

```
1000- 00 00 03 00 FA 55 53 45
1008- 52 53 2E 44 49 53 4B 00
1010- 00 00 00 00 00 00 00 00
1018- 00 00 00 00 00 00 00 00
 ...etc...
```

In the example above, if the byte at offset 6 (the second character of the volume name, "USERS.DISK") is to be changed to "O", the following would be entered.

```
1006:4F              (Change +$06 to $4F ("O"))
2009:81 N 2000G      (Change ZAP to write mode and do it)
```

Note that ZAP will remember the previous values in \$2004 through \$2009. If something is wrong with the block to be read or written (an I/O error, perhaps), ZAP will print an error message of the form:

RC=2B

A return code of \$2B, in this case, means that the diskette was write protected and a write operation was attempted. Other error codes are \$27 (I/O error), and \$28 (no device connected). Refer to the documentation on READ_BLOCK and WRITE_BLOCK in Chapter 6 for more information on these errors.

```
----- NEXT OBJECT FILE NAME IS ZAP.S.0
2000:        2000              ORG    $2000
2000:                          MSB    ON

2000:              ***********************************************************
2000:              *                                                         *
2000:              *  ZAP:   THIS PROGRAM WILL ALLOW ITS USER TO READ/WRITE  *
2000:              *         INDIVIDUAL BLOCKS FROM/TO THE DISKETTE          *
2000:              *                                                         *
2000:              *  INPUT: $2004   = UNIT NUMBER (DSSS0000)                *
2000:              *                   DEFAULTS TO SLOT 6, DRIVE 1 ($60)     *
2000:              *                   (SLOT 6, DRIVE 2 IS $E0)              *
2000:              *         $2005/6 = ADDRESS OF AREA IN MEMORY TO BE       *
2000:              *                   READ/WRITTEN.                         *
2000:              *                   DEFAULTS TO $1000                     *
2000:              *         $2007/8 = BLOCK NUMBER TO BE READ/WRITTEN       *
2000:              *                   DEFAULTS TO $0000                     *
```

```
2000:                *        $2009    = OPERATION TO BE PERFORMED:          *
2000:                *                        $80 = READ BLOCK                    *
2000:                *                        $81 = WRITE BLOCK                   *
2000:                *                    DEFAULTS TO READ BLOCK.                 *
2000:                *                                                            *
2000:                *   ENTRY POINT: $2000                                       *
2000:                *                                                            *
2000:                *   PROGRAMMER: DON D WORTH - 2/25/84                        *
2000:                *                                                            *
2000:                *************************************************************

2000:                *        FIXED LOCATIONS WE NEED

2000:          003C  A1L        EQU   $3C          MONITOR POINTERS
2000:          003D  A1H        EQU   $3D
2000:          003E  A2L        EQU   $3E
2000:          003F  A2H        EQU   $3F
2000:          BF00  MLI        EQU   $BF00        MACHINE LANGUAGE INTERFACE
2000:          FDED  COUT       EQU   $FDED        MONITOR PRINT VECTOR
2000:          FDDA  PRBYTE     EQU   $FDDA        MONITOR PRINT HEX BYTE
2000:          FDB3  XAM        EQU   $FDB3        MONITOR HEX DUMP SUBRTN

2000:                *        ENTRY POINT, JUMP AROUND PARMS

2000:4C 0A 20        ZAP        JMP   START        BR AROUND DATA

2003:                *        MLI READ/WRITE BLOCK PARAMETER LIST

2003:03              RWBLP      DFB   $03          PARM COUNT = 3
2004:60                         DFB   $60          UNIT NUMBER
2005:00 10           BUFF       DW    $1000        BUFFER ADDRESS
2007:00 00                      DW    $0000        BLOCK NUMBER
2009:80              OPER       DFB   $80          OPERATION TO BE PERFORMED

200A:                *        START OF CODE, CALL MLI

200A:AD 09 20        START      LDA   OPER         PASS OPERATION CODE
200D:8D 13 20                   STA   OP
2010:20 00 BF                   JSR   MLI          CALL MLI
2013:00              OP         DFB   $00
2014:03 20                      DW    RWBLP
2016:90 19    2031              BCC   EXIT         ALL WENT WELL???

2018:                *        IF ERROR OCCURS, PRINT MESSAGE

2018:48                         PHA                ; SAVE ERROR CODE
2019:A9 87                      LDA   #$87         BEEP THE SPEAKER
201B:20 ED FD                   JSR   COUT
201E:A9 D2                      LDA   #'R          PRINT THE "RC="
2020:20 ED FD                   JSR   COUT
2023:A9 C3                      LDA   #'C
2025:20 ED FD                   JSR   COUT
2028:A9 BD                      LDA   #'=
202A:20 ED FD                   JSR   COUT
202D:68                         PLA
202E:4C DA FD                   JMP   PRBYTE       PRINT THE HEX VALUE

2031:                *        WHEN FINISHED, DUMP SOME OF BLOCK IN HEX

2031:18              EXIT       CLC
2032:AD 05 20                   LDA   BUFF         DUMP $2000-$20B7
2035:85 3C                      STA   A1L
2037:69 AF                      ADC   #$AF
2039:85 3E                      STA   A2L
203B:AD 06 20                   LDA   BUFF+1
203E:85 3D                      STA   A1H
2040:69 00                      ADC   #0
2042:85 3F                      STA   A2H
2044:4C B3 FD                   JMP   XAM          EXIT VIA HEX DISPLAY
```

MAP—MAP FREESPACE ON A VOLUME

The MAP program is written in BASIC and calls a tiny assembly language subroutine to read blocks from a ProDOS volume. It first reads the Volume Directory key block to determine the length and location of the Volume Bit Map. It then reads the bit map and prints a map of the volume's freespace on the screen.

To run MAP against a disk volume, first LOAD the program into BASIC, place the disk to be MAPped in slot 6, drive 1, and then RUN the program. The output from such a run might look like this:

```
FREESPACE MAP FOR VOLUME /USERS.DISK/

UUUUUUUUUUUUUUUUUUUUUUUUUUUUUUUUUUUUUUUU
UUUUUUUUUUUUUUUUUUUUUUUUUUUUUUUUUUUUUUUU
UUUUUUUUUUUUUUUUUUUUUUUUUUUUUUUUUUUUUUUU
UUUUUUUUUUUUUUUUUUUUUUUUUUUUUUUUUUUUUUUU
UUUUUUUUUUUUUUUUUUUUUUUUUUUUUUUUU.......
........................................
........................................

U = USED BLOCK              . = FREE BLOCK

BLOCKS USED: 193     BLOCKS FREE: 87
```

The MAP program first reads a short machine language program from data statements and pokes it into memory at $300. The machine language program is as follows.

```
Ø3ØØ:    PHA      ;         SAVE REGISTERS UPON ENTRY
Ø3Ø1:    TYA
Ø3Ø2:    PHA
Ø3Ø3:    TXA
Ø3Ø4:    PHA
Ø3Ø5:    JSR      $BFØØ     CALL MLI
Ø3Ø8:    DFB      $8Ø       READ_BLOCK CALL
Ø3Ø9:    DW       $315      PARAMETERS AT $315
Ø3ØB:    STA      $314      SAVE RETURN CODE
Ø3ØE:    PLA      ;         RESTORE REGISTERS
Ø3ØF:    TAX
Ø31Ø:    PLA
Ø311:    TAY
Ø312:    PLA
```

```
Ø313:    RTS      ;        AND RETURN TO BASIC PROGRAM
Ø314:    DFB      $ØØ      RETURN CODE SAVED HERE
Ø315:    DFB      $Ø3      3 PARAMETERS
Ø316:    DFB      $6Ø      SLOT 6, DRIVE 1
Ø317:    DW       $4ØØØ    BLOCK BUFFER IS AT $4ØØØ
Ø319:    DW       Ø        BLOCK NUMBER FILLED IN BY BASIC PGM
```

MAP then calls the subroutine (see lines 1000-1020) to read the Volume Directory key block (BN = 2). It obtains the length of the volume name from +4 (eliminating the $F0 entry type), and peeks the volume name and prints it on the screen from +5 in the buffer. If the total number of blocks on the volume (+41/42) is not 280, then the message "NOT A PRODOS DISKETTE" is printed. Otherwise, the first block of the Volume Bit Map is read. A loop is then entered (lines 365-440) where each binary bit which is one in the bit map is counted and printed as a "." (free) and each that is zero is counted and printed as a "U" (in use). The totals for used and free blocks are then printed and the program exits. If an error occurs, it is printed in decimal and the program aborts execution. Possible errors are 39 (I/O error) and 40 (no device connected).

MAP will not currently work for volumes with more or less than 280 blocks but this can be easily changed by the reader.

```
10  REM
20  REM  THIS PROGRAM PRINTS A MAP OF
30  REM  A PRODOS DISKETTE VOLUME.
40  REM
50  REM  PROGRAMMER: DON D WORTH 2/22/84
60  REM
70  DATA   72,152,72,138,72,32,0,191,128,21,3,141,20,3,104,170,104,168
75  DATA  104,96,0,3,96
80  REM
90  REM  POKE BLOCK READ SUBROUTINE INTO MEMORY
95  REM
100 SB = 768: REM  SB=ADDR OF SUBROUTINE
105 BF = 16384: REM  BUFFER IS AT $4000
110  FOR I = SB TO SB + 22
120  READ X: POKE I,X
130  NEXT I
140  POKE I,0: POKE I + 1,BF / 256
150 BN = SB + 25:RC = SB + 20
160  REM
170  REM   READ THE VOLUME DIRECTORY KEY BLOCK TO FIND THE BIT MAP
190  REM
200  POKE BN,2
210  GOSUB 1000
230  REM
240  REM  PRINT THE VOLUME NAME
250  REM
260 L =  PEEK (BF + 4) - 240
265  HOME : PRINT "FREESPACE MAP FOR VOLUME /";
270  FOR I = 1 TO L
280  PRINT  CHR$ ( PEEK (BF + I + 4));
290  NEXT I
300  PRINT "/": PRINT
310  REM
320  REM  LOCATE AND READ BIT MAP BLOCK
330  REM
340  IF  PEEK (BF + 41) +  PEEK (BF + 42) * 256 <  > 280 THEN  PRINT  CHR$
     (7);"NOT A PRODOS DISKETTE": END
350  POKE BN, PEEK (BF + 39): POKE BN + 1, PEEK (BF + 40)
360  GOSUB 1000
362  REM
363  REM  PRINT BIT MAP
364  REM
365 U = 0:F = 0
370  FOR B = 0 TO 34
380 X =  PEEK (B + BF)
390  FOR I = 1 TO 8
400  IF X >  = 128 THEN X = X - 128: PRINT ".";:F = F + 1: GOTO 420
410  PRINT "U";:U = U + 1
420 X = X * 2
430  NEXT I
440  NEXT B
442  REM
443  REM  FINISH UP
444  REM
450  PRINT : PRINT : PRINT "U=USED BLOCK        .=FREE BLOCK"
455  PRINT : PRINT "BLOCKS USED: ";U;"    BLOCKS FREE: ";F
460  END
1000  REM
1001  REM  READ A BLOCK FROM DISK
1002  REM
1003  CALL SB
1010  IF  PEEK (RC) = 0 THEN  RETURN
1020  PRINT "I/O ERROR = "; PEEK (RC); CHR$ (7): END
```

FIB—FIND INDEX BLOCK UTILITY

From time to time one of your diskettes will develop an I/O error smack in the middle of a directory. When this occurs, any attempt to use the files described by that directory will result in an I/O ERROR message from ProDOS. Generally, when this happens, the data stored in the files on the diskette is still intact; only the pointers to the files are gone. If the data absolutely must be recovered, a knowledgeable Apple user can reconstruct the directory from scratch. Doing this involves finding the index blocks for each file, and then using ZAP to patch a directory entry into the Volume Directory for each file which is found. FIB is a utility which will scan a disk volume for index blocks. Although it may flag some blocks which are not index blocks as being such, it will never miss a valid index block. Therefore, after running FIB, the programmer must use ZAP to examine each block printed by FIB to see if it is really an index block. Additionally, FIB will find every index block image on the volume, even some which were for files which have since been deleted. Since it is difficult to determine which files are valid and which are old deleted files, it is usually necessary to restore all the files and copy them to another diskette, and later delete the duplicate or unwanted ones.

To run FIB, simply load the program and start execution at $2000. FIB will print the block number of each block it finds which bears a resemblance to an index block. For example:

```
CALL -151    (Get into the monitor)
BLOAD FIB    (Load the FIB program)
```

(Now insert the disk to be scanned into Slot 6, Drive 1)

```
2000G   (Run the FIB program on this diskette)
```

The output might look like this...

```
BLK=0008        BLK=0099
BLK=0027        BLK=00AF
BLK=0028        BLK=00B1
BLK=003C        BLK=00B4
BLK=006F        BLK=00B7
BLK=0097
```

Here 11 possible files were found. Of course, if some of the lost files were **seedlings**, they will not be represented here (seedlings are very difficult to locate once their directory entry is gone). And if some files were **tree** files, then three or more of the above block numbers could refer to index blocks for a single file. Also, if only one of several directories for a volume is damaged, some of the block numbers given may refer to files whose directory entries are still intact. If, after running FIB, you get an error message (RC = xx, see ZAP errors), you may need to reformat the offending track. Divide the block number by eight to determine which track has the error. An alternative is to use ZAP to copy all blocks without errors to another formatted disk and write zeroes on the blocks corresponding to I/O errors. In this way you can preserve undamaged blocks which are on the same track with damaged ones.

In the example above, ZAP should now be used to read block 8. At +$00 and +$100 are the LSB and MSB of the block number for the first data block of the file (assuming this is not the master index block for a tree file). This block can be read and examined to try to identify the file and its type. Usually a BASIC program can be identified (even though it is stored in tokenized form) from the text strings contained in the PRINT statements. An ASCII conversion chart (see page 16 in the *Apple II Reference Manual for IIe Only*) can be used to decode these character strings. Straight TXT type files will also contain ASCII text, with each line separated from the others with $0Ds (carriage returns). BIN type files are the hardest to identify and recover since their original address and length attributes were lost along with the directory entry. If you cannot identify a file, assume it is BAS (Applesoft BASIC). If this assumption turns out to be incorrect, you can always go back and ZAP the file type in the directory to try something else. Given below is an example ZAP to the Volume Directory to create an entry for the file whose index block is BLK = 0008. This ZAP assumes that the Volume Directory itself was lost

and that you are starting the entire volume from scratch. **Do not perform this patch to a diskette which is only partially damaged as you will wipe out the remainder of the valid directory entries in the process.**

```
CALL -151
BLOAD ZAP
```

(insert disk to be ZAPped)

```
1000:00 N 1001<1000.11FEM        (Zero entire block of memory)
1000:00 00 03 00 F5 46 49 58     (Store a dummy Volume Directory
1008:55 50                       header for volume /FIXUP)
1020:00 00 C3 27 0D 00 00 06
1028:00 18 01
102B:24 46 49 4C 45              (Make sapling entry for "FILE")
103B:FC                          (file is type BAS)
103C:08 00                       (key block is 8)
1040:00 xx 00                    (EOF mark, see below)
1049:E3                          (full access "unlocked")
104A:01 08                       (AUX_TYPE = $801 for BAS file)
1050:02 00                       (header pointer)
2007:02 00 81 N 2000G            (write new block image out as
                                 first Volume Directory block)
```

The "xx" above should be set to the number of non-zero block numbers found in the index block as a first cut at the end of file mark. If garbage is loaded at the end of the program, try a smaller number. You may be able to deduce the true EOF by examining the program image on disk. Remember that AUX_TYPE will be different for different file types. See Chapter 4 for more information.

As soon as the entry is created using the above procedure, the file should be immediately copied to another diskette. Do not attempt to use the file in place because the Volume Bit Map has not been updated and several other fields in the directory entry have been omitted. Also, you do not want to risk damaging other "lost" files on the disk. Repeat the above process for each index block found by FIB. As each file is recovered, it may be RENAMEd to its original name on the new diskette. Once all the files have been copied to another disk, and successfully tested, the damaged disk may be re-initialized.

```
----- NEXT OBJECT FILE NAME IS FIB.S.0
2000:        2000                 ORG   $2000
2000:                             MSB   ON

2000:             ***********************************************************
2000:             *                                                         *
2000:             *  FIB:  THIS PROGRAM SCANS AN ENTIRE VOLUME, SEARCHING *
2000:             *        FOR WHAT APPEAR TO BE INDEX BLOCKS AND PRINTS   *
2000:             *        THE BLOCK NUMBER OF EACH ONE IT FINDS. FIB WILL*
2000:             *        WORK FOR ANY SIZED VOLUME. SLOT 6, DRIVE 1 IS  *
2000:             *        ASSUMED.                                        *
2000:             *                                                         *
2000:             *  INPUT: NONE                                            *
2000:             *                                                         *
2000:             *  ENTRY POINT: $2000                                     *
2000:             *                                                         *
2000:             *  PROGRAMMER: DON D WORTH - 2/25/84                      *
2000:             *                                                         *
2000:             ***********************************************************

2000:             *        FIXED LOCATIONS WE NEED

2000:        0048 PTR      EQU   $48          WORK POINTER
2000:        1000 BUFFER   EQU   $1000        BLOCK BUFFER
2000:        BF00 MLI      EQU   $BF00        MACHINE LANGUAGE INTERFACE
2000:        FDED COUT     EQU   $FDED        MONITOR PRINT VECTOR
2000:        FDDA PRBYTE   EQU   $FDDA        MONITOR PRINT HEX BYTE
2000:        FDB3 XAM      EQU   $FDB3        MONITOR HEX DUMP SUBRTN

2000:             *        OFFSETS INTO VOL DIR HEADER

2000:        1029 TOTBLK   EQU   $1029
2000:        1027 BITMAP   EQU   $1027

2000:             *        ENTRY POINT, READ VOLUME DIRECTORY HEADER

2000:A9 02        FIB      LDA   #2           BLOCK = 2
2002:8D E9 20              STA   BLOCK
2005:A9 00                 LDA   #0
2007:8D EA 20              STA   BLOCK+1
200A:20 97 20              JSR   READ         READ VOL DIR BLOCK
200D:B0 35   2044          BCS   EXIT         IF ERROR, GIVE UP RIGHT NOW
200F:AD 29 10              LDA   TOTBLK
2012:8D ED 20              STA   LAST
2015:AD 2A 10              LDA   TOTBLK+1
2018:8D EE 20              STA   LAST+1
201B:4A                    LSR   A            COMPUTE TOTBLK/4096
201C:4A                    LSR   A
201D:4A                    LSR   A
201E:4A                    LSR   A            FOR NUM BIT MAP BLOCKS
201F:38                    SEC                ; AND ADD ONE TO THAT
2020:6D 27 10              ADC   BITMAP
2023:8D E9 20              STA   BLOCK
2026:8D EB 20              STA   FIRST
2029:A9 00                 LDA   #0
202B:6D 28 10              ADC   BITMAP+1
202E:8D EA 20              STA   BLOCK+1      POINT PAST THE BITMAP
2031:8D EC 20              STA   FIRST+1

2034:             *        SEE IF WE ARE AT END OF VOLUME

2034:AD EA 20     NEWBLK   LDA   BLOCK+1      WHEN WE REACH LAST BLOCK +1
2037:CD EE 20              CMP   LAST+1
203A:D0 13   204F          BNE   READIT
203C:AD E9 20              LDA   BLOCK
203F:CD ED 20              CMP   LAST
2042:D0 0B   204F          BNE   READIT
2044:60           EXIT     RTS                EXIT TO SYSTEM
2045:EE E9 20     NXTBLK   INC   BLOCK        INCREMENT BLOCK COUNT
2048:D0 EA   2034          BNE   NEWBLK
204A:EE EA 20              INC   BLOCK+1
204D:D0 E5   2034          BNE   NEWBLK       AND CONTINUE LOOP
```

```
204F:                  *     READ BLOCK AND CHECK FOR VALIDITY AS AN INDEX BLOCK

204F:20 97 20          READIT     JSR   READ            READ THIS BLOCK
2052:B0 F1    2045                BCS   NXTBLK          ERROR?

2054:A0 00                        LDY   #0
2056:B9 00 10          CHKNG1     LDA   BUFFER,Y        MAKE SURE ITS NOT ALL ZERO
2059:19 00 11                     ORA   BUFFER+$100,Y
205C:D0 05    2063                BNE   CHKNG2
205E:C8                           INY
205F:D0 F5    2056                BNE   CHKNG1
2061:F0 E2    2045                BEQ   NXTBLK          IF SO, SKIP IT

2063:A0 00             CHKNG2     LDY   #0
2065:B9 00 10          CHKING     LDA   BUFFER,Y        ALLOW ZERO ENTRIES
2068:D0 05    206F                BNE   COMPR
206A:B9 00 11                     LDA   BUFFER+$100,Y
206D:F0 0E    207D                BEQ   BLKOK
206F:A2 00             COMPR      LDX   #0              CHECK AGAINST FIRST
2071:20 86 20                     JSR   CMP             DO 16 BIT COMPARE
2074:90 CF    2045                BCC   NXTBLK          TOO SMALL FOR BLOCK NUMBER
2076:A2 02                        LDX   #2              CHECK AGAINST LAST
2078:20 86 20                     JSR   CMP
207B:B0 C8    2045                BCS   NXTBLK          TOO LARGE FOR BLOCK NUMBER
207D:C8                BLKOK      INY
207E:D0 E5    2065                BNE   CHKING

2080:20 BE 20                     JSR   PBLOCK          FOUND ONE, PRINT BLOCK NO.
2083:4C 45 20                     JMP   NXTBLK          THEN CONTINUE

2086:                  *          CMP: 16 BIT COMPARE

2086:B9 00 11          CMP        LDA   BUFFER+$100,Y CHECK MSB
2089:DD EC 20                     CMP   FIRST+1,X
208C:90 08    2096                BCC   RTS             ITS SMALLER
208E:D0 06    2096                BNE   RTS             ITS BIGGER
2090:B9 00 10                     LDA   BUFFER,Y        CHECK LSB
2093:DD EB 20                     CMP   FIRST,X
2096:60                RTS        RTS

2097:                  *          READ A BLOCK FROM DISK TO $1000

2097:20 00 BF          READ       JSR   MLI             CALL MLI
209A:80                           DFB   $80             READ CALL
209B:E5 20                        DW    RWBLP
209D:B0 01    20A0                BCS   ERROR           ERROR?
209F:60                           RTS

20A0:                  *          IF ERROR OCCURS, PRINT MESSAGE

20A0:48                ERROR      PHA                   ; SAVE ERROR CODE
20A1:A9 87                        LDA   #$87            BEEP THE SPEAKER
20A3:20 ED FD                     JSR   COUT
20A6:A9 D2                        LDA   #'R             PRINT THE "RC="
20A8:20 ED FD                     JSR   COUT
20AB:A9 C3                        LDA   #'C
20AD:20 ED FD                     JSR   COUT
20B0:A9 BD                        LDA   #'=
20B2:20 ED FD                     JSR   COUT
20B5:68                           PLA
20B6:20 DA FD                     JSR   PRBYTE          PRINT THE HEX VALUE
20B9:A9 A0                        LDA   #$A0            PRINT A BLANK
20BB:20 ED FD                     JSR   COUT            & FALL THRU TO PRINT BLOCK

20BE:                  *          PRINT CURRENT BLOCK NUMBER

20BE:A9 C2             PBLOCK     LDA   #'B             PRINT "BLK="
20C0:20 ED FD                     JSR   COUT
20C3:A9 CC                        LDA   #'L
20C5:20 ED FD                     JSR   COUT
```

```
20C8:A9 CB               LDA   #'K
20CA:20 ED FD            JSR   COUT
20CD:A9 BD               LDA   #'=
20CF:20 ED FD            JSR   COUT
20D2:AD EA 20            LDA   BLOCK+1      PRINT BLOCK NUMBER IN HEX
20D5:20 DA FD            JSR   PRBYTE       PRINT MSB
20D8:AD E9 20            LDA   BLOCK
20DB:20 DA FD            JSR   PRBYTE       AND LSB
20DE:A9 8D               LDA   #$8D
20E0:20 ED FD            JSR   COUT         NEW LINE
20E3:38                  SEC
20E4:60                  RTS

20E5:          *       MLI READ/WRITE BLOCK PARAMETER LIST

20E5:03          RWBLP   DFB   $03          PARM COUNT = 3
20E6:60          UNIT    DFB   $60          UNIT NUMBER
20E7:00 10       BUFF    DW    BUFFER       BUFFER ADDRESS
20E9:00 00       BLOCK   DW    $0000        BLOCK NUMBER

20EB:00 00       FIRST   DW    $0000        FIRST BLOCK AFTER BIT MAP
20ED:00 00       LAST    DW    $0000        LAST BLOCK ON DISK +1
```

TYPE—TYPE COMMAND

The TYPE program is an example of how to add commands to the ProDOS BASIC Interpreter. TYPE may be installed as a command by BRUNning TYPE or using the "–" smart RUN command. Once installed, the user may enter:

TYPE filename[,Sslot][,Ddrive]

The BI will not recognize "TYPE" as one of its commands and will pass control to the installed external command handler. The handler will locate and open the file, read its contents and print them on the screen or output device. The user may suspend the listing with any keypress and resume it with any other. A control-C will abort the listing.

TYPE's operation begins when it is BRUN. Its first task is to allocate a page of memory between the BI and its buffers. It will copy the resident part of its program into this page. TYPE next stores the address of the newly allocated page in the BI's EXTERNCMD vector in the BI Global Page. Each time the BI sees a command it doesn't recognize, it will call the address in the EXTERNCMD vector before treating it as an invalid command. The transient portion of TYPE finishes up by copying and relocating the fixed addresses in the resident portion up to its new home in the newly allocated BI buffer. The transient portion then exits to ProDOS.

When an unknown command line is encountered, control passes to the resident code at TYPENT. TYPENT compares the command to the string "TYPE", and if there is a match, it claims the command and returns to the BI to allow it to parse the filename and any other keywords given. If no SYNTAX ERROR occurs, control returns from the BI at the label TYPBAK. (If TYPENT does not recognize the command, it passes control on to the original contents of EXTERNCMD, in case there are other external command handlers installed.) When control returns to TYPBAK, the MLI is called to open the file, using the BI's General Purpose buffer at HIMEM for an I/O buffer. The file is then read, 256 bytes at a time using $200 for a data buffer, and its contents are copied to the COUT screen output vector. At End of File, TYPENT exits to the BI through the MLI CLOSE function call.

TYPE may be used as a model for small command handlers. It is written in such a way that it may coexist with numerous other external command handlers by preserving the original value it finds in the EXTERNCMD vector. Suggestions for additional external commands might include a file COPY command or a file hex/ASCII DUMP command. Note that if the installed, resident portion is longer than 256 bytes, the relocation code will have to be rewritten and will be a bit more complex.

```
----- NEXT OBJECT FILE NAME IS TYPE.S.0
2000:        2000               ORG   $2000

2000:             ************************************************************
2000:             *                                                          *
2000:             *    TYPE: WHEN BRUN, THIS PROGRAM INSTALLS AN EXTERNAL    *
2000:             *          PRODOS BASIC INTERPRETER COMMAND BETWEEN THE    *
2000:             *          BI AND ITS BUFFERS. THE NEW COMMAND IS          *
2000:             *          INVOKED AS FOLLOWS:                             *
2000:             *                                                          *
2000:             *          TYPE <PATHNAME>[,S#][,D#]                       *
2000:             *                                                          *
2000:             *          THE TYPE COMMAND COPIES THE CONTENTS OF THE     *
2000:             *          INDICATED FILE TO THE SCREEN.                   *
2000:             *                                                          *
2000:             *          THE RESIDENT PORTION OF THE TYPE COMMAND        *
2000:             *          REQUIRES ONLY 256 BYTES OF RAM.                 *
2000:             *                                                          *
2000:             *    PROGRAMMER: DON D WORTH - 2/21/84                     *
2000:             *                                                          *
2000:             ************************************************************
```

```
2000:                 *          FIXED LOCATIONS WE NEED

2000:          0048     PTR       EQU   $48            WORK ZPAGE POINTER
2000:          0073     HIMEM     EQU   $73            HIMEM (START OF GP BUFFER)
2000:          0200     IN        EQU   $200           INPUT LINE BUFFER
2000:          BF00     MLI       EQU   $BF00          MACHINE LANGUAGE INTERFACE
2000:          C000     KBD       EQU   $C000          KEYBOARD LATCH
2000:          C010     KBDSTB    EQU   $C010          KEYBOARD CLEAR STROBE
2000:          FDED     COUT      EQU   $FDED          MONITOR PRINT VECTOR

2000:                 *          SELECTED THINGS FROM THE BI GLOBAL PAGE

0000:                             DSECT
BE00:          BE00               ORG   $BE00          START OF BI GLOBAL PAGE

BE00:4C 00 00           BIENTRY   JMP   $0000          WARM ENTRY INTO PRODOS BI
BE03:4C 00 00           DOSCMD    JMP   $0000          COMMAND EXECUTER
BE06:4C 00 00           EXTCMD    JMP   $0000          EXTERNAL COMMAND VECTOR
BE09:4C 00 00           ERROUT    JMP   $0000          EXIT WITH ERROR
BE0C:4C 00 00           PRNTERR   JMP   $0000          PRINT ERROR MESSAGE
BE0F:00                 ERRCODE   DFB   0              ERROR CODE

BE50:          BE50               ORG   $BE50
BE50:00 00              XTADDR    DW    $0000          EXEC ADDR OF EXTERNAL CMD
BE52:00                 XLEN      DFB   0              LENGTH OF CMD STRING -1
BE53:00                 XCNUM     DFB   0              BI COMMAND NUMBER

BE54:          0001     FN1       EQU   $01            FILE NAME EXPECTED
BE54:          0004     SD        EQU   $04            SLOT/DRIVE PERMITTED
BE54:00 00              PBITS     DW    0              ALLOWED PARAMETERS BITS
BE56:00 00              FBITS     DW    0              PARAMETERS FOUND BITS

BE6C:          BE6C               ORG   $BE6C
BE6C:00 00              VPATH1    DW    $0000          ADDR OF PATHNAME 1 BUFFER
BE6E:00 00              VPATH2    DW    $0000          ADDR OF PATHNAME 2 BUFFER

BE70:          BE70     GOSYS     EQU   *              MLI CALL HANDLER

BECB:          BECB               ORG   $BECB
BECB:03                 SOPEN     DFB   $03            OPEN PARAMETER LIST
BECC:00 00                        DW    $0000
BECE:00 00              OSYSBUF   DW    $0000          BUFFER ADDR
BED0:00                 OREFNUM   DFB   $00            REF NUM RETURNED

BED5:          BED5               ORG   $BED5
BED5:          BED5     SREAD     EQU   *              READ/WRITE PARM LIST
BED5:          BED5     SWRITE    EQU   *
BED5:04                           DFB   $04            PARM COUNT = 4
BED6:00                 RWRFNUM   DFB   $00            REFNUM
BED7:00 00              RWDATA    DW    $0000          BUFFER ADDR
BED9:00 00              RWCOUNT   DW    $0000          REQUEST LENGTH
BEDB:00 00              RWTRANS   DW    $0000          TRUE LENGTH

BEDD:          BEDD     SCLOSE    EQU   *              CLOSE/FLUSH PARM LIST
BEDD:          BEDD     SFLUSH    EQU   *
BEDD:01                           DFB   $01            PARM COUNT = 1
BEDE:00                 CFRFNUM   DFB   $00            REFNUM

BEF5:          BEF5               ORG   $BEF5
BEF5:4C 00 00           GETBUFR   JMP   $0000          ALLOCATE BI BUFFER

2000:                             DEND

2000:                 *          THIS PART OF THE PROGRAM GETS CONTROL WHEN THE
2000:                 *          BRUN COMMAND IS ISSUED. IT RELOCATES THE RESIDENT
2000:                 *          PART OF THE CODE TO THE TOP OF MEMORY

2000:A9 01              TYPE      LDA   #1             WE NEED 1 PAGE
2002:20 F5 BE                     JSR   GETBUFR        BUY MEMORY FOR RESIDENT CODE
2005:90 10     2017               BCC   GOTBUF         GOT IT
```

```
2007:A0 00                        LDY   #0
2009:B9 76 20          ERLP       LDA   MSG,Y          NO BUFFER, PRINT MESSAGE
200C:20 ED FD                     JSR   COUT
200F:C8                           INY
2010:C9 8D                        CMP   #$8D
2012:D0 F5    2009                BNE   ERLP
2014:4C 00 BE          EXIT       JMP   BIENTRY        AND LEAVE

2017:85 49             GOTBUF     STA   PTR+1          PTR --> BUFFER
2019:AE 08 BE                     LDX   EXTCMD+2
201C:8D 08 BE                     STA   EXTCMD+2       EXTCMD --> BUFFER
201F:8E 40 21                     STX   NXTCOM+2
2022:AE 07 BE                     LDX   EXTCMD+1       BUT SAVE OLD EXTRNCMD VECTOR
2025:8E 3F 21                     STX   NXTCOM+1
2028:A0 00                        LDY   #0
202A:84 48                        STY   PTR
202C:8C 07 BE                     STY   EXTCMD+1

202F:B9 00 21          COPY       LDA   TYPENT,Y       COPY RESIDENT CODE TO BUFFER
2032:91 48                        STA   (PTR),Y
2034:8C 8F 20                     STY   SAVE           SAVE YREG
2037:48                           PHA
2038:29 03                        AND   #$03           ISOLATE BIT OFFSET OF OPCODE
203A:A8                           TAY
203B:68                           PLA
203C:4A                           LSR   A
203D:4A                           LSR   A              DIVIDE BY 4 (BYTE OFFSET)
203E:AA                           TAX
203F:BD 90 20                     LDA   OPTAB,X        GET 4 OPCODES' LENGTHS
2042:88                OPLOOP     DEY
2043:30 04    2049                BMI   OPDONE         SHIFT OUT THE 2 BIT LEN
2045:4A                           LSR   A
2046:4A                           LSR   A
2047:D0 F9    2042                BNE   OPLOOP
2049:29 03             OPDONE     AND   #$03           ISOLATE LENGTH
204B:F0 26    2073                BEQ   COPIED         0 LENGTH OP ($FF) SIGNALS END
204D:AA                           TAX
204E:AC 8F 20                     LDY   SAVE           RESTORE YREG
2051:E0 03                        CPX   #3
2053:F0 0C    2061                BEQ   RELOC          RELOCATE ALL 3 BYTE OPS
2055:C8                           INY
2056:CA                           DEX
2057:F0 D6    202F                BEQ   COPY           1 BYTE OP?
2059:B9 00 21                     LDA   TYPENT,Y       NO, THAT LEAVES 2 BYTE OPS
205C:91 48             STMSB      STA   (PTR),Y
205E:C8                           INY
205F:D0 CE    202F                BNE   COPY           CONTINUE COPYING

2061:                  *          RELOCATE ABSOLUTE ADDRESSES IN INSTRUCTIONS

2061:C8                RELOC      INY
2062:B9 00 21                     LDA   TYPENT,Y       COPY LSB OF ADDR
2065:91 48                        STA   (PTR),Y
2067:C8                           INY
2068:B9 00 21                     LDA   TYPENT,Y
206B:C9 21                        CMP   #<TYPENT       THIS ADDR WITHIN TYPENT?
206D:D0 ED    205C                BNE   STMSB          NO
206F:A5 49                        LDA   PTR+1          YES, USE MSB OF NEW HOME
2071:D0 E9    205C                BNE   STMSB          ALWAYS TAKEN

2073:                  *          RESIDENT CODE HAS BEEN INSTALLED, WE CAN EXIT

2073:4C 00 BE          COPIED     JMP   BIENTRY        DONE, EXIT

2076:                  *          INSTALLATION DATA

2076:                             MSB   ON
2076:CE CF A0 D2       MSG        ASC   'NO            ROOM FOR NEW COMMAND'
208D:87 8D                        DFB   $87,$8D
```

```
208F:00                SAVE      DFB   0              SAVE AREA FOR YREG

2090:                  *       EACH BYTE CONTAINS THE LENGTHS OF 4 6502 OPCODES
2090:                  *         FOR EXAMPLE, AT +0 IS A $59.
2090:                  *         IN BINARY $59 = 01011001 OR
2090:                  *                         01 01 10 01  (1,1,2,1)
2090:                  *         THESE ARE THE LENGTHS (IN REVERSED ORDER) FOR BRK,
2090:                  *         ORA (N,X), AND TWO UNDEFINED OPCODES.

2090:59 69 59 7D       OPTAB     DFB   $59,$69,$59,$7D OPCODE LENGTH TABLE
2094:5A 69 5D 7D                 DFB   $5A,$69,$5D,$7D
2098:5B 6A 59 7F                 DFB   $5B,$6A,$59,$7F
209C:5A 69 5D 7D                 DFB   $5A,$69,$5D,$7D
20A0:59 69 59 7F                 DFB   $59,$69,$59,$7F
20A4:5A 69 5D 7D                 DFB   $5A,$69,$5D,$7D
20A8:59 69 59 7F                 DFB   $59,$69,$59,$7F
20AC:5A 69 5D 7D                 DFB   $5A,$69,$5D,$7D
20B0:59 6A 55 7F                 DFB   $59,$6A,$55,$7F
20B4:5A 6A 5D 5D                 DFB   $5A,$6A,$5D,$5D
20B8:6A 6A 59 7F                 DFB   $6A,$6A,$59,$7F
20BC:5A 6A 5D 7F                 DFB   $5A,$6A,$5D,$7F
20C0:5A 6A 59 7F                 DFB   $5A,$6A,$59,$7F
20C4:5A 69 5D 7D                 DFB   $5A,$69,$5D,$7D
20C8:5A 6A 59 7F                 DFB   $5A,$6A,$59,$7F
20CC:5A 69 5D 3D                 DFB   $5A,$69,$5D,$3D ONLY $FF GIVES 0 LEN


20D0:                  *       NOW STARTS THE RESIDENT CODE WHICH IS MOVED TO HIGH
20D0:                  *       MEMORY.

20D0:                  *       TYPENT IS CALLED BY THE BI WHENEVER IT DOESN'T
20D0:                  *       RECOGNIZE A COMMAND. WE TAKE A LOOK AT IT SO SEE IF
20D0:                  *       IT MIGHT BE THE "TYPE" COMMAND.

2100:          2100              ORG   TYPE+256       MUST BE PAGE ALIGNED
2100:D8                TYPENT    CLD                  ; IDENTIFY TO BI
2101:AD 6C BE                    LDA   VPATH1         COPY COMMAND LINE PTR
2104:85 48                       STA   PTR
2106:AD 6D BE                    LDA   VPATH1+1
2109:85 49                       STA   PTR+1
210B:A0 01                       LDY   #1
210D:B1 48             COMPR     LDA   (PTR),Y        COMPARE COMMAND STRING
210F:D9 AC 21                    CMP   NAME-1,Y       TO "TYPE"
2112:D0 29     213D              BNE   NOTIT          NOT IT, VECTOR ON
2114:C8                          INY
2115:C0 05                       CPY   #5
2117:90 F4                       BCC   COMPR          CHECK ALL 4 CHARS

2119:                  *       IT HAS BEEN DETERMINED THAT THIS COMMAND IS MINE.
2119:                  *       RETURN TO THE BI TO PARSE THE PATHNAME OPERAND

2119:88                          DEY
211A:8C 52 BE                    STY   XLEN           STORE COMMAND LINE INDEX
211D:A9 00                       LDA   #0
211F:8D 53 BE                    STA   XCNUM          COMMAND NUMBER 0 (EXTERN)
2122:A9 04                       LDA   #SD            SLOT/DRIVE PERMITTED
2124:8D 55 BE                    STA   PBITS+1
2127:A9 01                       LDA   #FN1           WE NEED PATHNAME1
2129:8D 54 BE                    STA   PBITS
212C:AD 44 21          WHERE     LDA   TYPBAK         <USED TO FIND TYPBAK>
212F:AD 2D 21                    LDA   WHERE+1        TELL BI WHERE TO RETURN
2132:8D 50 BE                    STA   XTADDR
2135:AD 2E 21                    LDA   WHERE+2
2138:8D 51 BE                    STA   XTADDR+1
213B:18                          CLC                  ; INDICATE COMMAND WAS FOUND
213C:60                          RTS                  ; BACK TO BI FOR MORE PARSING

213D:                  *       IF WE DON'T CLAIM A COMMAND, PASS IT THROUGH TO ANY
213D:                  *       OTHER EXTERNAL COMMAND HANDLERS

213D:38                NOTIT     SEC                  ; INDICATE COMMAND NOT FOUNI
213E:4C 00 00          NXTCOM    JMP   $0000          <OLD EXTCMD VECTOR>
```

```
2141:4C 09 BE        TYPERR    JMP   ERROUT          VECTOR TO BI ERROR EXIT

2144:                *         ONCE THE COMMAND HAS BEEN PARSED, THE BI CALLS THE
2144:                *         FOLLOWING CODE TO FINISH HANDLING THE COMMAND

2144:A4 74           TYPBAK    LDY   HIMEM+1         MSB OF BUFFER AREA
2146:8C CF BE                  STY   OSYSBUF+1       COPY TO OPEN LIST
2149:A9 00                     LDA   #0
214B:8D CE BE                  STA   OSYSBUF
214E:A9 C8                     LDA   #$C8            MLI: OPEN
2150:20 70 BE                  JSR   GOSYS           OPEN THE FILE
2153:B0 EC    2141             BCS   TYPERR          ERROR?
2155:AD D0 BE                  LDA   OREFNUM         COPY REF NUM
2158:8D D6 BE                  STA   RWRFNUM         TO READ LIST
215B:8D DE BE                  STA   CFRFNUM         AND CLOSE LIST

215E:                *         FILE IS OPEN, READ 256 BYTES AT A TIME

215E:A0 00           TYPLP     LDY   #0
2160:8C D7 BE                  STY   RWDATA
2163:8C D9 BE                  STY   RWCOUNT
2166:C8                        INY
2167:8C DA BE                  STY   RWCOUNT+1       256 BYTES AT A TIME
216A:C8                        INY
216B:8C D8 BE                  STY   RWDATA+1        TO $200
216E:A9 CA                     LDA   #$CA            MLI: READ
2170:20 70 BE                  JSR   GOSYS           READ 256 BYTES TO $200
2173:90 0E    2183             BCC   TYPPRT          ALL WENT WELL
2175:C9 05                     CMP   #5              EOF ERROR?
2177:D0 C8    2141             BNE   TYPERR          NO, REAL ERROR
2179:A9 8D           TYQUIT    LDA   #$8D
217B:20 ED FD                  JSR   COUT            PRINT A FINAL NEWLINE
217E:A9 CC                     LDA   #$CC            MLI: CLOSE
2180:4C 70 BE                  JMP   GOSYS           EXIT THROUGH CLOSE

2183:                *         COPY READ BUFFER TO SCREEN

2183:A0 00           TYPPRT    LDY   #0
2185:B9 00 02        TYPPLP    LDA   $200,Y          COPY BYTE BY BYTE
2188:09 80                     ORA   #$80            MSB ON FOR COUT
218A:20 ED FD                  JSR   COUT            TO OUTPUT VECTOR
218D:AD 00 C0                  LDA   KBD             CHECK FOR INTERVENTION
2190:10 13    21A5             BPL   TYPON           NOTHING, CONTINUE
2192:8D 10 C0                  STA   KBDSTB          CLEAR STROBE
2195:C9 83                     CMP   #$83            CONTROL-C?
2197:F0 E0    2179             BEQ   TYQUIT          YES, EXIT NOW
2199:AD 00 C0        TYPWT     LDA   KBD             WAIT FOR A SECOND KEYPRESS
219C:10 FB    2199             BPL   TYPWT
219E:8D 10 C0                  STA   KBDSTB          CLEAR STROBE
21A1:C9 83                     CMP   #$83            CONTROL-C?
21A3:F0 D4    2179             BEQ   TYQUIT          YES, ABORT
21A5:C8              TYPON     INY                   ; ELSE, CONTINUE TYPING
21A6:CC DB BE                  CPY   RWTRANS         UNTIL BUFFER EMPTY
21A9:D0 DA    2185             BNE   TYPPLP
21AB:F0 B1    215E             BEQ   TYPLP           THEN GO READ ANOTHER


21AD:                          MSB   OFF
21AD:54 59 50 45     NAME      ASC   'TYPE'                   COMMAND NAME
21B1:FF FF FF                  DFB   $FF,$FF,$FF     END OF PROGRAM FLAGS
```

DUMBTERM—DUMB TERMINAL PROGRAM

DUMBTERM is an example of how to program under ProDOS using interrupts. DUMBTERM acts as a simple, line-at-a-time terminal emulation program which interfaces to a California Computer Systems CCS 7710 serial card. The same program can be written for an Apple Super Serial card (but interrupts are not as reliable for that card). The main portion of the program merely loops, checking the keyboard and the serial card for incoming data. If a keypress is found, it is sent out over the serial line. If incoming serial data is found, it is displayed on the screen.

The meat of the program lies within the communications subroutines in the last half of the listing. COMINT initializes the CCS card for interrupts after passing the address of its interrupt handler (COMIRQ) to ProDOS via the ALLOC_INTERRUPT MLI call. Each time an interrupt occurs, the COMIRQ handler is called by ProDOS and it examines the CCS status register to determine whether the interrupt was raised by the CCS card. If not, COMIRQ returns to ProDOS with the carry flag set to indicate that it is not claiming the interrupt. This gives other interrupt handlers a chance to service the interrupt. If the interrupt was generated by the CCS card and incoming data is available, a character is read and stored in a 256-byte circular buffer and COMIRQ exits to ProDOS.

The buffer is called circular because a pair of index pointers are used (start of data, end of data) to mark the actual data within the buffer and these pointers may wrap at the end of the buffer back to its beginning. Thus, conceptually the buffer has no beginning or end. This means that the main program may be doing something else but the interrupt routine can buffer up to 256 characters coming in from the serial port before it will lose data. If the main part of the program was ever vigilant and constantly checked for incoming serial data, there would be no need for an **interrupt exit**. However, each time the COUT screen output subroutine is called, there is a potential that control will not return before the next character is available. This is because the Apple scrolls the screen by moving every line up a byte at a time, one by one. The process of scrolling a 40-column screen lasts over one character time at 1200 baud (120 characters per second) on the serial port. Thus, without an interrupt exit, a character would be lost each time the screen is scrolled up one line.

Ideally this should be all there is to it. On an Apple II Plus, DUMBTERM works well under most circumstances and with most 80-column cards. Unfortunately this is not the case on an Apple IIe. Due to an error in programming the Apple IIe ROM, the entire process of scrolling the 40-column screen in PR#0 mode is disabled from interrupts! Thus the interrupt exit is useless in this mode. For 80-column scrolls, the ROM also disables interrupts while scrolling the bank switched text page, and the interrupt exit is again useless (at 1200 baud anyway). The only mode where the exit is reliable is the 40-column mode with PR#3 (control-Q). There are ways of avoiding these problems for 1200 baud. One is to change the window size (so that the monitor has less data to scroll). This is done by storing a new bottom line value at $23. In PR#0 40-column mode, this value should be $15. In 80-column mode, it must be $0E. Another solution would be to reproduce the scrolling code from the monitor into your own program and "sniff" for interrupts (i.e. enable for interrupts and disable again) more frequently than Apple does. It is also worth noting that some 80-column cards, such as the ALS Smarterm, "scroll" by moving a hardware "top of screen" pointer. No CPU time is required to scroll this way and terminal programs are much easier to write.

DUMBTERM is also an example of a simple Interpreter or System Program. It sets up the stack register and ProDOS version fields in the System Global Page upon entry, and it exits upon sensing a control-C keypress using the MLI QUIT call.

```
----- NEXT OBJECT FILE NAME IS DUMBTERM.S.0
2000:        2000                ORG   $2000

2000:              ************************************************************
2000:              *                                                          *
2000:              * DUMBTERM: THIS PROGRAM ACTS AS A DUMB TERMINAL           *
2000:              *           THROUGH A CCS 7710 SERIAL CARD USING           *
2000:              *           THE PRODOS INTERRUPT HANDLER FOR INPUT         *
2000:              *           INTERRUPTS.  THIS PROGRAM FOLLOWS THE RULES    *
2000:              *           FOR A PRODOS INTERPRETER.                      *
2000:              *                                                          *
2000:              * ASSUMPTIONS: CCS7710 CARD IN SLOT 1                      *
2000:              *              8 DATA BITS, 1 STOP, NO PARITY              *
2000:              *              BAUD RATE SET BY DIP SWITCHES ON CARD       *
2000:              *                                                          *
2000:              * ENTRY POINT: $2000                                       *
2000:              *                                                          *
2000:              * PROGRAMMER: DON D WORTH 3/8/84                           *
2000:              *                                                          *
2000:              ************************************************************
```

```
2000:          0087   BELL     EQU   $87          BELL CHARACTER
2000:          000D   CR       EQU   $0D          RETURN
2000:          008D   RETURN   EQU   $8D          PRINTABLE RETURN
2000:          00A0   SPACE    EQU   $A0          BLANK

2000:                 *       ZPAGE DEFINITIONS

2000:          003C   A1L      EQU   $3C          MONITOR POINTER
2000:          003D   A1H      EQU   $3D
2000:          003E   A2L      EQU   $3E          MONITOR POINTER
2000:          003F   A2H      EQU   $3F

2000:                 *       OTHER ADDRESSES

2000:          BF00   MLI      EQU   $BF00        PRODOS ENTRY POINT
2000:          BF98   MACHID   EQU   $BF98        PRODOS MACHINE ID
2000:          BFFC   IBAKVER  EQU   $BFFC        MLI VERSION WANTED
2000:          BFFD   IVERS    EQU   $BFFD        MY VERSION
2000:          C000   KBD      EQU   $C000        KEYBOARD STROBE
2000:          C010   KBDRES   EQU   $C010        KEYBOARD RESET
2000:          FDED   COUT     EQU   $FDED        MONITOR OUTPUT SUBROUTINE
2000:          FD0C   RDKEY    EQU   $FD0C        MONITOR INPUT SUBROUTINE
2000:          FC58   HOME     EQU   $FC58        MONITOR HOME
2000:          FB39   TEXT     EQU   $FB39        SET TEXT MODE

2000:                 *       START OF DUMB TERMINAL EMULATOR

2000:A2 FF            DTERM    LDX   #$FF         SET UP STACK POINTER
2002:9A                        TXS
2003:A9 00                     LDA   #0
2005:8D FC BF                  STA   IBAKVER      VERSION 0 FOR EVERYBODY
2008:8D FD BF                  STA   IVERS
200B:20 62 20                  JSR   COMINT       INITIALIZE SERIAL PORT
200E:20 58 FC                  JSR   HOME         CLEAR SCREEN
2011:A9 02                     LDA   #$02
2013:2C 98 BF                  BIT   MACHID       80 COLUMN CARD PRESENT?
2016:F0 03     201B            BEQ   BEGIN        NO
2018:20 00 C3                  JSR   $C300        INITIALIZE 80 COLUMN CARD

201B:                 *
201B:                 *       NOTE: NO NEED TO SET BIT MAP HERE SINCE NOT DOING
201B:                 *             DYNAMIC MEMORY ALLOCATION. AND WE WILL LEAVE
201B:                 *             THE POWERUP BYTE SO THAT RESET FORCES REBOOT.
201B:                 *
201B:          201B   BEGIN    EQU   *
201B:                 *
201B:                 *       --- SPECIAL NOTE ---
201B:                 *
201B:                 *       IF AN APPLE ][E IS USED, THERE MAY BE DATA
201B:                 *       ERRORS AT 1200 BAUD WHEN SCROLLING.  IF THIS
201B:                 *       OCCURS, INSERT THESE INSTRUCTIONS AT THIS POINT:
201B:                 *
201B:                 *       LDA     #$0E          SET WINDOW 14 LINES HIGH
201B:                 *       STA     $23
201B:                 *
201B:                 *       (LDA #$15 IF YOU HAVE NO 80 COL CARD IN YOUR ][E.)
201B:                 *

201B:                 *       MAIN TERMINAL LOOP

201B:AD F4 20         LOOP     LDA   ERRORS       HAVE ANY ERRORS OCCURED?
201E:F0 0A     202A            BEQ   NOERRS       NO
2020:A9 87                     LDA   #BELL        YES, BEEP AT HIM
2022:20 ED FD                  JSR   COUT
```

```
2025:A9 00                    LDA   #0            AND CLEAR ERROR COUNTER
2027:8D F4 20                 STA   ERRORS
202A:AD 00 C0       NOERRS    LDA   KBD           FIRST TEST KEYBOARD
202D:10 0F    203E            BPL   NOKEY         NOTHING YET?
202F:29 7F                    AND   #$7F
2031:C9 03                    CMP   #3            CONTROL-C?
2033:F0 1D    2052            BEQ   EXIT
2035:AD 00 C0                 LDA   KBD           RELOAD CHARACTER
2038:8D 10 C0                 STA   KBDRES        CLEAR KEYBOARD
203B:20 CC 20                 JSR   COMOUT        SEND THE CHARACTER OUT

203E:20 B1 20       NOKEY     JSR   COMTIN        TEST FOR AVAILABLE INPUT
2041:F0 D8    201B            BEQ   LOOP          NONE, CHECK KEYBOARD AGAIN
2043:20 BA 20                 JSR   COMINP        GET NEXT INPUT CHARACTER
2046:09 80                    ORA   #$80          MSB ON FOR OUTPUT
2048:C9 8A                    CMP   #$8A          LINE FEED?
204A:F0 CF    201B            BEQ   LOOP          YES, SKIP IT
204C:20 ED FD                 JSR   COUT          ELSE, PRINT IT
204F:4C 1B 20                 JMP   LOOP          AND CONTINUE LOOP

2052:               *       IF CONTROL-C IS TYPED, EXIT

2052:20 D9 20       EXIT      JSR   COMCLS        CLOSE DOWN COMM LINE
2055:20 00 BF                 JSR   MLI           MLI: QUIT CALL
2058:65                       DFB   $65
2059:5B 20                    DW    QPARMS
205B:04             QPARMS    DFB   4             QUIT PARMLIST
205C:00                       DFB   0
205D:00 00                    DW    0
205F:00                       DFB   0
2060:00 00                    DW    0

2062:               ***************************************************
2062:               *                                                 *
2062:               *       CCS 7710 COMMUNICATIONS SUBROUTINES       *
2062:               *                                                 *
2062:               ***************************************************

2062:         C09E  CCCOM     EQU   $C09E         CCS COMMAND REG
2062:         C09E  CCSTS     EQU   $C09E         CCS STATUS REG
2062:         C09F  CCDTA     EQU   $C09F         CCS DATA REG

2062:               *       COMINT: INITIALIZE THE COMM LINE

2062:A9 00          COMINT    LDA   #0
2064:8D F5 20                 STA   CIRCS         START CIRCULAR BUFFER PTRS
2067:8D F6 20                 STA   CIRCE
206A:20 00 BF                 JSR   MLI           ALLOCATE INTERRUPT EXIT
206D:40                       DFB   $40
206E:F0 20                    DW    APARMS
2070:A9 23                    LDA   #$23          RESET ACIA
2072:8D 9E C0                 STA   CCCOM
2075:A9 15                    LDA   #$15          8 BITS/1 STOP/NO PAR/NO INTS
2077:8D 9E C0                 STA   CCCOM
207A:AE 9F C0                 LDX   CCDTA         THROW AWAY ANY GARBAGE
207D:09 80                    ORA   #$80          ENABLE INTERRUPTS
207F:8D 9E C0                 STA   CCCOM
2082:60                       RTS

2083:               *       COMIRQ: INTERRUPT EXIT

2083:AD 9E C0       COMIRQ    LDA   CCSTS         CHECK STATUS
2086:30 02    208A            BMI   COMME         INTERRUPT WAS FOR ME?
2088:38                       SEC                 ; INDICATE NOT MY INTERRUPT
2089:60                       RTS
208A:48             COMME     PHA
208B:29 70                    AND   #$70          ANY ERRORS OCCURED?
208D:F0 03    2092            BEQ   COMNE         NO
208F:EE F4 20                 INC   ERRORS        YES, BUMP ERROR COUNT
2092:68             COMNE     PLA
```

```
2093:29 01                     AND   #$01          CHECK FOR INCOMING DATA
2095:F0 18    20AF             BEQ   CLAIM         NONE, IGNORE OTHER INTERUPTS
2097:AD 9F C0                  LDA   CCDTA         GET INCOMING BYTE
209A:AE F6 20                  LDX   CIRCE
209D:9D F7 20                  STA   CIRC,X        STORE IT AT END OF BUFFER
20A0:E8                        INX
20A1:8E F6 20                  STX   CIRCE         UPDATE END POINT
20A4:EC F5 20                  CPX   CIRCS         WRAPPED BACK TO START?
20A7:D0 06    20AF             BNE   CLAIM         NO, DID NOT OVERRUN
20A9:EE F4 20                  INC   ERRORS        OVERRUN ERROR, BUMP COUNT
20AC:CE F6 20                  DEC   CIRCE         BACK UP END POINT
20AF:18             CLAIM      CLC                 ; CLAIM THE INTERRUPT
20B0:60                        RTS

20B1:               *        COMTIN: TEST FOR AVAILABLE INPUT
20B1:               *                IF NEQ, DATA IS AVAILABLE

20B1:78             COMTIN     SEI                 ; DISABLE FROM INTERRUPTS
20B2:AE F5 20                  LDX   CIRCS         CHECK CIRCULAR BUFFER
20B5:EC F6 20                  CPX   CIRCE         SEE IF ITS EMPTY
20B8:58                        CLI                 ; REENABLE
20B9:60                        RTS

20BA:               *        COMINP: WAIT FOR NEXT INPUT, RETURN IN AREG

20BA:20 B1 20       COMINP     JSR   COMTIN        TEST STATUS
20BD:F0 FB    20BA             BEQ   COMINP        NOTHING YET?
20BF:78                        SEI                 ; DISABLE TO MESS WITH CIRC
20C0:AE F5 20                  LDX   CIRCS
20C3:BD F7 20                  LDA   CIRC,X        GET INPUT CHARACTER
20C6:E8                        INX
20C7:8E F5 20                  STX   CIRCS         BUMP START POINTER FORWARD
20CA:58                        CLI                 ; REENABLE FOR INTERRUPTS
20CB:60                        RTS

20CC:               *        COMOUT: OUTPUT A BYTE FROM AREG

20CC:48             COMOUT     PHA
20CD:AD 9E C0       COMOL      LDA   CCSTS         CHECK STATUS
20D0:29 02                     AND   #$02          ISOLATE TX BUFFER BIT
20D2:F0 F9    20CD             BEQ   COMOL         NOT READY YET
20D4:68             COMOIT     PLA
20D5:8D 9F C0                  STA   CCDTA         SEND BYTE
20D8:60                        RTS

20D9:               *        COMCLS: CLOSE COMM PORT

20D9:A9 23          COMCLS     LDA   #$23          STOP INTERRUPTS/DTR OFF
20DB:8D 9E C0                  STA   CCCOM
20DE:58                        CLI                 ; JUST FOR SAFETY SAKE
20DF:A9 01                     LDA   #1
20E1:8D F0 20                  STA   APARMS        CHANGE PARMLIST
20E4:20 00 BF                  JSR   MLI
20E7:41                        DFB   $41           DEALLOC_INTERRUPT
20E8:F0 20                     DW    APARMS
20EA:A9 02                     LDA   #2
20EC:8D F0 20                  STA   APARMS        LEAVE THINGS AS I FOUND THEM
20EF:60                        RTS

20F0:               *        DATA

20F0:02             APARMS     DFB   2             ALLOC_INTERRUPT PARMS
20F1:00                        DFB   0
20F2:83 20                     DW    COMIRQ

20F4:00             ERRORS     DFB   0             ERROR STATISTICS
20F5:00             CIRCS      DFB   0             START OF DATA IN CIRC
20F6:00             CIRCE      DFB   0             END OF DATA IN CIRC
20F7:         0100  CIRC       DS    256           CIRCULAR INPUT BUFFER
```

APPENDIX **B**

DISKETTE PROTECTION SCHEMES

Protected software, that software which is modified in some way to prevent it from being copied or duplicated, has existed since very early in the history of the Apple II. This was even true of tape based software before disk drives were widely used. It is not known who protected the first piece of Apple software, but it has become a widespread practice. So has the practice of copying or **breaking** protected software. It should be pointed out that the following discussion will not take sides in the sometimes controversial subject of software protection. Rather, it will provide an informative look at the methods used to protect software and how those methods have been circumvented. This seems appropriate since almost all protection schemes now involve a modified or customized disk operating system.

At this time, ProDOS is still relatively new and it is unclear if it will influence the current practice of protecting software. In that a ProDOS disk is identical to earlier operating systems (DOS 3.3) at a byte level, it is certainly possible and probable that protection will exist. However, since ProDOS can and will support other storage devices (i.e. hard disks etc.), and with the current trend in sharing data between different applications, additional challenges exist for software developers. It is possible that the percentage of protected software may decrease somewhat with the introduction of ProDOS. The following discussion will deal with software protection in general on the Apple II family of computers.

A BRIEF HISTORY OF APPLE SOFTWARE PROTECTION

The first protected software was tape based and appeared in the latter part of 1978, and protected disks followed shortly thereafter. Early protection schemes often were quite effective as there was relatively little technical information available. Almost any modification that rendered the normal means of copying useless was sufficient in most cases—most schemes did in fact consist of relatively minor changes to the normal format of data. Individuals were able to discover and disable these protection methods on a program by program basis, with little or no thought given to some automated means of reproducing protected software.

It was not until perhaps a year later, in late 1979, that a significant event occurred in disk protection. An extremely popular product was introduced that employed a considerably improved protection method. This marked the beginning of an escalating battle between those protecting software and those trying to copy it. The protection methods used became more and more complex and involved, increasing time and expense for developers to create. The copiers also were increasing their efforts. Programs appeared that were designed to copy particular software products—a major development in that it defeated a great number of different schemes with a single basic technique. These programs are referred to as **nibble copiers** and were introduced in early 1981.

Throughout this process, it is clear that both sides made use of the work of their counterparts. Protection schemes started to reflect a working knowledge of breaking techniques, and were often designed to circumvent a particular method or copier. The people breaking protection methods were also studying the various methods employed to stop them and producing increasingly effective tools. This produced a kind of ebb and flow seen in many competitive areas where each side gains a temporary advantage only to see it lost. Nibble copiers have had numerous revisions to cope with advancements in protection methods.

Another significant milestone was the introduction of a **hardware card** that could copy software from the Apple's memory, thus bypassing most existing protection methods. While it is hard to single out advancements in protection methods, the mere presence of the numerous copy programs, hardware devices, bulletin boards, classes, and magazines aimed at defeating protection methods indicates the constant advancement of protection. Also, the fact that software developers continue to protect software in the face of escalating costs indicates protection is still cost effective.

The cycle will no doubt continue. As new sophisticated schemes are developed, they will be broken by equally sophisticated schemes.

PROTECTION METHODS

It seems reasonable at this time to say that it is impossible to protect a program on disk in such a way that it can't be broken. This is, in large part, due to the nature of the Apple computer and its disk drive. It is an extremely well documented machine, with numerous publications available on both hardware and software functions. It is indeed difficult to hide anything (necessary in protecting software) from anyone who is willing to invest sufficient time to find it.

Most disk protection methods fall into two different types of schemes. The first involves **format alterations**, altering some portion of the disk from its normal format (Chapter 3 and APPENDIX C provide descriptions of the normal format). The second involves creating an identifiable mark or **signature** that can be used to verify the disk.

FORMAT ALTERATION

A great number of ways exist to alter the format of normal data. They range from a single byte changed to an entirely different format. A special case is **changing the location** of data, and not necessarily the structure of the data itself. An early example of this was moving the directory information from its normal location to a different track altogether. Later, tracks themselves were moved when "half" tracks became popular (but data must be a full track apart from other data, a restriction imposed by hardware). Some disks now even use quarter tracks. Although these methods were effective for a while, most nibble copiers are equipped to handle them.

A more elaborate technique used is known as **spiral tracks.** Data is staggered on alternating half tracks producing, as its name indicates, a spiral of sorts. Each half track contains approximately one third of a track of data. The actual amount will vary in different protection schemes. Note that no data is within one full track from any other data. If the relationship of the different segments is critical, this method of protection can be quite difficult to deal with. Several copy programs are capable of handling this, but may require parameters and additional time to reproduce a disk protected in this manner.

As with location changes, **format changes** range from simple to complex. Almost all early changes were merely minor modifications to existing operating systems. The most common change was a change to the code that would read and write the Address Field. This was reasonable because the Address Field is never rewritten, and the only special code required was the code to read the modified Address Field.

The Address Field normally starts with the bytes $D5/$AA/$96. If any of these bytes were changed, a standard operating system would not be able to locate that particular Address Field, causing an error. After the Address Field comes the address information itself (volume, track, sector, and checksum). Some common techniques include changing the order of this information, doubling the sector numbers, or altering the checksum with some constant. Any of the above would cause an error on a standard operating system. The Address Field ends with two closing bytes ($DE/$AA), which can be changed or switched also. Similar kinds of changes can be made to the Data Field. These techniques worked well until automated programs appeared.

The first automated programs were good but generally made the assumption that the data portions had been modified and that the various gaps between the data portions were normal. This prompted modification of the gaps and eventually a radically different format in an attempt to circumvent the copy programs. These formats generally involved either different numbers of otherwise normal sectors on a track, or special sectors with Address and Data Fields combined. As with other advancements, this worked well for a time, but current nibble copiers make as few assumptions about the data format as possible and can generally deal with such techniques.

SIGNATURE

The earliest example of a signature was probably an unused track (track 3 was commonly "un"used). The software verifies the signature by trying to read a sector on the unused track. If an error occurred, the signature was verified. As simple as this seems now, it was reasonably effective. While this is a fairly obvious example of a signature, later methods were much more difficult to detect. In fact, most signatures have been uncovered by finding and examining the code that verified it. Once a method was known, an algorithm could be developed to deal with it.

There are three common signatures used currently in protecting disks. The first to appear involves counting the number of bytes on a given track. This is commonly known as **nibble counting**. The reasoning was that no two drives spin at precisely the same speed, and therefore would not reproduce a track precisely. While this is in fact true, a number of programs now provide the means to reproduce this type of signature.

Next to arrive was a method that was dependent on the positional relationship between different portions of the disk. This is commonly known as **synchronized tracks**. It generally involves reading a specific sector, then moving the disk arm to another track (often with nonstandard timing), and finding a particular sector first. The angle between the two sectors is arbitrary, but will always provide just enough time to move the arm and allow for any settling time needed. This relationship between tracks would not normally be maintained when copying the disk, and the signature would thus be removed. This also is provided for in many current copy programs, sometimes requiring parameters for a particular disk.

The final method involves writing extra zero bits at given locations on a disk. These can be thought of as **special sync bytes**. When the disk is read, these extra bits are normally discarded. Figure B.1 shows two different bit patterns that produce the same data when read. A special routine looks for the extra bits and thus verifies the signature. There exist some variations to this method which have proved quite difficult for "nibble" copy programs to handle. Parameters were generally required, but recent advancements in nibble copiers appear to be able to locate and reproduce these extra bits.

We have dealt primarily with disk protection schemes and nibble copiers, but several other methods of protection exist. These are protection methods which do not allow a program to be taken out of memory and patched to disable the protection scheme. It is worth mentioning that copies produced by a nibble copier are themselves protected, but software broken in some other way may be copied by normal means.

11111111 ⟶ FF   1111111100 ⟶ FF

Figure B.1 Comparison of a Normal FF Byte and a Special Sync Byte

MEMORY PROTECTION

It has long been realized that software is vulnerable as it is being loaded into memory, and when it resides entirely in memory. This has prompted a number of techniques, the earliest of which involved **reset protection**. When the Reset key was pressed (on early Apples), the software could be interrupted and was then resident in memory. Several memory locations were altered during a reset, and many programs were dependent on the values contained in those locations. The later Apple computers provide some measure of protection in that they make it much harder to interrupt software programs. The hardware boards designed to copy software from memory have made memory protection very difficult. The boards generate a Non-Maskable Interrupt and pass control to on-board software. It is not possible to prevent this interrupt from software. About the only defense is simply to never have the entire program in memory at one time. This is often inconvenient but may be the only effective defense.

CODE PROTECTION

Hiding the code that reads the unusual disk format or checks for a particular signature has become increasingly popular. Early schemes rarely tried to hide anything because there were few people who knew where to look or even what to look for. But it is clear now that most of the advancements in nibble copiers resulted from the examination of the actual code that provided the protection. Signature schemes would have been effective much longer if it had been possible to hide the code that verified them. While it is impossible to prevent the code from being found, it can be made more difficult. The general method used is some sort of encryption of the code. It is decrypted just before execution, and either encrypted again or destroyed just after execution.

THE IDEAL PROTECTION SCHEME

There are thousands of programs available for the Apple II family of machines, and it is safe to say that they all have been copied despite a vast array of protection schemes. It seems reasonable to assume that this fact will not change. Nevertheless, it may be possible to devise a reasonably effective method. It would have to address the three primary ways that software is broken— nibble copiers, hardware boards that copy memory, and what we call the "front door" method.

NIBBLE COPIERS

Nibble copy programs have an advantage of sorts in that they need only respond to existing protection methods. This clearly requires considerable skill but not necessarily creativity. In fairness though, it should be noted that at least one of the nibble copiers has included capabilities that may effectively deal with yet to be created protection schemes. The best that one should hope for is a protection method that requires parameters to be input by the user of the copier. If the method could be varied so that each variation required a different set of parameters, it would be considered a victory.

HARDWARE BOARDS

It is not possible through software to detect the presence of these boards, nor prevent them from saving an image of memory onto a disk. For this reason, they are particularly effective with programs that are totally loaded into memory and require no additional disk accesses. The only good defense is to never have the entire program in memory at one time. While this could create some difficulties such as decreased performance for particular programs, it is nevertheless necessary for single program products. Modular software requiring constant disk access may already provide sufficient protection.

FRONT DOOR METHOD

The process by which a disk is loaded into memory is well defined for normal disks. Certain facts remain true of protected disks regardless of the method employed. First the disk must contain at least one sector (Track 0, Sector 0) which can be read by the program in the PROM on the disk controller card. Second the code that reads the protected disk must be on the disk. This means that it is possible to trace the boot process by disassembling the code involved in each step of that process. While this can be a formidable task, it is nevertheless theoretically possible to break all protection schemes with this method. The main defense against use of this method is to make it require a great deal of time to accomplish. This could primarily be done in several ways.

One way is to write the code in separate modules or layers. Each layer typically decodes the next layer and recodes the previous layer. It is also vital to verify critical layers to ensure they have not been patched. A second way is to use an interpreted language which introduces an additional level of obscurity and a considerable amount of additional code. Neither of these can be entirely effective, but are important nevertheless.

APPENDIX C

NIBBLIZING

This appendix covers in great detail the encoding of data (nibblizing) on the Disk II family of drives (Disk II, IIe, and IIc). Some of this discussion may relate in a general way to encoding techniques on other computers made by Apple. But the details relate specifically to ProDOS and its device driver for a Disk II (or equivalent).

Before starting an explanation of encoding, it is fair to ask why data must be encoded at all? It seems reasonable that the data could simply be written to the disk as it is without any encoding. The reason this can't be done involves the hardware itself. Apple's design of the original Disk II was innovative and used a unique method of recording the data. While this allowed Apple to produce an excellent product, it did require some additional work to be done in software. It is not possible to read all 256 possible byte values from a diskette. This was clearly not an insurmountable problem, but it did require that the data stored on the disk be restricted to bytes with certain characteristics.

ENCODING TECHNIQUES

Three different techniques have been used. The first one, which is currently used in Address Fields, involves writing a data byte as two **disk bytes**, one containing the odd bits, and the other containing the even bits. This method is often referred to as "**4 and 4**" encoding, depicting the fact that an 8-bit byte is split into two 4-bit pieces. It requires two disk bytes for each byte of data, thus 512 disk bytes would be needed for each 256-byte sector of data. Had this technique been used for sector data, no more than 10 sectors would have fit on a track. This amounts to about 88K of data per diskette, typical for 5 1/4 inch single sided, single density drives.

Fortunately, other techniques for writing data to diskettes were devised that allowed more sectors per track. The earliest technique involved 13 sectors per track. This initial method involved a "**5 and 3**" split of the data bits, versus the "4 and 4" mentioned earlier. Each byte written to the disk contains five valid bits rather than four. This required 410 disk bytes to store a 256-byte sector. Currently, of course, ProDOS features 16 sectors per track and uses a "**6 and 2**" split of data bits thereby requiring 342 disk bytes per 256-byte sector. This allows 140K of data per diskette.

The two different encoding techniques ("4 and 4" and "6 and 2") will now be covered in some detail. The hardware (in order to insure the integrity of the data) imposes a number of restrictions upon how data can be stored and retrieved. It requires that a disk byte have the **high bit set** (the first bit is a "1"), and in addition, it can have **no more than two consecutive zero bits**. Further, each byte can have at most **one pair of consecutive zero bits**.

"4 AND 4" ENCODING

The odd-even "4 and 4" technique meets these requirements—each data byte is represented as two bytes, one containing the even data bits and the other the odd data bits, (shifted one bit right). Figure C.1 illustrates this transformation. It should be noted that the unused bits are all set to "1" to guarantee meeting the two requirements.

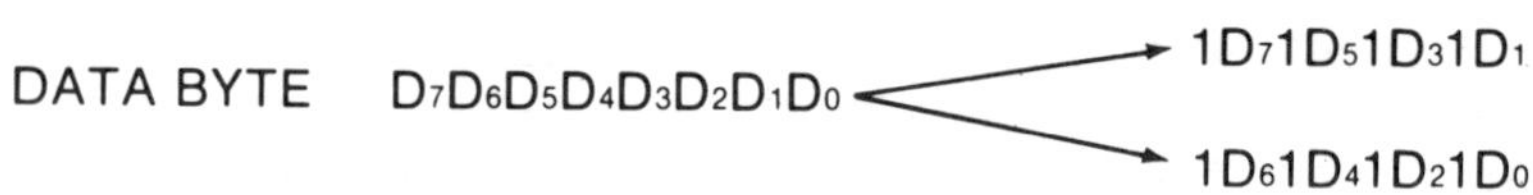

Figure C.1 "4 and 4" Encoding Technique

No matter what value the original data byte has, this technique insures that the high bit is set and that there cannot be two consecutive zero bits. The "4 and 4" technique is used to store the information (volume, track, sector, checksum) contained in the Address Field. It is quite easy to decode the data, since the byte with the odd bits is simply shifted left and logically ANDed with the byte containing the even bits. This is illustrated in Figure C.2.

	$D_7\ 1\ D_5\ 1\ D_3\ 1\ D_1\ 1$	(shifted left)
AND	$1\ D_6\ 1\ D_4\ 1\ D_2\ 1\ D_0$	
	$D_7 D_6 D_5 D_4 D_3 D_2 D_1 D_0$	

Figure C.2 "4 and 4" Decoding Technique

It is important that the least significant bit is a 1 when the odd-bits byte is left shifted. The entire operation is carried out in the device driver for the Disk II.

"6 AND 2" ENCODING

The major difficulty with the above technique is that it takes up a lot of room on the track. Since each disk byte actually contains only four bits of real data, half the bits are wasted. To overcome this deficiency, the "6 and 2" encoding technique was developed. It is so named because, instead of splitting the bytes in half as in the "4 and 4" technique, they are split "6 and 2". The two bits split off from each byte are grouped together to form additional 6-bit bytes. (They are stored in an area called the Auxiliary Data Buffer.) This means that only two bits are lost in each disk byte. The 6-bit bytes used take the form XXXXXXOO and have values from $00 to $FC, each being a multiple of four, for a total of 64 different values. Figure C.3 shows the 6-bit bytes.

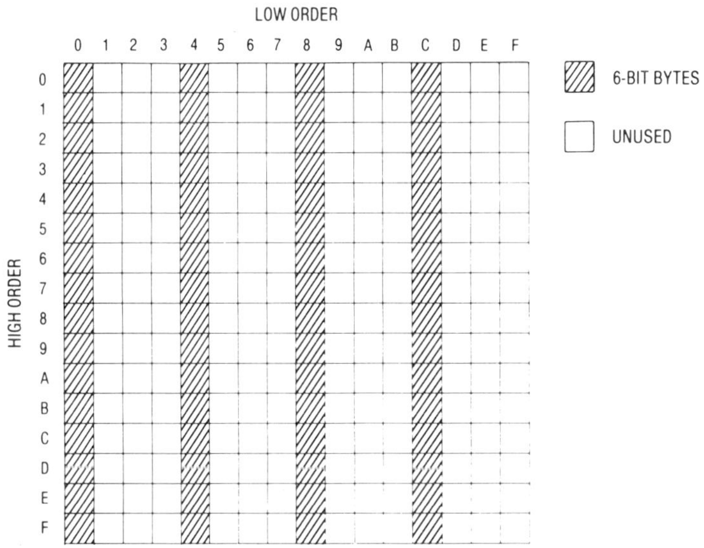

Figure C.3 Valid 6-Bit Bytes

It was necessary to map these 64 6-bit bytes into disk bytes so that they can be stored on the disk. However, there are 72 different bytes ranging in value from $95 up to $FF that meet the requirements for valid disk bytes (i.e. the high bit set and one pair of consecutive zero bits at most). After removing the two reserved bytes, $AA and $D5, 70 disk bytes remain, and only 64 are needed. An additional requirement was introduced to force the mapping to be one to one, namely, that there must be at least two adjacent bits set, excluding bit 7. This produces exactly 64 valid disk bytes. A table of valid (and invalid) disk bytes is presented in Figure C.4.

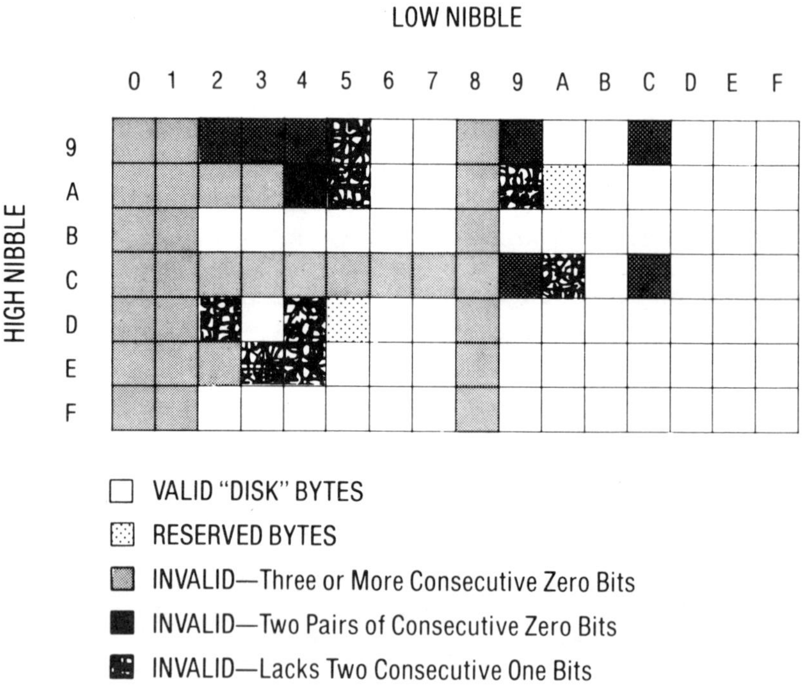

Figure C.4 Valid "Disk Bytes"

The process of converting 8-bit data bytes to disk bytes is a fairly involved process. It has three separate components, two of which we have already mentioned. We will now detail the entire operation required to convert 256 bytes of data into data suitable for diskette storage. An overview of the process is diagrammed in Figure C.5.

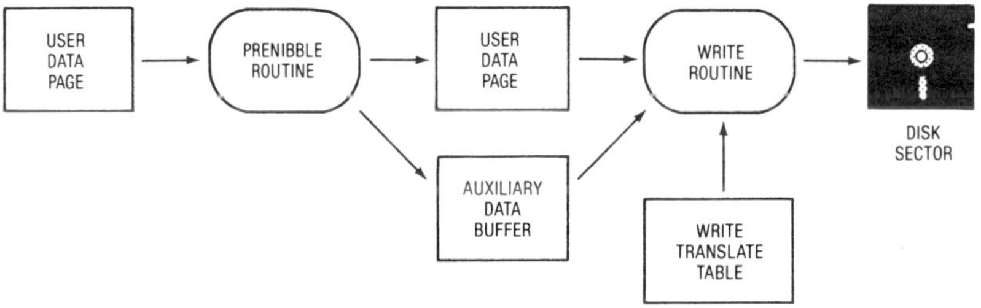

Figure C.5a Writing to the Diskette

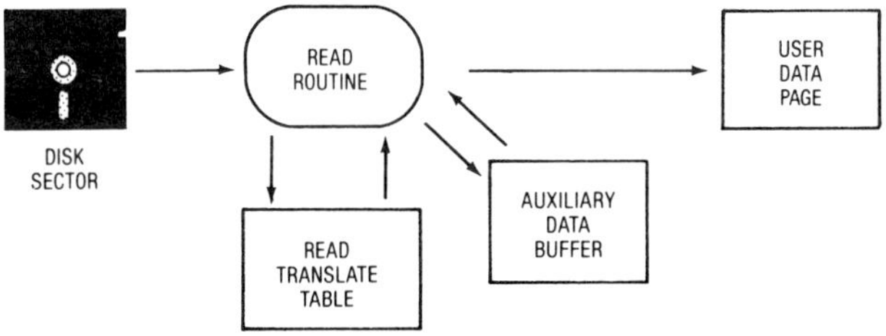

Figure C.5b Reading from the Diskette

THE ENCODING PROCESS

First, the 256 bytes that will make up a sector must be **converted** to 342 6-bit bytes. The number 342 results from finding the total number of bits (256 x 8 = 2048) and dividing by the number of bits per byte (2048 / 6 = 341.33). Four of the bits are not used. This operation is done by the "prenibble" routine in the Disk II device driver. The code that performs this operation is fairly involved, as it requires a good deal of bit rearrangement. The results of the operation can however be easily illustrated. Figure C.6 shows how the Auxiliary Data Buffer is formed. The 256-byte User Data Page (containing 8-bit bytes), is passed to the Disk II device driver by ProDOS. Two bits are taken from each byte and put into the Auxiliary Data Buffer. The bits are rearranged slightly during this process. The two bits from each byte are reversed and the order in which they are stored in the Auxiliary Data Buffer is also reversed. The way in which these bits are rearranged and then stored is arbitrary—it could have been done differently. The method chosen can be executed rapidly with a small amount of code. The 256-byte User Data Page is in fact unchanged as the bits are copied rather than removed, these bits

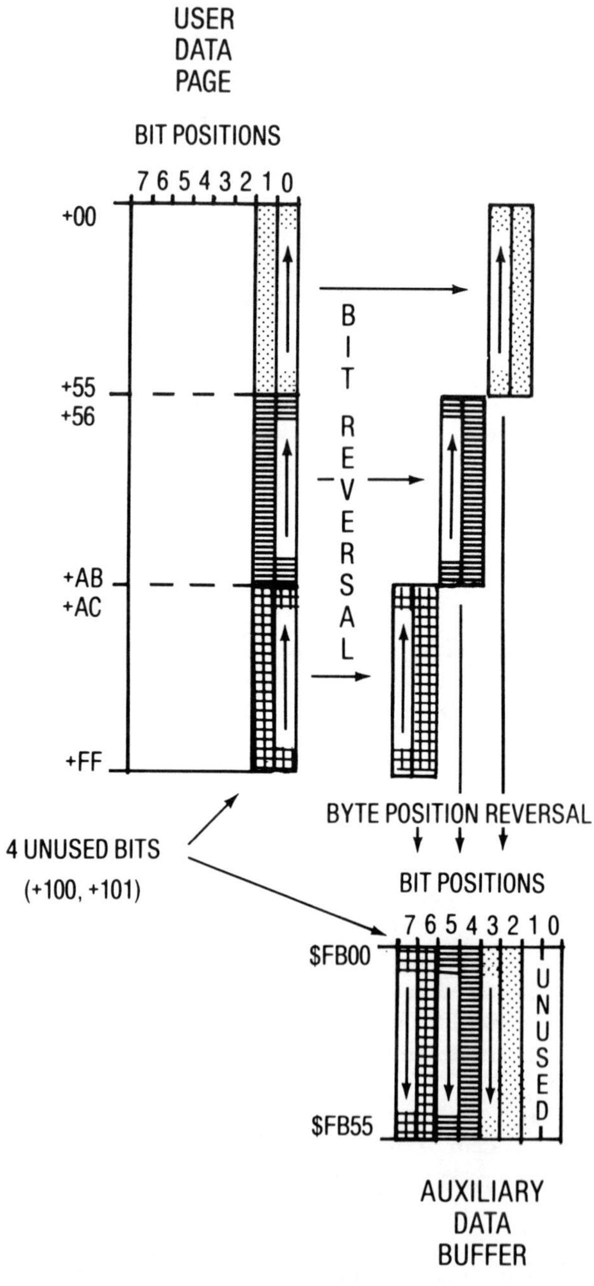

Figure C.6a Forming the Auxiliary Data Buffer

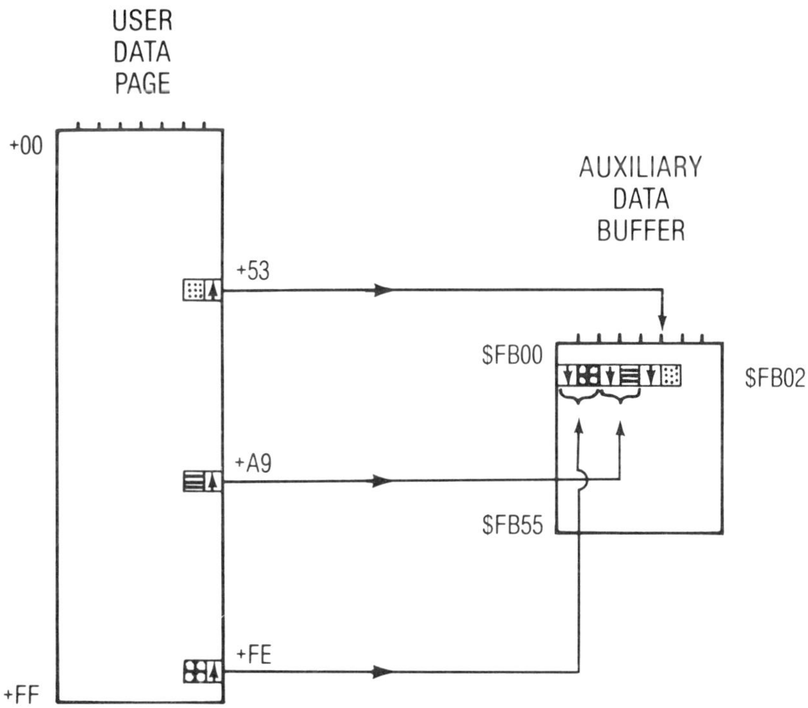

Figure C.6b Forming One Byte of the Auxiliary Data Buffer

are ignored (stripped out) when the data is written to the disk. This double usage of the User Data Page eliminates the need for an additional buffer. The Auxiliary Data Buffer contains four areas, one unused and the other three containing segments of the last two bits of the User buffer as is graphically illustrated.

The result of the first step is 342 6-bit bytes. The next step is that of creating a simple checksum that will be used to verify the integrity of the data. Like the Address Field, it also involves **exclusive-ORing** the information, but, due to time constraints during reading bytes, it is implemented differently. The entire block of data is exclusive-ORed with itself offset by one byte. This adds one byte, bringing the block of data to 343 bytes. This process is reversible and, while it cannot aid in recovering damaged data, it does provide a reasonable check on whether the data has been read correctly. The operation of exclusive-ORing the data block with itself is carried out a pair of bytes at a time. This enables the process to be carried out on the fly, that is, while the data is being

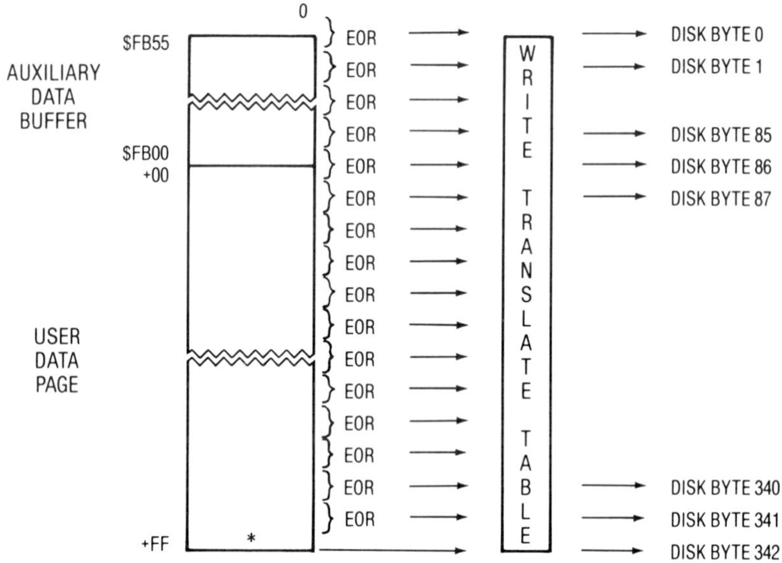

* Last data byte is used as checksum.

Figure C.7 Writing from Buffers to Disk

read or written. This step and the next are actually done together and are depicted in Figure C.7.

The last step is to **translate** these 343 6-bit bytes to 8-bit disk bytes. This operation is performed using a data table in the Disk II device driver. Figure C.8 shows the mapping of 6-bit bytes to disk

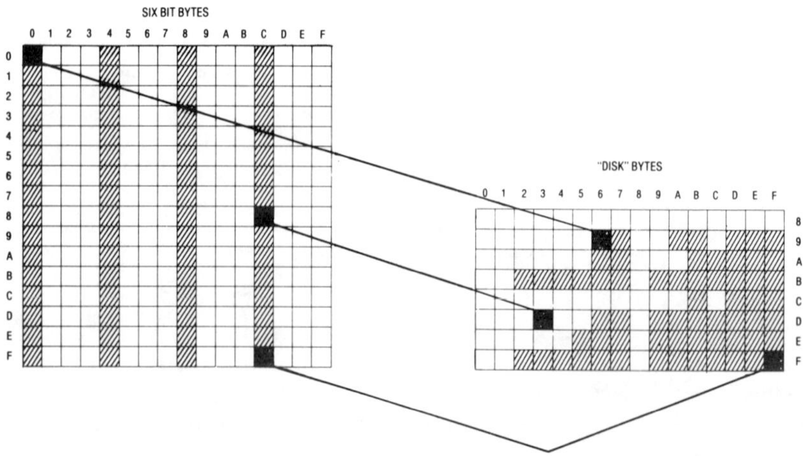

Figure C.8 Relationship of 6-Bit Bytes to Disk Bytes

bytes in greater detail. Three bytes are highlighted to graphically show how the translation is made. We see for example the $00 becomes $96, $8C becomes $D3, and $FC becomes $FF.

00<->96	40<->B4	80<->D6	C0<->ED
04<->97	44<->B5	84<->D7	C4<->EE
08<->9A	48<->B6	88<->D9	C8<->EF
0C<->9B	4C<->B7	8C<->DA	CC<->F2
10<->9D	50<->B9	90<->DB	D0<->F3
14<->9E	54<->BA	94<->DC	D4<->F4
18<->9F	58<->BB	98<->DD	D8<->F5
1C<->A6	5C<->BC	9C<->DE	DC<->F6
20<->A7	60<->BD	A0<->DF	E0<->F7
24<->AB	64<->BE	A4<->E5	E4<->F9
28<->AC	68<->BF	A8<->E6	E8<->FA
2C<->AD	6C<->CB	AC<->E7	EC<->FB
30<->AE	70<->CD	B0<->E9	F0<->FC
34<->AF	74<->CE	B4<->EA	F4<->FD
38<->B2	78<->CF	B8<->EB	F8<->FE
3C<->B3	7C<->D3	BC<->EC	FC<->FF

Figure C.9 "6 and 2" Write Translate Table

A tabular representation of the same mapping is shown in Figure C.9. It should be noted that this is in fact a **two way mapping**. When bytes are read from the disk they are converted back to 6-bit bytes using this same table.

The reason for this transformation can be better understood by examining how the information is retrieved from the disk. The read routine must read a byte, transform it, and store it—all in under 32 cycles (the time taken to write a byte) or the information will be lost. By using the checksum computation to decode data, the transformation shown in Figure C.10 greatly facilitates the time constraint. As the data is being read from a sector, the accumulator contains the cumulative result of all previous bytes, exclusive-ORed together. The value of the accumulator after any exclusive-OR operation is the actual data byte for that point in the series. This process is diagrammed in Figure C.10.

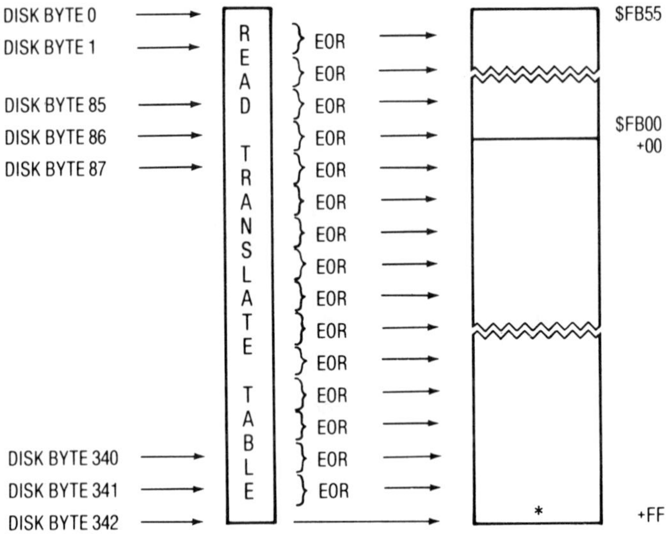

* Last data byte is used as checksum.

Figure C.10 Reading from Disk into the Buffers

While containing specific information, the preceding discussion might still be viewed as somewhat of a theoretical presentation. The follow section will show each stage of the transformation that takes place as 256 bytes of data are prepared prior to being written to disk. The data chosen is real data that exists on the ProDOS System disk which will enable the reader to verify the following transformation.

STAGE 1

The first stage consists of creating an auxiliary buffer thereby converting the 256 bytes of data to 342 bytes. Each byte in the auxiliary buffer is made up of bits from three different bytes of the original 256-byte data. Please note that the original 256 bytes are still unchanged. Figure C.11 illustrates the results of stage 1, highlighting several bytes to aid in following this process.

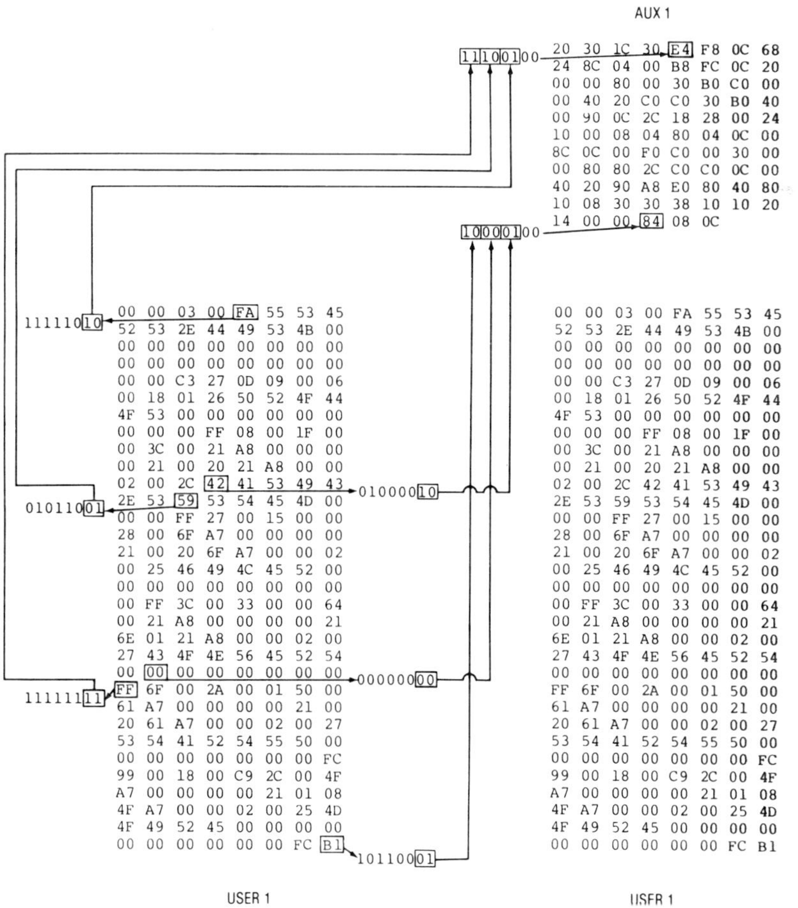

Figure C.11 Example: Forming the Auxiliary Data Buffer

STAGE 2

The second stage is to create a checksum by exclusive-ORing the entire 342-byte data block with itself, offset by one byte. If it were not offset, the results would be undesirable (all zeroes). An additional byte is created in this process. While the last byte is in fact unchanged by the process and is independent of the preceding data, it serves as the checksum as seen in Figure C.12.

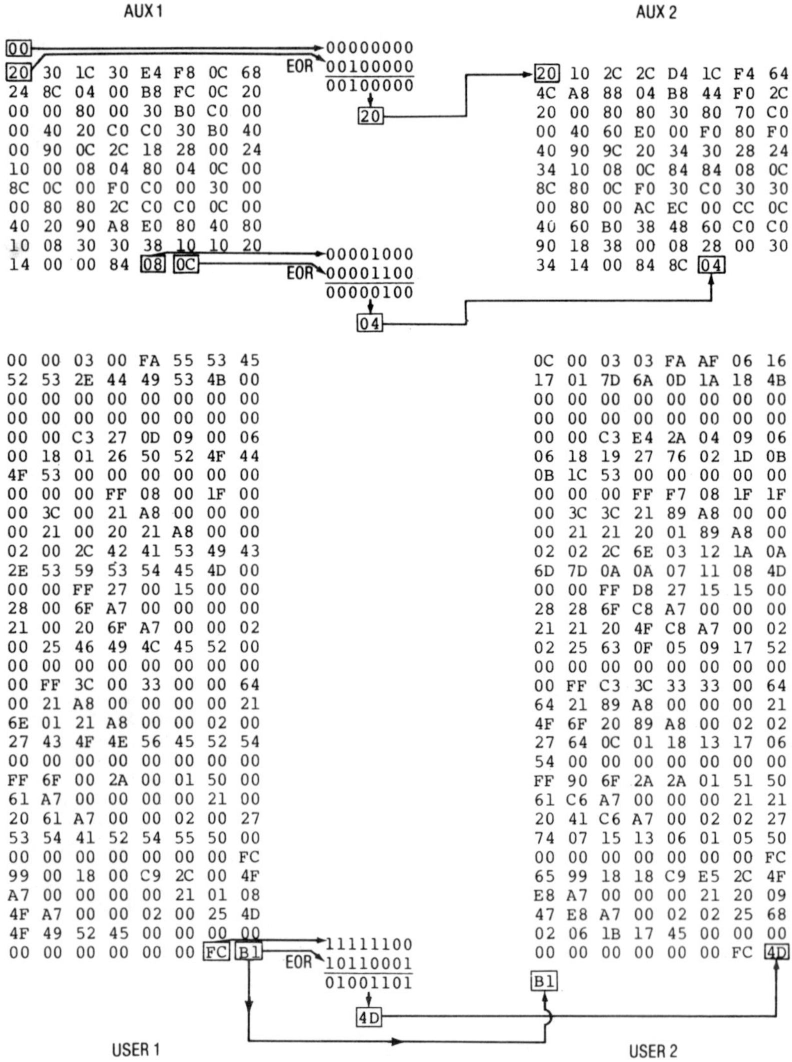

Figure C.12 Example: The Exclusive ORing Operation

STAGE 3

The third and last stage is to translate the 343 6-bit bytes into disk bytes. This is done with a simple lookup table as shown in Figure C.13. Please note that during this step the last two bits are removed from all bytes before using the table.

AUX 2

10 AND FC = 10

```
20 10 2C 2C D4 1C F4 64
4C A8 88 04 B8 44 F0 2C
20 00 80 80 30 80 70 C0
00 40 60 E0 00 F0 80 F0
40 90 9C 20 34 30 28 24
34 10 08 0C 84 84 08 0C
8C 80 0C F0 30 C0 30 30
00 80 00 AC EC 00 CC 0C
40 60 B0 38 48 60 C0 C0
90 18 38 00 08 28 00 30
34 14 00 84 8C 04
```

WRITE TRANSLATE TABLE

```
00 <-> 96
04 <-> 97
08 <-> 9A
0C <-> 9B
10 <-> 9D
   :
48 <-> B6
   :
B0 <-> E9
   :
F0 <-> FC
F4 <-> FD
F8 <-> FE
FC <-> FF
```

AUX 3

```
A7 9D AD AD F4 A6 FD BE
B7 E6 D9 97 EB B5 FC AD
A7 96 D6 D6 AE D6 CD ED
96 B4 BD F7 96 FC D6 FC
B4 DB DE A7 AF AE AC AB
AF 9D 9A 9B D7 D7 9A 9B
DA D6 9B FC AE ED AE AE
96 D6 96 E7 FB 96 F2 9B
B4 BD E9 B2 B6 BD ED ED
DB 9F B2 96 9A AC 96 AE
AF 9E 96 D7 DA 97
```

4B AND FC = 48

```
0C 00 03 03 FA AF 06 16
17 01 7D 6A 0D 1A 18 4B
00 00 00 00 00 00 00 00
00 00 00 00 00 00 00 00
00 00 C3 E4 2A 04 09 06
06 18 19 27 76 02 1D 0B
0B 1C 53 00 00 00 00 00
00 00 00 FF F7 08 1F 1F
00 3C 3C 21 89 A8 00 00
00 21 21 20 01 89 A8 00
02 02 2C 6E 03 12 1A 0A
6D 7D 0A 0A 07 11 08 4D
00 00 FF D8 27 15 15 00
28 28 6F C8 A7 00 00 00
21 21 20 4F C8 A7 00 02
02 25 63 0F 05 09 17 52
00 00 00 00 00 00 00 00
00 FF C3 3C 33 33 00 64
64 21 89 A8 00 00 00 21
4F 6F 20 89 A8 00 02 02
27 64 0C 01 18 13 17 06
54 00 00 00 00 00 00 00
FF 90 6F 2A 2A 01 51 50
61 C6 A7 00 00 00 21 21
20 41 C6 A7 00 02 02 27
74 07 15 13 06 01 05 50
00 00 00 00 00 00 00 FC
65 99 18 18 C9 E5 2C 4F
E8 A7 00 00 00 21 20 09
47 E8 A7 00 02 02 25 68
02 06 1B 17 45 00 00 00
00 00 00 00 00 00 FC 4D
D1
```

B1 AND FC = B0

USER 2

```
9B 96 96 96 FE E7 97 9E
9E 96 D3 BF 9B 9F 9F B6
96 96 96 96 96 96 96 96
96 96 96 96 96 96 96 96
96 96 ED F9 AC 97 9A 97
97 9F 9F AB CE 96 A6 9A
9A A6 B9 96 96 96 96 96
96 96 96 FF FD 9A A6 A6
96 B3 B3 A7 D9 E6 96 96
96 A7 A7 A7 96 D9 E6 96
96 96 AD CB 96 9D 9F 9A
CB D3 9A 9A 97 9D 9A B7
96 96 FF F5 AB 9E 9E 96
AC AC CB EF E5 96 96 96
A7 A7 A7 B7 EF E5 96 96
96 AB BD 9B 97 9A 9E B9
96 96 96 96 96 96 96 96
96 FF ED B3 AE AE 96 BE
BE A7 D9 E6 96 96 96 A7
B7 CB A7 D9 E6 96 96 96
AB BE 9B 96 9F 9D 9E 97
BA 96 96 96 96 96 96 96
FF DB CB AC AC 96 B9 B9
BD EE E5 96 96 96 A7 A7
A7 B4 EE E5 96 96 96 AB
CE 97 9E 9D 97 96 97 B9
96 96 96 96 96 96 96 FF
BE DD 9F 9F EF F9 AD B7
FA E5 96 96 96 A7 A7 9A
B5 FA E5 96 96 96 AB BF
96 97 9F 9E B5 96 96 96
96 96 96 96 96 96 FF B7
E9
```

USER 3

Figure C.13 Example: Translation, the Final Step Before Writing

APPENDIX D

THE LOGIC STATE SEQUENCER

Because there is such a close relationship between the disk hardware and the software that controls it, it seems appropriate to examine the firmware that directly responds to the software, that is, the Logic State Sequencer ROM. The code on this ROM actually controls the reading and writing of bits. While the information presented here should enable one to understand the process involved, it is nevertheless intended to be an overview and not a complete analysis.

The Disk II family of drives uses a unique method of storing data on a disk. They use a method named GCR (Group Code Recording), unlike most current disk drives that use FM (Frequency Modulation) or MFM (Modified Frequency Modulation). This enables writing data bytes without the use of clock bits and thereby greatly increases the amount of data that can be stored on a given track. Apple has recently put the Disk Controller Card into a Custom Integrated Circuit. Versions of the Disk Drive Controller Unit (IWM—Integrated Woz/Wendell Machine) are now used on the Apple IIc and the Macintosh. The following discussion is based on the original controller card, but should apply functionally to the new chip as well.

LOGIC STATE SEQUENCER ROM

The Logic State Sequencer is a 256-byte ROM on the disk controller card. The "program" stored there controls the data register, providing the actual means of reading and writing bits. The program on the ROM is unlike traditional software such as BASIC or machine language—it is a simple language with only six different functions or commands available. What makes it different and difficult to follow is how the flow of the program is determined. Traditional languages typically execute instructions in sequence until they encounter a control statement (such as GOTO or GOSUB) that indicates a new location. In the state machine, each byte is both a command (operating on the data register) and a control statement. What is unique is that the location of the next command to execute is only partially determined by the control statement.

The program flow is additionally controlled by four external inputs, two provided by software and two provided by hardware. The software inputs are controlled by four memory locations, $C08C through $C08F. The locations are slot dependent (adding the slot number times 16 to the base address gives the appropriate address). Because of the nature of the state machine (timing), this is normally done with the X-register containing the offset (i.e. the slot number times 16). The two inputs provided by the hardware are the presence or absence of a read pulse and the status of the high bit of the data register.

Each of the 256 bytes in the ROM is an available location that can be accessed with the appropriate control statements. Eight bits are needed to indicate all of the locations. Four of these bits are provided by each byte in the ROM and the remaining four bits are provided by the external inputs described earlier. The four bits in the control statement contained in each byte of the ROM indicate what will be called for the next "sequence," and the four bits from the external inputs indicate what will be called for the next "state." Figure D.1 depicts the ROM as a two dimensional array, with "sequence" and "state" each providing one dimension of the address of a given element.

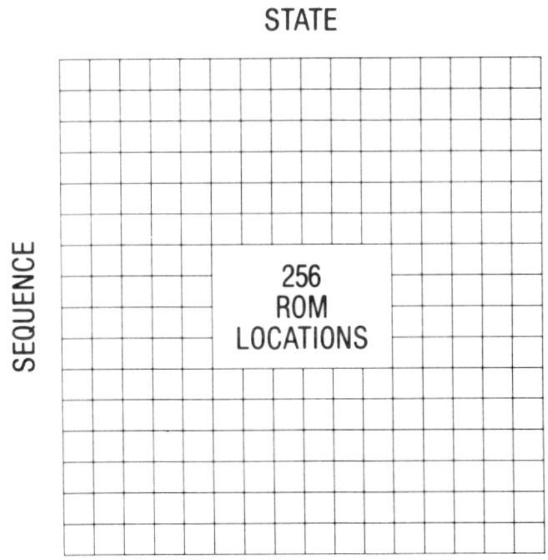

Figure D.1 Sequencer ROM is Addressed by a 4-Bit Input (STATE) and a 4-Bit Control Statement (SEQUENCE)

The 16 sequences are simply the hex numbers 0 through F, and are supplied by the high order nibble of each byte in the ROM. The low order nibble is the command number. For example, the byte "18" would execute command number 8 (no operation) and proceed to sequence 1. Each byte or instruction takes two cycles to execute, but the state machine is running twice as fast as the 6502, so only one 6502 cycle per state machine instruction is required. The six available commands that control the data register are listed in Table D.1.

Table D.1 Commands Which Control the Data Register.

CODE	OPERATION	DATA REGISTER BEFORE	DATA REGISTER AFTER
0	Clear	XXXXXXXX*	00000000
8	No operation	ABCDEFGH	ABCDEFGH
9	Shift left (bringing in a 0)	ABCDEFGH	BCDEFGH0
A	Shift right (WRITE protected)	ABCDEFGH	11111111
	(not WRITE protected)	ABCDEFGH	0ABCDEFG
B	Load	XXXXXXXX*	YYYYYYYY*
D	Shift left (bringing in a 1)	ABCDEFGH	BCDEFGH1

*XXXXXXXX and YYYYYYYY denote valid, but different bytes.

The logic of the state machine is difficult to follow even though relatively few operations are carried out on the data register. Figure D.2 graphically illustrates the logic.

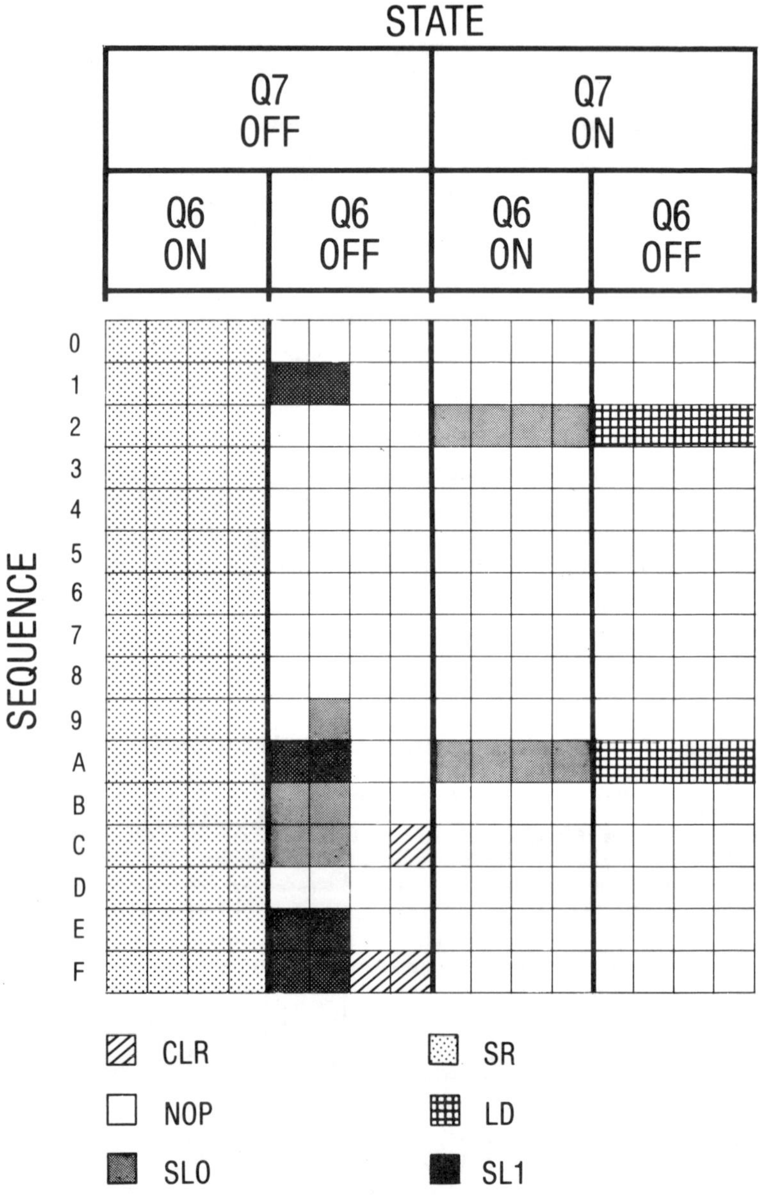

Figure D.2 Sequencer Commands

To make the task easier, the contents of the ROM will be analyzed in four parts, corresponding to the four software states. As mentioned above, the locations $C08C—C08F (plus the slot number times 16) partially control the state machine. These four locations control two switches, Q6 and Q7. If one of these addresses is accessed, the appropriate switch will be set as indicated in Table D.2.

Table D.2 State Switches

ADDRESS	SWITCH Q6	SWITCH Q7
$C08C	OFF	—
$C08D	ON	—
$C08E	—	OFF
$C08F	—	ON

The first state examined will be with switch Q6 on and Q7 off. This can be described as checking the write protect switch and initializing the state machine for writing. Table D.3 lists the contents of this portion of the state machine ROM. All the instructions are identical ($0A), each shifting the data register right (command A), bringing in the status of the write protect switch, and then going to sequence 0. This readies the hardware for writing since it is necessary to be in sequence 0 in order to write correctly.

Table D.3 STATE: Q6 ON and Q7 OFF (Check Write Protect)

	HIGH BIT CLEAR		HIGH BIT SET	
SEQUENCE	PULSE	NO PULSE	PULSE	NO PULSE
0	0A	0A	0A	0A
1	0A	0A	0A	0A
2	0A	0A	0A	0A
3	0A	0A	0A	0A
4	0A	0A	0A	0A
5	0A	0A	0A	0A
6	0A	0A	0A	0A
7	0A	0A	0A	0A
8	0A	0A	0A	0A
9	0A	0A	0A	0A
A	0A	0A	0A	0A
B	0A	0A	0A	0A
C	0A	0A	0A	0A
D	0A	0A	0A	0A
E	0A	0A	0A	0A
F	0A	0A	0A	0A

The next state examined is with switches Q6 and Q7 off (see Table D.4). This reads data from the disk, shifting in the appropriate bits as a "Pulse" or "No Pulse" is detected by the hardware. Additionally, once the high bit of the data register is set, the data is retained until a read pulse is detected (0 bits or "No Pulses" are ignored).

When switch Q7 is turned on (write mode), the presence or absence of a read pulse is ignored. For this reason, the ROM contains two identical 64-byte sections. Therefore, Table D.5 is presented in a slighly different format. Only two operations are carried out, loading the data register from the data bus, and shifting the data out one bit at a time, so that it can be written to the disk. Note that only sequences 2 and A carry out any action on the data register.

Table D.4 STATE: Q6 OFF and Q7 OFF (Read)

SEQUENCE	HIGH BIT CLEAR PULSE	HIGH BIT CLEAR NO PULSE	HIGH BIT SET PULSE	HIGH BIT SET NO PULSE
0	18	18	18	18
1	2D	2D	38	38
2	D8	38	08	28
3	D8	48	48	48
4	D8	58	D8	58
5	D8	68	D8	68
6	D8	78	D8	78
7	D8	88	D8	88
8	D8	98	D8	98
9	D8	29	D8	A8
A	CD	BD	D8	B8
B	D9	59	D8	C8
C	D9	D9	D8	A0
D	D8	08	E8	E8
E	FD	FD	F8	F8
F	DD	4D	E0	E0

Table D.5 State: Q7 ON (Write)

SEQUENCE	Q6 OFF HIGH BIT CLEAR	Q6 OFF HIGH BIT SET	Q6 ON HIGH BIT CLEAR	Q6 ON HIGH BIT SET
0	18	18	18	18
1	28	28	28	28
2	39	39	3B	3B
3	48	48	48	48
4	58	58	58	58
5	68	68	68	68
6	78	78	78	78
7	08	88	08	88
8	98	98	98	98
9	A8	A8	A8	A8
A	B9	B9	BB	BB
B	C8	C8	C8	C8
C	D8	D8	D8	D8
D	E8	E8	E8	E8
E	F8	F8	F8	F8
F	88	08	88	08

This discussion should provide a general understanding of the Logic State Sequencer. For a comprehensive look at the disk hardware, an excellent source is *Understanding the Apple II* by Jim Sather, published by Quality Software.

SEQUENCER EXAMPLE

Table D.6 follows the state machine through a number of steps during the read process. It is assumed that a $D5 has just been read and is now in the data register. The state machine is executing the instruction at column 4 and sequence 2 of Table D.4 and will continue to loop until a read pulse is detected. The instruction being executed is a $28 which performs a NOP (8 = No OPeration) and remains at sequence 2. In our example, the next byte to be read is an $AA (only the first 5 bits are shown in Table D.6). If the reader can understand this example, it should be possible to construct a similar table for any other read or write example. Note that the column number is controlled by the contents of the MSB of the data register and the presence or absence of a Read Pulse.

Table D.6 A Sequencer Example

	DATA	READ	REFER TO TABLE D.4			NEXT	
STEP	REGISTER	PULSE	COLUMN	SEQUENCE	BYTE	SEQUENCE	ACTION**
1	11010101	NO	4	2	28	2	NOP
2	11010101	YES	3	2	08	0	NOP
3	11010101	NO	4	0	18	1	NOP
4	11010101	NO	4	1	38	3	NOP
5	11010101	NO	4	3	48	4	NOP
6	11010101	NO	4	4	58	5	NOP
7	11010101	NO	4	5	68	6	NOP
8	11010101	NO	4	6	78	7	NOP
9	11010101	NO	4	7	88	8	NOP
10	11010101	NO*	4	8	98	9	NOP
11	11010101	NO	4	9	A8	A	NOP
12	11010101	NO	4	A	BB	B	NOP
13	11010101	NO	4	B	C8	C	NOP
14	11010101	NO	4	C	A0	A	CLR
15	00000000	NO	2	A	BD	B	SL1
16	00000001	NO	2	B	59	5	SL0
17	00000010	NO	2	5	68	6	NOP
18	00000010	YES	1	6	D8	D	NOP
19	00000010	NO	2	D	08	0	NOP
20	00000010	NO	2	0	18	1	NOP
21	00000010	NO	2	1	2D	2	SL1
22	00000101	NO	2	2	38	3	NOP
23	00000101	NO	2	3	48	4	NOP
24	00000101	NO	2	4	58	5	NOP
25	00000101	NO	2	5	68	6	NOP
26	00000101	NO*	2	6	78	7	NOP
27	00000101	NO	2	7	88	8	NOP
28	00000101	NO	2	8	98	9	NOP
29	00000101	NO	2	9	29	2	SL0
30	00001010	NO	2	2	38	3	NOP
31	00001010	NO	2	3	38	4	NOP
32	00001010	NO	2	4	58	5	NOP
33	00001010	NO	2	5	68	6	NOP
34	00001010	YES	1	6	D8	D	NOP
35	00001010	NO	2	D	08	0	NOP
36	00001010	NO	2	0	18	1	NOP
37	00001010	NO	2	1	2D	2	SL1
38	00010101	NO	2	2	38	3	NOP

*Normal time to detect a read pulse (if one exists).

**See Table D.1. Notation used here is borrowed from *Understanding the Apple II* by Jim Sather.

Notes

GLOSSARY

access time. The time required to locate and read or write data on a direct access storage device, such as a diskette drive.

address. The numeric location of a piece of data in memory, usually given as a hexadecimal number from $0000 to $FFFF (65,535 decimal). A disk address is the location of a data sector, expressed in terms of its track and sector numbers.

algorithm. A sequence of steps which may be performed by a program or other process, which will produce a given result.

alphanumeric. An alphabetic character (A-Z) or a numeric digit (0-9). In the past, the term referred to the class of all characters and digits.

analog. Having a value which is continuous, such as a voltage or electrical resistance, as opposed to digital.

AND. The logical process of determining whether two bits are both "1"s. 0 AND 1 results in 0 (false), 1 AND 1 results in 1 (true).

arm. The portion of a disk drive which suspends the read/write head over the disk's surface. The arm can be moved radially to allow access to different tracks.

ASCII (American Standard Code for Information Interchange). A hexadecimal to character conversion code assignment, such that the 256 possible values of a single byte may each represent a alphabetic, numeric, special, or control character. ASCII is used when interfacing to peripherals, such as keyboards, printers, or video text displays.

assembly language. Also known as machine language. The native programming language of the individual computer. Assembly language is oriented to the machine, and is not humanized, as is BASIC, PASCAL, or FORTRAN. An assembler is used to convert assembly language statements to an executable program.

bank switched memory. Also called the language card. An additional 16K of memory which may only be accessed by "throwing" hardware switches to cause portions of the bank switched memory to temporarily replace the Monitor ROM memory in the machine. This is necessary because an Apple can only address 64K, and all addresses are already used with 48K, 4K of I/O and 12K of Monitor ROM.

base. The number system in use. Decimal is base 10, since each digit represents a power of 10 (1,10,100,...). Hexadecimal is base 16 (1,16,256,...). Binary is base 2 (1,2,4,8,...).

BI (BASIC Interpreter). Also called the BASIC System Program. The BI accepts user commands such as CATALOG and LOAD, and translates them into calls to the ProDOS Machine Language Interface (MLI).

binary. A number system based upon powers of 2. Only the digits 0 and 1 are used. For example, 101 in binary is 1 units digit, 0 twos, and 1 fours, or 5 in decimal.

bit cell. The space on a diskette which passes beneath the read/write head in a 4-microsecond interval. A bit cell contains a signal which represents the value of a single binary 0 or 1 (bit).

bit map. A table where each binary bit represents the allocation of a unit of storage. ProDOS uses bit maps to keep track of memory use (System Bit Map) and of disk use (Volume Bit Map).

bit slip marks. The epilogue of a disk field, used to double check that the disk head is still in read sync and the sector has not been damaged.

block. An arbitrary unit of disk space composed of two sectors or 512 bytes. ProDOS reads and writes a block at a time to improve performance and to allow support for larger devices.

BRK, Break. An assembly language instruction which can be used to force an interrupt and immediate suspension of execution of a program.

buffer. An area of memory used to temporarily hold data as it is being transferred to or from a peripheral, such as a disk drive.

carry flag. A 6502 processor flag which indicates that a previous addition resulted in a carry. Also used as an error indicator by many system programs.

catalog. A directory of the files on a diskette. See directory.

chain. A linked list of data elements. Data is chained if its elements need not be contiguous in storage and each element can be found from its predecessor via an address or block pointer.

checksum/CRC. A method for verifying that data has not been damaged. When data is written, the sum of all its constituent bytes is stored with it. If, when the data is later read, its sum no longer matches the checksum, it has been damaged.

clobbered. Damaged or destroyed. A clobbered sector is one which has been overwritten such that it is unrecoverable.

coldstart. A restart of a program which reinitializes all of its parameters, usually erasing any work which was in progress at the time of the restart.

contiguous. Physically next to. Two bytes are contiguous if they are adjoining each other in memory or on the disk.

control block. A collection of data which is used by the operating system to manage resources. Examples of control blocks used by ProDOS are the Volume Control Block (VCB) or a Volume Directory Header.

control character. A special ASCII code which is used to perform a unique function on a peripheral, but does not generate a printable character. Carriage return, line feed, form feed, and a bell are all control characters.

controller card. A hardware circuit board which is plugged into an Apple connector which allows communication with a peripheral device, such as a disk or printer. A controller card usually contains a small driver program in ROM.

CSWL. A vector in zero page, through which output data is passed for display on the CRT or for printing.

cycle. The smallest unit of time within the central processor of the computer. Each machine language instruction requires two or more cycles to complete. One cycle on the Apple is about one microsecond (one millionth of a second).

data type. The type of information stored in a byte. A byte might contain a printable ASCII character, binary numeric data, or a machine language instruction.

decimal. A number system based upon powers of 10. Digits range from 0 to 9.

deferred commands. ProDOS commands which may (or must) be invoked from within an executing BASIC program. OPEN, APPEND, READ, WRITE, and CLOSE are all examples of deferred commands.

digital. Discrete values as opposed to continuous (analog) values. Only digital values may be stored in a computer. Analog measurements from the real world, such as a voltage or the level of light outside, must be converted into a numerical value which, of necessity, must be "rounded off" to a discrete value.

direct access. Peripheral storage allowing rapid access of any piece of data, regardless of its placement on the medium. Magnetic tape is generally not considered direct access, since the entire tape must be read to locate the last byte. A diskette is direct access, since the arm may be rapidly moved to any track and sector.

directory. A catalog of files stored on a diskette. The directory must contain each file's name and its location on the disk as well as other information regarding the type of data stored there. In ProDOS, a directory is a file in itself and one directory can describe other, subdirectories.

disk initialization. The process which places track formatting information, including sectors and gaps, on a blank diskette. During diskette initialization, the ProDOS FILER also places a copy of the boot loader in Block 0 and creates an empty Volume Directory in Blocks 2 through 5. The Volume Bit Map is also initialized in Block 6.

displacement. The distance from the beginning of a block of data to a particular byte or field. Displacements are usually given beginning with 0, for the first byte, 1 for the second, etc. Also known as an offset.

DOS. Also called DOS 3.2 and DOS 3.3. An earlier disk operating system for the Apple, DOS was designed to support BASIC programming using the Disk II drive only. When hard disks became available, Apple introduced ProDOS.

driver. A program which provides an input stream to another program or an output device. A printer driver accepts input from a user program in the form of lines to be printed, and sends them to the printer.

dump. An unformatted or partially formatted listing of the contents of memory or a diskette in hexadecimal. Used for diagnostic purposes.

encode. To translate data from one form to another for any of a number of reasons. In ProDOS, data is encoded from 8-bit bytes to 6-bit bytes for storage.

entry point (EPA). The entry point address is the location within a program where execution is to start. This is not necessarily the same as the load point (or lowest memory address in the program).

EOF (End Of File). A 3-byte number ranging from 0 to 16,777,216 (16 megabytes), which represents the offset to the end of the file. If the file is sequential (contains no "holes"), the EOF is also the length of the file in bytes.

epilogue. The last three bytes of a field on a track. These unique bytes are used to insure the integrity of the data which precedes them.

Exclusive OR. A logical operation which compares two bits to determine if they are different. 1 EOR 0 results in 1. 1 EOR 1 results in 0.

field. A group of contiguous bytes forming a single piece of data, such as a person's name, his age, or his social security number. In disk formatting, a group of bytes surrounded by gaps.

file. A named collection of data on a diskette or other mass storage medium. Files can contain data or programs.

file buffers. In Apple ProDOS, a pair of 512-byte buffers used by the BASIC Interpreter to manage one open file. Included are a buffer containing the block image of the current index block and one containing the image of the current data block. File buffers are allocated by the BI as needed by moving Applesoft's HIMEM pointer down in memory.

file descriptive entry. A single entry in a disk directory which describes one file. Included are the name of the file, its data type, its length, its access restrictions, its creation date, its location on the diskette, etc.

file type. The type of data held by a file. Valid ProDOS file types include Binary (BIN), Applesoft (BAS), Text (TXT), and System (SYS) files. ProDOS supports up to 256 different file types.

firmware. A middle ground between hardware and software. Usually used to describe micro-code or programs which have been stored in read-only memory (ROM).

gap. The space between fields of data on a diskette. Gaps on an Apple diskette contain self-sync bytes.

garbage collection. The process of combining many small embedded free spaces into one large area. For example, Applesoft performs garbage collection on its string storage to recover memory allocated to strings which have been deleted.

Global Page. A 256-byte area of memory set aside by ProDOS to contain system variables of general interest. Two Global Pages are currently defined: the System Global Page at $BF00; and the BI Global Page at $BE00. The structure of the Global Pages is rigidly defined, allowing external programs to communicate with ProDOS without depending upon release dependent locations. See also vectors.

hard error. An unrecoverable Input/Output error. The data stored in the disk sector can never be successfully read again.

head. The read/write head on a diskette drive. A magnetic pickup, similar in nature to the head on a stereo tapedeck, which rests on the spinning surface of the diskette.

hexadecimal/HEX. A numeric system based on powers of 16. Valid hex digits range from 0 to 9 and A to F, where A is 10, B is 11, ..., F is 15. Standard Apple practice is to indicate a number as hexadecimal by preceding it with a dollar sign. $B30 is 11-256s plus 3-16s plus 0-1s, or 2864 in decimal. Two hexadecimal digits can be used to represent the contents of one byte. Hexadecimal is used with computers because it easily converts to binary.

high memory. Those memory locations which have high address values. $FFFF is the highest memory location. Also called the "top" of memory.

HIMEM. Applesoft's zero page address which identifies the first byte past the available memory which can be used to store BASIC programs and their variables.

immediate command. A ProDOS command which may be entered at any time, especially when ProDOS is waiting for a command from the keyboard. The opposite of deferred commands.

index. A displacement into a table or block of storage.

index block. A block containing a table of block numbers describing the order and location of the blocks of data within a file. A sapling file has one index block describing up to 256 data blocks. A tree file has a master index block which points to other index blocks, which in turn point to the data blocks in the file.

instruction. A single step to be performed in an assembly language or machine language program. Instructions perform such operations as addition, subtraction, store, or load.

integer. A "whole" number with no fraction associated with it, as opposed to floating point.

intercept. A program which logically places itself in the execution path of another program, or pair of programs. A video intercept is used to re-direct program output from the screen to a printer, for example.

interleave. The practice of selecting the order of sectors on a diskette track to minimize access time due to rotational delay. Also called "skewing" or interlacing.

interpreter. A program which translates user written commands or program statements directly into their intended function. Applesoft is an interpreter. The ProDOS BASIC Interpreter translates ProDOS commands into functions such as loading, saving, reading or writing files. Another name for ProDOS Interpreters is System Programs.

interrupt. A hardware signal which causes the computer to halt execution of a program and enter a special handler routine. Interrupts are used to service real-time clock time-outs, BRK instructions, and RESET.

I/O (Input/Output) error. An error which occurs during transmission of data to or from a peripheral device, such as a disk or cassette tape.

JMP. A 6502 assembly language instruction which causes the computer to begin executing instructions at a different location in memory. Similar to a GOTO statement in BASIC.

JSR. A 6502 assembly langauge instruction which causes the computer to "call" a subroutine. Similar to a GOSUB statement in BASIC.

K. A unit of measurement, usually applied to bytes. 1 K bytes is equivalent to 1024 bytes.

Kernel. That part of ProDOS which provides the basic operating system support functions. The Kernel resides in the Language Card or bank switched memory and consists of the MLI, interrupt handler, and diskette and calendar/clock device drivers.

key block. The first block of a ProDOS file.

KSWL. A vector in zero page through which input data is passed from the keyboard or a remote terminal.

label. A name associated with a location in a program or in memory. Labels are used in assembly language much like statement numbers are used in BASIC.

language card. An additional 16K of RAM added to an Apple II or Apple II Plus using a card in slot 0. The card gets its name from its original use with the Apple UCSD PASCAL system and for loading other versions of BASIC. Apple IIe's have this additional memory built in. See also bank switched memory.

latch. A component into which the Input/Output hardware can store a byte value, which will hold that value until the central processor has time to read it (or vice versa).

link. An address or block pointer in an element of a linked chain of data or buffers.

list. A one dimensional sequential array of data items.

load point (LP). The lowest address of a loaded assembly language program—the first byte loaded. Not necessarily the same as the entry point address (EPA).

locked. A file is locked if it is restricted from certain types of access—usually one which is read only. ProDOS provides control over file access through the use of directory entry bits.

logical. A form of arithmetic which operates with binary "truth" or "false", 1 or 0. AND, OR, NAND, NOR, and Exclusive OR are all logical operations.

LOMEM. Applesoft's zero-page address which identifies the first byte of the available memory which can be used to store BASIC programs and their variables.

loop. A programming construction in which a group of instructions or statements are repeatedly executed.

low memory. The memory locations with the lowest addresses. $0000 is the lowest memory location. Also called the "bottom" of memory.

LSB/Lo order. Least Significant Bit or Least Significant Byte. The 1's bit in a byte or the second pair of hexadecimal digits forming an address. In the address $8030, $30 is the Lo order part of the address.

mark. A 3-byte "byte number" or position within a ProDOS file. When a file is being read by the MLI, a current mark is maintained as well as the EOF mark. See also EOF.

microsecond. A millionth of a second. Equivalent to one cycle of the Apple II central processor. Also written as "μsec".

MLI (Machine Language Interface). The MLI is part of the ProDOS Kernel which resides in the language card or bank switched memory. The MLI performs such functions as OPENing a file, WRITING to a file, or DESTORYing a file.

monitor. A machine language program which always resides in the computer and which is the first to receive control when the machine is powered up. The Apple monitor resides in ROM and allows examination and modification of memory at a byte level.

MSB/Hi order. Most Significant Bit or Most Significant Byte. The 128's bit of a byte (the left-most) or the first pair of hexadecimal digits in an address. In the byte value $83, the MSB is on (is a 1).

nibble/nybble. A portion of a byte, usually 4 bits and represented by a single hexadecimal digit. $FE contains two nibbles, $F and $E.

null. Empty, having no length or value. A null string is one which contains no characters. The null control character ($00) produces no effect on a printer (also called an idle).

object code. A machine language program in binary form, ready to execute. Object code is the output of an assembler.

object module. A complete machine language program in object code form, stored as a file on a diskette.

offset. The distance from the beginning of a block of data to a particular byte or field. Offsets are usually given beginning with 0, for the first byte, 1 for the second, etc. Also known as a displacement.

opcode, operation code. The three letter mnemonic representing a single assembly language instruction. JMP is the opcode for the jump instruction.

operating system. A machine language program which manages the memory and peripherals automatically, simplifying the job of the applications programmer.

OR. The logical operation comparing two bits to determine if either of them are 1. 1 OR 1 results in 1 (true), 1 OR 0 results in 1, 0 OR 0 results in 0 (false).

overhead. The space required by the system, either in memory or on the disk, to manage either. The boot blocks, Volume Directory, and Volume Bit Map are part of a diskette's overhead.

page. 256 bytes of memory which share a common high order address byte. Zero page is the first 256 bytes of memory ($0000 through $00FF).

parallel. A communication mode which sends all of the bits in a byte at once, each over a separate line or wire. Opposite of serial.

parameter list. An area of storage set aside for communication between a calling program and a subroutine. The parameter list contains input and output variables which will be used by the subroutine.

parity. A scheme which allows detection of errors in a single data byte, similar to checksums but on a bit level rather than a byte level. An extra parity bit is attached to each byte which is a sum of the bits in the byte. Parity is used in expensive memory to detect or correct single bit failures, and when sending data over communications lines to detect noise errors.

parse. The process of interpreting character string data, such as a command with keywords.

patch. A small change to the object code of an assembly language program. Also called a "zap".

pathname. A string describing the path ProDOS must follow to find a file. A fully qualified pathname consists of the volume name followed by one or more directory names followed by the name of the file itself. If a partial pathname is given, a default prefix is attached to it to form a complete pathname. See also prefix.

physical record. A collection of data corresponding to the smallest unit of storage on a peripheral device. For disks, a physical record is a sector.

pointer. The address or memory location of a block of data or a single data item. The address "points" to the data. A pointer may also be a block number, such as the pointer to the Volume Bit Map in the Volume Directory Header.

prefix. A system maintained default character string which is automatically attached to file names entered by the user to form a complete pathname. See also pathname.

prologue. The three bytes at the beginning of a disk field which uniquely identify it from any other data on the track.

PROM (Programmable Read Only Memory). PROMs are usually used on controller cards associated with peripherals to hold the driver program which interfaces the device to applications programs.

prompt. An output string which lets the user know that input is expected. An "*" is the prompt character for the Apple monitor.

pseudo-opcode. A special assembly language opcode which does not translate into a machine instruction. A pseudo-opcode instructs the assembler to perform some function, such as skipping a page in an assembly listing or reserving data space in the output object code.

RAM (Random Access Memory). Computer memory which will allow storage and retrieval of values by address.

random access. Direct access. The capability to rapidly access any single piece of data on a storage medium without having to sequentially read all of its predecessors.

recal. Recalibrate the disk arm so that the read/write head is positioned over track zero. This is done by pulling the arm as far as it will go to the outside of the diskette until it hits a stop, producing a "clacking" sound.

reference number (REF NUM). An arbitrary number assigned to an open file by the MLI to simplify identification in later calls.

register. A named temporary storage location in the central processor itself. The 6502 has 5 registers; the A, X, Y, S, and P registers. Registers are used by an assembly language program to access memory and perform arithmetic.

relocatable. The attribute of an object module file which contains a machine language program and the information necessary to make it run at any memory location.

return code. A numeric value returned from a subroutine, indicating the success or failure of the operation attempted. A return code of zero usually means there were no errors. Any other value indicates the nature of the error, as defined by the design of the subroutine.

ROM (Read Only Memory). Memory which has a permanent value. The Apple monitor and Applesoft BASIC are stored in ROM.

sapling. A ProDOS file which requires only one index block (2 to 256 data blocks). A sapling ranges from 513 bytes to 131,072 bytes in length. See also seedling and tree.

search. The process of scanning a track for a given sector.

sector. The smallest updatable unit of data on a disk track. One sector on an Apple Disk II contains 256 data bytes.

sector address. A disk field which identifies the following sector data field in terms of its volume, track, and sector number.

sector data. A disk field which contains the actual sector data in nibbilized form.

seedling. A ProDOS file which has only a single data block (512 bytes). A seedling file does not require index blocks. See also sapling and tree.

seek. The process of moving the disk arm to a given track.

self-sync. Also called "auto-sync" bytes. Special disk bytes which contain more than 8 bits, allowing synchronization of the hardware to byte boundaries when reading.

sequential access. A mode of data retrieval where each byte of data is read in the order in which it was written to the disk.

serial. A communication mode which sends data bits one at a time over a single line or wire. As opposed to parallel.

shift. A logical operation which moves the bits of a byte either left or right one position, moving a 0 into the bit at the other end.

skewing. The process of interleaving sectors. See interleave.

soft error. A recoverable I/O error. A worn diskette might produce soft errors occasionally.

SOS (Sophisticated Operating System). The standard operating system for the Apple III computer.

source code. A program in a form which is understandable to humans; in character form as opposed to internal binary machine format. Source assembly code must be processed by an assembler to translate it into machine or "object" code.

sparse file. A file with random organization (see random access) which contains areas which were never initialized. A sparse file might have an End Of File mark of 16 megabytes but only contain several hundred bytes.

state machine. A process (in software or hardware) which defines a unique target state, given an input state and certain conditions. A state machine approach is used in the ProDOS BASIC Interpreter to keep track of its video intercepts and by the hardware on the disk controller card to process disk data.

strobe. The act of triggering an I/O function by momentarily referencing a special I/O address. Strobing $C030 produces a click on the speaker. Also called "toggling".

subroutine. A program whose function is required repeatedly during execution, and therefore is called by a main program in several places.

system disk. A ProDOS volume which contains the system files necessary to allow ProDOS to be booted into memory. Normally, the PRODOS and BASIC.SYSTEM files are necessary. A STARTUP program may also be present.

system program. A ProDOS program, written in machine language, which acts as an intermediary between the user and the ProDOS Kernel. BASIC.SYSTEM, FILER, and CONVERT are all examples of System Programs. See also interpreter and BI.

table. A collection of data entries, having similar format, residing in memory. Each entry might contain the name of a program and its address, for example. A "lookup" can be performed on such a table to locate any given program by name.

toggle. The act of triggering an I/O function by momentarily referencing a special I/O address. Toggling $C030 produces a click on the speaker. Also called "strobe".

tokens. A method where human recognizable words may be coded to single binary byte values for memory compression and faster processing. BASIC statements are tokenized, where hex codes are assigned to words like IF, PRINT, and END.

track. One complete circular path of magnetic storage on a diskette. There are 35 concentric tracks on an Apple diskette.

translate table. A table of single byte codes which are to replace input codes on a one-for-one basis. A translate table is used to convert from 6-bit codes to disk codes.

tree. A ProDOS file which requires several index blocks (131,073 to 16,777,216 bytes of data). See also index block, seedling, and sapling.

TTL (Transistor to Transistor Logic). A standard for the interconnection of integrated circuits which also defines the voltages which represent 0's and 1's.

unlocked. A file which allows all types of access (READ, WRITE, DELETE, RENAME, etc.). See also locked.

utility. A program which is used to maintain, or assist in the development of, other programs or disk files.

vector. A collection of pointers or JMP instructions at a fixed location in memory which allows access to a relocatable program or data.

volume. An identification for a diskette, disk platter, or cassette, containing one or more files.

Volume Directory. The first directory on a disk volume. Also called the "root" directory. All other directories must be reached by first reading the Volume Directory.

warmstart. A restart of a program which retains, as much as is possible, the work which was in progress at the time.

ZAP. From the IBM mainframe utility program, SUPERZAP. A program which allows updates to a disk at a byte level, using hexadecimal.

zero page. The first 256 bytes of memory in a 6502 based machine. Zero page locations have special significance to the central processor, making their management and assignment critical.

INDEX

FREQUENTLY USED TABLES

The most frequently used tables in Beneath Apple ProDOS are repeated here at the end of the book for easy reference.

ProDOS and SOS File Types

TYPE (Hex)	NAME	OS	MEANING
$ØØ		both	Typeless file
$Ø1	BAD	both	Bad blocks file
$Ø2	PCD	SOS	Pascal code file
$Ø3	PTX	SOS	Pascal text file
$Ø4	TXT	both	ASCII text file
$Ø5	PDA	SOS	Pascal data file
$Ø6	BIN	both	Binary file
$Ø7	FNT	SOS	Font file
$Ø8	FOT	both	Graphics screen file
$Ø9	BA3	SOS	Business BASIC program file
$ØA	DA3	SOS	Business BASIC data file
$ØB	WPF	SOS	Word processor file
$ØC	SOS	SOS	SOS System file
$ØD-$ØE		SOS	SOS reserved
$ØF	DIR	both	Directory file
$1Ø	RPD	SOS	RPS data file
$11	RPI	SOS	RPS index file
$12		SOS	AppleFile discard file
$13		SOS	AppleFile model file
$14		SOS	AppleFile report format file
$15		SOS	Screen library file
$16-$18		SOS	SOS reserved
$19	ADB	ProDOS	AppleWorks Data Base file
$1A	AWP	ProDOS	AppleWorks Word Processing file
$1B	ASP	ProDOS	AppleWorks Spreadsheet file
$1C-$AF		ProDOS	Reserved for future use
$BØ	SRC	ProDOS	APW Source file
$B1	OBJ	ProDOS	APW Object file
$B2	LIB	ProDOS	APW Library file
$B3	S16	ProDOS	ProDOS 16 application program file
$B4	RTL	ProDOS	APW run-time library file
$B5	EXE	ProDOS	ProDOS 16 SHELL application file
$B6		ProDOS	ProDOS 16 permanent initialization file
$B7		ProDOS	ProDOS 16 temporary initialization file
$B8		ProDOS	New desk accessory
$B9		ProDOS	Classic desk accessory
$BA		ProDOS	Tool set file
$BB-$BE		ProDOS	Reserved for ProDOS 16 load files
$BF		ProDOS	ProDOS 16 document file
$CØ-$E1		ProDOS	ProDOS reserved
$E2		ProDOS	AppleTalk INIT file
$E3-$EE		ProDOS	ProDOS reserved
$EF	PAS	ProDOS	PASCAL AREA on a ProDOS volume
$FØ	CMD	ProDOS	ProDOS 8 CI added command file
$F1-$F8		ProDOS	ProDOS 8 user defined file types
$F9		ProDOS	ProDOS 8 reserved
$FA	INT	ProDOS	Integer BASIC program file
$FB	IVR	ProDOS	Integer BASIC variables file
$FC	BAS	ProDOS	Applesoft program file
$FD	VAR	ProDOS	Applesoft variables file
$FE	REL	ProDOS	EDASM relocatable object module file
$FF	SYS	ProDOS	ProDOS 8 system program file

ProDOS Hardware Addresses

	"OFF" SWITCHES		"ON" SWITCHES	
SWITCH	BASE ADDRESS	FUNCTION	BASE ADDRESS	FUNCTION
Q0	$C080	Phase 0 off	$C081	Phase 0 on
Q1	$C082	Phase 1 off	$C083	Phase 1 on
Q2	$C084	Phase 2 off	$C085	Phase 2 on
Q3	$C086	Phase 3 off	$C087	Phase 3 on
Q4	$C088	Drive off	$C089	Drive on
Q5	$C08A	Select drive 1	$C08B	Select drive 2
Q6	$C08C	Shift data register	$C08D	Load data register
Q7	$C08E	Read	$C08F	Write

Four Way Q6/Q7 Switches

Q6	Q7	FUNCTION
Off	Off	Enable read sequencing.
Off	On	Shift data register every four cycles while writing.
On	Off	Check write protect and initialize sequencer for writing.
On	On	Load data register every four cycles while writing.

Address Ranges For Slots

SLOT NUMBER	ADDRESS RANGE
0	$C080—$C08F
1	$C090—$C09F
2	$C0A0—$C0AF
3	$C0B0—$C0BF
4	$C0C0—$C0CF
5	$C0D0—$C0DF
6	$C0E0—$C0EF
7	$C0F0—$C0FF

 Also See Pages 6-2 to 6-3

ProDOS Block Conversion Table for Diskettes

PHYSICAL SECTOR →	0&2	4&6	8&A	C&E	1&3	5&7	9&B	D&F
TRACK 0	000	001	002	003	004	005	006	007
TRACK 1	008	009	00A	00B	00C	00D	00E	00F
TRACK 2	010	011	012	013	014	015	016	017
TRACK 3	018	019	01A	01B	01C	01D	01E	01F
TRACK 4	020	021	022	023	024	025	026	027
TRACK 5	028	029	02A	02B	02C	02D	02E	02F
TRACK 6	030	031	032	033	034	035	036	037
TRACK 7	038	039	03A	03B	03C	03D	03E	03F
TRACK 8	040	041	042	043	044	045	046	047
TRACK 9	048	049	04A	04B	04C	04D	04E	04F
TRACK A	050	051	052	053	054	055	056	057
TRACK B	058	059	05A	05B	05C	05D	05E	05F
TRACK C	060	061	062	063	064	065	066	067
TRACK D	068	069	06A	06B	06C	06D	06E	06F
TRACK E	070	071	072	073	074	075	076	077
TRACK F	078	079	07A	07B	07C	07D	07E	07F
TRACK 10	080	081	082	083	084	085	086	087
TRACK 11	088	089	08A	08B	08C	08D	08E	08F
TRACK 12	090	091	092	093	094	095	096	097
TRACK 13	098	099	09A	09B	09C	09D	09E	09F
TRACK 14	0A0	0A1	0A2	0A3	0A4	0A5	0A6	0A7
TRACK 15	0A8	0A9	0AA	0AB	0AC	0AD	0AE	0AF
TRACK 16	0B0	0B1	0B2	0B3	0B4	0B5	0B6	0B7
TRACK 17	0B8	0B9	0BA	0BB	0BC	0BD	0BE	0BF
TRACK 18	0C0	0C1	0C2	0C3	0C4	0C5	0C6	0C7
TRACK 19	0C8	0C9	0CA	0CB	0CC	0CD	0CE	0CF
TRACK 1A	0D0	0D1	0D2	0D3	0D4	0D5	0D6	0D7
TRACK 1B	0D8	0D9	0DA	0DB	0DC	0DD	0DE	0DF
TRACK 1C	0E0	0E1	0E2	0E3	0E4	0E5	0E6	0E7
TRACK 1D	0E8	0E9	0EA	0EB	0EC	0ED	0EE	0EF
TRACK 1E	0F0	0F1	0F2	0F3	0F4	0F5	0F6	0F7
TRACK 1F	0F8	0F9	0FA	0FB	0FC	0FD	0FE	0FF
TRACK 20	100	101	102	103	104	105	106	107
TRACK 21	108	109	10A	10B	10C	10D	10E	10F
TRACK 22	110	111	112	113	114	115	116	117

Also See Page 3-17

DIRECTORY HEADERS

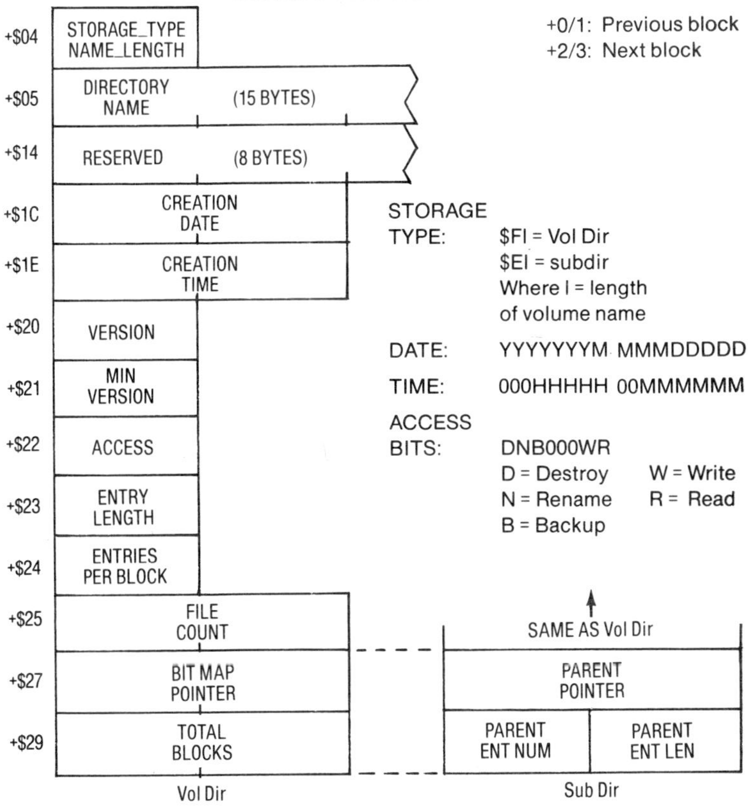

 Also See Pages 4-8 to 4-9

FILE DESCRIPTIVE ENTRY

Offset	Field
+$00	STORAGE_TYPE NAME_LENGTH
+$01	FILE NAME (15 BYTES)
+$10	FILE TYPE
+$11	KEY BLOCK POINTER
+$13	BLOCKS IN USE
+$15	EOF MARK
+$18	CREATE DATE
+$1A	CREATE TIME
+$1C	VERSION
+$1D	MIN VERSION
+$1E	ACCESS
+$1F	AUX TYPE
+ $21	MODIFY DATE
+$23	MODIFY TIME
+$25	DIR HEAD POINTER

STORAGE TYPE: $1l = Seedling
$2l = Sapling
$3l = Tree
$Dl = Dir
Where l = length of volume name

FILE TYPE: $04 = TXT
$06 = BIN
$0F = DIR
$FC = BAS
$FD = VAR
$FF = SYS

DATE: YYYYYYYM MMMDDDDD
TIME: 000HHHHH 00MMMMMM
ACCESS BITS: DNB000WR
D = Destroy W = Write
N = Rename R = Read
B = Backup

AUX TYPE: TXT = Record Len
BIN, BAS, VAR } Load Address
SYS = Default Parms ($2000)

Also See Pages 4-10 to 4-13

VOLUME BIT MAP

01234567 89 . . . ⟶

↑ if bit is 1, Block 0 is free
0, Block 0 is in use

Volume Bit Map for a Disk II diskette is in Block 6 and is 35 bytes in length.

 Also See Page 4-5

SYSTEM GLOBAL PAGE FORMAT

ADDR	CONTENTS
BF00	JMP to MLI
BF03	JMP to $BFF6
BF06	JMP to Date/Time Address (or RTS if no clock)
BF09	JMP to System Error
BF0C	JMP to System Death
BF0F	System Error number
BF10-2F	Device Driver address table
BF10-11	Slot 0 reserved
BF12-13	Slot 1, Drive 1
BF14-15	Slot 2, Drive 1
BF16-17	Slot 3, Drive 1
BF18-19	Slot 4, Drive 1
BF1A-1B	Slot 5, Drive 1
BF1C-1D	Slot 6, Drive 1
BF1E-1F	Slot 7, Drive 1
BF20-21	Slot 0 reserved
BF22-23	Slot 1, Drive 2
BF24-25	Slot 2, Drive 2
BF26-27	/RAM
BF28-29	Slot 4, Drive 2
BF2A-2B	Slot 5, Drive 2
BF2C-2D	Slot 6, Drive 2
BF2E-2F	Slot 7, Drive 2
BF30	Slot/Drive last device
BF31	Count (-1) active devices
BF32-3F	List of active devices (ID)
BF40-4F	Copyright Notice
BF50-55	Bank in RAM call IRQ ($FFD8)
BF56-57	Temporary storage ($FF9B)
BF58-6F	Bitmap low 48K of memory
BF70-7F	Open File buffer address table
BF70-71	Open file 1
BF72-73	Open file 2
BF74-75	Open file 3
BF76-77	Open file 4
BF78-79	Open file 5
BF7A-7B	Open file 6
BF7C-7D	Open file 7
BF7E-7F	Open file 8
BF80-87	Interrupt address table
BF80-81	Priority 1
BF82-83	Priority 2
BF84-85	Priority 3
BF86-87	Priority 4
BF88	A register savearea
BF89	X register savearea
BF8A	Y register savearea
BF8B	S register savearea
BF8C	P register savearea
BF8D	Bank ID byte (ROM/RAM)
BF8E-8F	Interrupt return address
BF90-91	Date
BF92-93	Time
BF94	Current File Level
BF95	Backup Bit
BF96-97	Currently Unused
BF98	Machine ID byte
BF99	Slot ROM bit map
BF9A	Prefix Flag (0 = no Prefix)
BF9B	MLI active Flag
BF9C-9D	Last MLI call return address
BF9E	MLI X register savearea
BF9F	MLI Y register savearea
BFA0-CF	Lang. card entry/exit routines
BFD0-F3	Interrupt entry/exit routines
BFF4	Storage for byte at $E000
BFF5	Storage for byte at $D000
BFF6-F9	Call System Death ($D1E4)
BFFC	Interpreter minimum Version
BFFD	Interpreter Version number
BFFE	Kernel minimum version
BFFF	Kernel version number

MACHINE IDENTIFICATION BYTE ($BF98)

```
00.. 0... II
01.. 0... II+
10.. 0... IIe
11.. 0... III emulation
00.. 1... Future expansion
01.. 1... Future expansion
10.. 1... IIc
11.. 1... Future expansion
```

```
..00 .... unused
..01 .... 48K
..10 .... 64K
..11 .... 128K
.... .X.. Reserved
.... ..0. no 80-column card
.... ..1. 80-column card
.... ...0 no compatible clock
.... ...1 compatible clock
```

 Also See Pages 8-5 to 8-8

BI GLOBAL PAGE FORMAT

ADDR	CONTENTS
BE00	JMP to WARMDOS
BE03	JMP to command parse
BE06	JMP to user parser
BE09	JMP to error handler
BE0C	JMP to error printer
BE0F	Error code number
BE10-1F	Output vectors
BE20-2F	Input vectors
BE30-31	Current output vec
BE32-33	Current input vec
BE34-35	Output intercept addr
BE36-37	Input intercept addr
BE38-3B	STATE intercepts
BE3C	Default slot
BE3D	Default drive
BE3E-40	A,X,Y savearea
BE41	TRACE active flag
BE42	STATE (0=immediate)
BE43	EXEC active flag
BE44	READ active flag
BE45	WRITE active flag
BE46	PREFIX active flag
BE47	DIR file READ flag
BE48	not used
BE49	STRINGS space count
BE4A	Buffered write count
BE4B	Command line length
BE4C	Previous character
BE4D	Open file count
BE4E	EXEC file closing flag
BE4F	CATALOG line state
BE50-51	External cmd handler
BE52	Command name length
BE53	Number of command
BE54-55	PBITS (permitted)
BE56-57	FBITS (found)
BE58-59	A keyword value
BE5A-5C	B keyword value
BE5D-5E	E keyword value
BE5F-60	L keyword value
BE61	S keyword value
BE62	D keyword value
BE63-64	F keyword value
BE65-66	R keyword value
BE67	V keyword value
BE68-69	@ keyword value
BE6A	T keyword value
BE6B	PR#/IN# slot value
BE6C-6D	Pathname 1 addr
BE6E-6F	Pathname 2 addr
BE70	GOSYSTEM MLI interf.
BE85	Last MLI call number
BE86-87	Last MLI parmlist addr
BEA0	CREATE parmlist
BEAC	GET_PREFIX parmlist
BEAF	RENAME parmlist
BEB4	GET_FILE_INFO parmlist
BEC6	ONLINE parmlist
BECB	OPEN parmlist
BED1	SET_NEWLINE parmlist
BED5	READ parmlist
BEDD	CLOSE parmlist
BEDF	reserved
BEF5	JMP to GETBUFR
BEF8	JMP to FREEBUFR
BEFB	Original HIMEM MSB

COMMAND NUMBERS:

$00 = external	$07 = BRUN	$0E = BLOAD	$15 = WRITE	$1C = VERIFY
$01 = IN#	$08 = EXEC	$0F = BSAVE	$16 = APPEND	$1D = CATALOG
$02 = PR#	$09 = LOAD	$10 = CHAIN	$17 = CREATE	$1E = RESTORE
$03 = CAT	$0A = LOCK	$11 = CLOSE	$18 = DELETE	$1F = POSITION
$04 = FRE	$0B = OPEN	$12 = FLUSH	$19 = PREFIX	
$05 = BYE	$0C = READ	$13 = NOMON	$1A = RENAME	
$06 = RUN	$0D = SAVE	$14 = STORE	$1B = UNLOCK	

PBITS/FBITS BIT ASSIGNMENTS:

$8000 Prefix needed	$0080 AD keyword ok
$4000 Slot number only	$0040 B keyword ok
$2000 Deferred command	$0020 E keyword ok
$1000 File name optional	$0010 L keyword ok
$0800 Create file	$0008 @ keyword ok
$0400 T keyword ok	$0004 S or D ok
$0200 Path 2 expected	$0002 F keyword ok
$0100 Path 1 expected	$0001 R keyword ok

 Also See Pages 8-2 to 8-6

MLI CALLS

```
JSR $BFØØ
DFB function_code
DW  addr_of_parms
```

On return carry flag set if error and A reg has return code.

Also See Page 0-12

$40 ALLOC_INTERRUPT

Offset	Field
+0	$02
+1	PRIORITY * (shaded)
+2/+3	ADDRESS OF HANDLER

$41 DEALLOC_INTERRUPT

Offset	Field
+0	$01
+1	PRIORITY

$65 QUIT

Offset	Field
+0	$04
+1	RESERVED
+2/+3	RESERVED
+4	RESERVED
+5/+6	RESERVED

$80 READ_BLOCK

Offset	Field
+0	$03
+1	UNIT NUMBER
+2/+3	ADDRESS OF DATA BUFFER
+4/+5	BLOCK NUMBER

UNIT BITS: DSSS0000

* Shaded fields are outputs only or do not need initialization.

$81 WRITE_BLOCK

Offset	Field
+0	$03
+1	UNIT NUMBER
+2/+3	ADDRESS OF DATA BUFFER
+4/+5	BLOCK NUMBER

UNIT BITS: DSSS 0000

$82 GET_TIME

NO PARAMETER LIST

$C0 CREATE

Offset	Field
+0	$07
+1/+2	ADDRESS OF PATHNAME
+3	ACCESS BITS
+4	FILE TYPE
+5/+6	AUXILIARY FILE TYPE
+7	STORAGE TYPE
+8/+9	CREATION DATE
+A/+B	CREATION TIME

ACCESS: DNB000WR
FILE TYPE: (see next panel)
AUX_TYPE: TXT=Rec Len
BIN, BAS, VAR = Address
STORAGE TYPE:
$01—Seedling
$02—Sapling
$03—Tree
$0D—Directory
DATE: YYYYYYYM MMMDDDDD
TIME: 000HHHHH 00MMMMMM
PATHNAME Buffer must start with one byte length followed by name (MSB off)

 Also See Pages 6-15 to 6-25

$C1 DESTROY

Offset	Field
+0	$01
+1/+2	ADDRESS OF PATHNAME

$C2 RENAME

Offset	Field
+0	$02
+1/+2	ADDRESS OF OLD PATHNAME
+3/+4	ADDRESS OF NEW PATHNAME

$C3 SET_FILE_INFO

Offset	Field
+0	$07
+1/+2	ADDRESS OF PATHNAME
+3	ACCESS BITS
+4	FILE TYPE
+5/+6	AUXILIARY FILE TYPE
+7	NOT USED
+8/+9	NOT USED
+A/+B	DATE OF LAST MODIFICATION
+C/+D	TIME OF LAST MODIFICATION

$C4 GET_FILE_INFO

Offset	Field
+0	$0A
+1/+2	ADDRESS OF PATHNAME
+3	ACCESS BITS
+4	FILE TYPE
+5/+6	AUXILIARY FILE TYPE
+7	STORAGE TYPE
+8/+9	BLOCKS USED
+A/+B	DATE OF LAST MODIFICATION
+C/+D	TIME OF LAST MODIFICATION
+E/+F	CREATION DATE
+10/+11	CREATION TIME

GET_FILE_INFO on Vol Dir returns blocks on Volume in AUX_TYPE, blocks in use by all files in blocks used.

$C5 ONLINE

Offset	Field
+0	$02
+1	UNIT NUMBER
+2/+3	ADDRESS OF DATA BUFFER

UNIT BITS:
DSSS 0000
or
0000 0000

Also See Pages 6-26 to 6-38

$C6 SET_PREFIX

Offset	Field
+0	$01
+1/+2	ADDRESS OF PATHNAME

$C7 GET_PREFIX

Offset	Field
+0	$01
+1/+2	ADDRESS OF PATHNAME

$C8 OPEN

Offset	Field
+0	$03
+1/+2	ADDRESS OF PATHNAME
+3/+4	ADDRESS OF FILE BUFFER
+5	REFERENCE NUMBER

$C9 NEWLINE

Offset	Field
+0	$03
+1	REFERENCE NUMBER
+2	AND MASK
+3	NEWLINE CHARACTER

$00 DISABLE
$FF MATCH
$7F IGNORE MSB

$CA READ

Offset	Field
+0	$04
+1	REFERENCE NUMBER
+2/+3	ADDRESS OF DATA BUFFER
+4/+5	REQUESTED LENGTH
+6/+7	ACTUAL LENGTH

$CB WRITE

Offset	Field
+0	$04
+1	REFERENCE NUMBER
+2/+3	ADDRESS OF DATA BUFFER
+4/+5	REQUESTED LENGTH
+6/+7	ACTUAL LENGTH

$CC CLOSE

Offset	Field
+0	$01
+1	REFERENCE NUMBER

$CD FLUSH

Offset	Field
+0	$01
+1	REFERENCE NUMBER

$CE SET_MARK

Offset	Field
+0	$02
+1	REFERENCE NUMBER
+2/+3/+4	NEW FILE POSITION

$CF GET_MARK

Offset	Field
+0	$02
+1	REFERENCE NUMBER
+2/+3/+4	FILE POSITION

 Also See Pages 6-39 to 6-54

$D0 SET_EOF

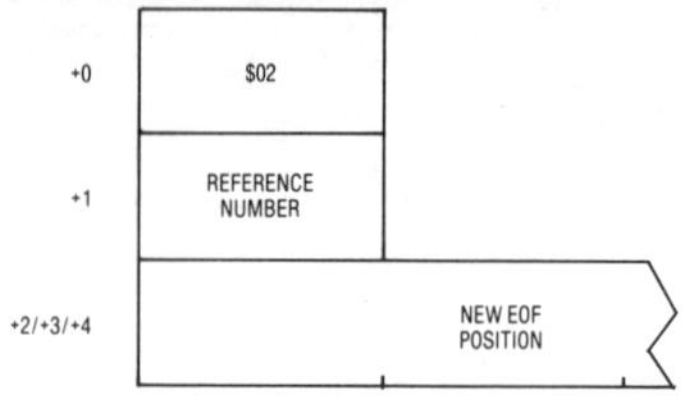

$D2 SET_BUF

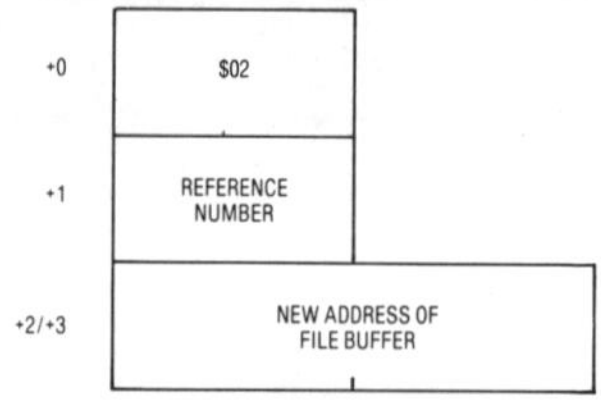

$D1 GET_EOF

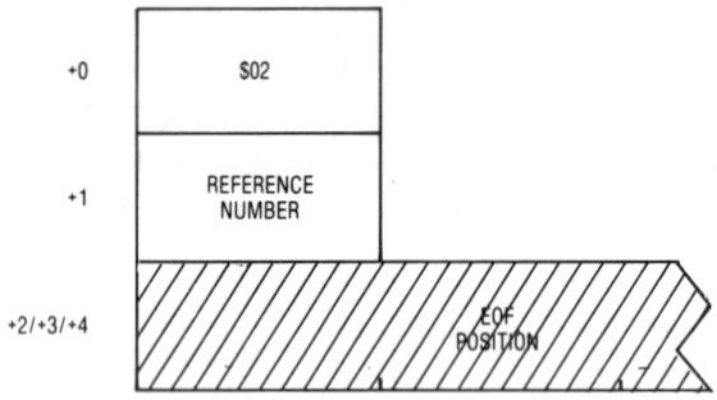

$D3 GET_BUF

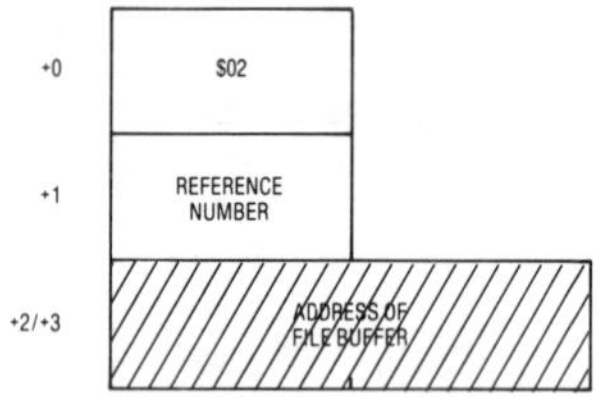

MLI ERROR CODES

Code	Error	Code	Error
$00	No error	$48	Disk full
$01	Invalid MLI function	$49	Vol DIR full
$04	Invalid parameter count	$4A	Incompatible ProDOS version
$25	Interrupt table full	$4B	Unsupported storage type
$27	I/O error	$4C	End of file
$28	No device connected	$4D	Position past EOF
$2B	Write protected	$4E	Access error
$2E	Volume switched	$50	File already open
$40	Invalid pathname syntax	$51	File count bad
$42	Too many files open	$52	Not a ProDOS disk
$43	Invalid REF NUM	$53	Bad parameter
$44	Nonexistent path	$55	VCB overflow
$45	Volume not mounted	$56	Bad buffer addr.
$46	File not found	$57	Duplicate volume
$47	Duplicate file name	$5A	Bad vol. bit map

 Also See Pages 6-54 to 6-61